Through
Seasons of the Heart

with
JOHN POWELL, S.J.

A book of daily readings
selected from the writings and programs
of John Powell, S.J.

TABOR PUBLISHING

Other Books and Programs by John Powell, S.J.

Why Am I Afraid To Love?
Why Am I Afraid To Tell You Who I Am?
A Reason To Live, A Reason To Die
He Touched Me
The Secret Of Staying In Love
My Vision and My Values (an audio program)
Fully Human, Fully Alive
Free To Be Me (a video program)
Families (a video program)
Unconditional Love
Jesus As I Know Him (a video program)
The Fully Alive Experience (an audio program)
The Silent Holocaust
The Growing Edge Of Life (an audio program)
Faith In Search Of God (a video program)
The Christian Vision
Reverence For Life (a video program)
Will The Real Me Please Stand Up?

Send all inquiries to:
Tabor Publishing
200 E. Bethany Drive
Allen, Texas 75002-3804

Printed in the United States of America
ISBN 1-55924-197-7

5 6 7 8   95 94 93

Cover painting by Bosc
Cover and Interior Design: Design Office/Peter Martin

Photographs
Winter, © Ed Buryn/Jeroboam, Inc.
Spring, Lawrence Cameron/Jeroboam, Inc.
Summer, Mitchell Payne/Jeroboam, Inc.
Autumn, © Frank Siteman/Jeroboam, Inc.

I am very indebted to my colleague and friend, Loretta Brady. It was her idea to publish a book of daily readings taken from my writings and audio visual programs. I am grateful to her for her patience and perseverance in selecting and editing these readings. With my encouragement Loretta has in several instances changed the wording and punctuation from the original texts. These changes have in some cases supplied context, and in others the changes have helped the flow and continuity.

In reading and listening to my various words and works that have been published over the last twenty years, Loretta picked out four themes: (1) Becoming a Person (2) Becoming a Loving Person (3) Becoming a Communicator (4) Becoming a Believer. In her selection of readings for each day, she has skillfully woven these four themes into each season of the year: Spring, Summer, Autumn, and Winter. Through Seasons of the Heart.

As I was reading over the final version of these selections, I was on the verge of blushing at least several times. I was painfully aware of the discrepancy between my lip-service and my lifestyle. My noisy conscience kept nudging me, "If you really mean that, why don't you practice it better?" So I knew all along I would have to say this to you: The ideals presented in these selections are precisely this for me: ideals. Unfortunately, they are not my accomplishments. But, as you will read in the pages to follow: "Please be patient. God is not finished with me yet."

In 1966, my old friend from high school days, Dick Leach, made a retreat I preached at the Jesuit Retreat House in Barrington, Illinois. He was persistent in urging me to get some of the contents of that retreat into print. Part of his persistence was his promise to publish whatever I would and could write. So we started with a handshake and became a team. Argus Press became Argus Communications and has recently been renamed Tabor Publishing.

It is now twenty years since that handshake. Nearly thirteen million copies of ten Tabor books are now in print. They have been translated into ten foreign languages. Audio and video programs produced and published by Tabor have reached many millions. It is indeed a happy twentieth anniversary.

No one is more surprised by all this than I am. Somewhere deep down inside me is a shy little boy, who keeps blinking into the light and asking: "Is all this really happening to me?" My heart keeps repeating the words of the psalmist, "What can I ever give to the Lord in return for all the things which he has given to me?" Thank you, Lord.

And thank you, Loretta. Thank you, Dick Leach. Thank you, Dear Readers. Please remember me as loving you!

John Powell, S.J.
Loyola University of Chicago
Autumn, 1986

Winter

*T*he most important of all our perceptions is the way we perceive ourselves. There is a story in American Indian folklore that illustrates this truth very clearly. According to the legend, an Indian brave came upon an eagle's egg which had somehow fallen unbroken from an eagle's nest. Unable to find the nest, the brave put the egg in the nest of a prairie chicken, where it was hatched by the brooding mother hen. The fledgling eagle, with its proverbial strong eyes, saw the world for the first time. Looking at the other prairie chickens, he did what they did. He crawled and scratched at the earth, pecked here and there for stray grains and husks, now and then rising in a flutter a few feet above the earth and then descending again. He accepted and imitated the daily routine of the earthbound prairie chickens. And he spent most of his life this way.

Then, as the story continues, one day an eagle flew over the brood of prairie chickens. The now aging eagle, who still thought he was a prairie chicken, looked up in awed admiration as the great bird soared through the skies. "What is that?" he gasped in astonishment. One of the old prairie chickens replied, "I have seen one before. That is the eagle, the proudest, strongest, and most magnificent of all the birds. But don't you ever dream that you could be like that. You're like the rest of us and we are prairie chickens." And so, shackled by this belief, the eagle lived and died thinking he was a prairie chicken.

Our lives are shaped by the way we perceive ourselves. The all-important attitudes by which we perceive and evaluate ourselves tell us who we are and describe the appropriate behavior for such a person. We live and die according to our self-perception.

From *The Christian Vision*

*T*hrough the eyes of our minds you and I look out at reality (ourselves, other people, life, the world, and God). However, we see these things differently. Your vision of reality is not mine and, conversely, mine is not yours. Both of our visions are limited and inadequate, but not to the same extent. We have both mis-interpreted and distorted reality, but in different ways. We have each seen something of the available truth and beauty to which the other has been blind. The main point is that it is the dimensions and clarity of this vision that determine the dimensions of our worlds and the quality of our lives. To the extent that we are blind or have distorted reality, our lives and our happiness have been diminished. Conse-quently, if we are to change—to grow—there must first be a change in this basic vision, or perception of reality.

It has been generally agreed that true and full human living is based on three components, like legs on a tripod: intrapersonal dynamics, interpersonal relationships, and a frame of reference. In my previous attempts to write, I have been mostly concerned with the first two. My present concern is with the third: a frame of reference, a basic per-ception of reality through which we integrate, evaluate, and interpret new persons, events, and ideas. As a flexible person continues to inte-grate the "new," his or her basic perception or vision is itself changed. But it is always this vision, however modified, that controls the qual-ity and participation in human life.

From *Fully Human, Fully Alive*

*E*very baby born into this world is a living question mark. The first question asked is about self: Who am I? The baby proceeds to discover physical reality: hands, feet, and so forth. There is an experience of wetness and hunger. Then comes the discovery of personal emotional reality: security, insecurity, the need for gratification and attention. Somewhere in the course of this ongoing awareness of self, the infant gradually discovers that he or she is not the whole of reality, that all other beings are not merely extensions of self. This initiates the startling discovery of *otherness*. Who are they? Some are warm; some are cold. Some can be manipulated by crying; others cannot.

The thing that all people have in common for the baby is that they are there. They are a part of the world. He or she must learn to relate to them. Thus, from the first days of life, the infant must begin the work of interpreting and adjusting to reality. As the eyes of the small body start to draw physical reality into focus, the small mind begins its own work of understanding, interpreting, and evaluating. It is the beginning of a vision which will shape a human life.

The human body is instinctively adaptive. The pores close in cold weather. The pupils of the eyes contract in bright light. So, as the baby grows up, he or she will develop a whole repertoire of psychologically adaptive reactions comparable to those of the body. As each new being in this world is perceived, some adjustment to it must be made. This process will eventually constitute the personalized interpretation of and adjustment to reality by a unique human being.

From *Fully Human, Fully Alive*

*E*veryone is born with unique and unconditional value. Each of us is mysterious and unrepeatable in the whole course of human history; made after the image and likeness of God himself. But we can know ourselves only as reflected in the eyes of others. Consequently, our basic endowment of self-appreciation is largely the gift of our parents. However, if we have perceived from them—as all of us have to some extent—that their love for us was only conditional, that it was turned on only when we met their conditions and turned off when we failed to meet them, that their love was not based on what we are but conditioned on our performance, we can only conclude that our value is somehow outside ourselves. There is no cause within for true self-love, self-esteem, self-appreciation. There is no occasion for celebration.

When worthiness of love becomes a matter of passing tests and fulfilling conditions, we begin to experience more failure than success. In the experience of repeated failure, there is conflict, fear, frustration, pain, and ultimately some form of self-hatred. So we spend the rest of our lives trying to escape this pain through some form of pretense. We try to assume an appearance that will please others and gain us loving acceptance. We give up on being ourselves and try to be someone else, someone who will be worthy of recognition and love.

From *The Secret of Staying In Love*

*T*he importance of one's self-image is aptly illustrated in the fairy tale *Rapunzel.* It is the story of a young girl, imprisoned in a tower with an old witch. The young girl is in fact very beautiful, but the old witch insistently tells her that she is ugly. It is, of course, a stratagem of the witch to keep the girl in the tower. The moment of Rapunzel's liberation occurs one day when she is gazing from the window of the tower. At the base of the tower stands her Prince Charming. She throws her hair, long and beautiful tresses, out the window (the root-ends, of course, remain attached to her scalp), and he braids the hair into a ladder and climbs up to rescue her. Rapunzel's imprisonment is really not that of the tower. She is imprisoned by the fear of her own ugliness that the witch has described so often and so effectively. However, when Rapunzel sees in the mirroring eyes of her lover that she is beautiful, she is freed from the real tyranny of her own imagined ugliness.

This is true not only in the case of Rapunzel but with all of us. We desperately need to see in the mirror of another's eyes our own goodness and beauty, if we are to be truly free. Until this moment, we, too, will remain locked inside the prison towers of ourselves. And if the thrust of love requires us to be outside ourselves and to be preoccupied with the happiness and fulfillment of others, we will not love very much until we have had this vision.

From *Why Am I Afraid To Love?*

*T*here are many things inside every one of us which we would like to share. All of us have our own secret past, our secret shames and broken dreams, our secret hopes. Over and against this need and desire to share these secrets and to be understood, every one of us must weigh fear and risk. Whatever my secrets are, they seem, more than anything else, to be deeply and uniquely a part of me. No one has ever done the precise things that I have done, no one has ever thought my thoughts, or dreamed my dreams. I am not sure that I could even find the words to share these things with another, but what I am even less sure of is this: how would they sound to another?

The person who has a good self-image, who really and truly accepts him or herself, will be greatly helped at this time of dilemma. It is not very likely, however, that someone, who has never really shared him or herself, could have the support of a good self-image. Most of us have experienced and done things, have lived with sensations and feelings, that we feel we would never dare tell another. To the other, I might appear deluded or even evil, ridiculous or vain. My whole life could appear as a hideous deceit.

From *Why Am I Afraid To Tell You Who I Am?*

*M*emories. People are made of memories. Half of what we are is determined by our memories. The things that happen today in our families are the memories of tomorrow. Whenever we invest any kindness, any encouragement, any sympathy in another, it's a lifetime investment. It will yield rich dividends all throughout that person's life.

Some memories happen, but other memories must be planned. Yes, some memories happen: like the first day at school, various things that are just part of daily life. But other memories have to be planned: like Christmases and outings and birthdays. I think it is really important to plan things because they keep playing as memories in one's mind and heart always. Half of what we are is indeed determined by the memories we have inside us.

From the video program, *Families*

*T*here is no doubt that the attitude each of us has toward him or herself is the most important of all our attitudes. We have compared an attitude to a lens of the mind. To continue with this comparison, the lens or the attitude one has toward self is *always* over the eyes of the mind. Other lenses or attitudes may be superimposed when we are reacting to something else, but this lens-vision of "self" will affect favorably or unfavorably the way we see everything else. Depending on what we are dealing with, our various attitudes are always ready to interpret, evaluate, and dictate an appropriate response. However, it is important to realize that the attitude toward self is *always* in play, always affecting our other attitudes, always coloring the way we see every part of reality. It is, without a doubt, the basic or fundamental attitude in each and every one of us.

Perhaps the most critical function and result of this attitude toward self is this: Each of us acts out his or her self-image. For example, if I perceive myself as a loser, I act like a loser. I approach each new person or situation with a loser mentality. All my expectations are colored by this "loser" perception of myself. And, as we all know, the expectation is often the mother of the result. Our expectations of failure give birth to our actual failures. And when in fact we do lose or fail, we are then confirmed in our original self-defeating attitude. "You see, I told you I was no good! I failed again." It is indeed a vicious circle.

From *The Christian Vision*

*S*ome years ago, a psychologist named Carl Rogers offered a revolutionizing thought to counselors. He said that everybody really has the same problem. We do, however, have different symptoms. Whatever the symptoms are, the real problem is always the same, according to Rogers. We do not understand, accept and love ourselves. This problem may squirt out in one symptom or another, but the problem remains radically the same. We do not offer ourselves understanding, acceptance and love. And so Rogers suggests that instead of focusing on the symptom, we must simply accept people wherever they are. What we have to be saying to others in our lives is this: "I accept you. I understand you. I care about you." If we can extend acceptance like this to one another, we will all individually grow in self-understanding and self-acceptance.

Think about your husbands and wives, your children, your parents, your friends. In a sense, we hold the destiny of those we love in our hands. If we accept and love them, they will be empowered to accept and love themselves. We are like a mirror standing in front of them, saying: "Look! You're beautiful. You're really okay. Of course, you have problems, and I'm not denying that. What I'm trying to say is that you are okay. I accept you wherever you are. I care about you." According to the Rogerian concept, when people are empowered by others to understand, accept and love themselves: the symptomatic problems (whatever they are) will miraculously disappear! This is not something to be debated. It has to be put to work in our lives.

From the audio program, *My Vision And My Values*

*O*nce a wise old teacher was speaking to a group of young and eager students. He gave them the assignment to go out and find by the side of some lonely road a small, unnoticed flower. He asked them to study the flower for a long time. "Get a magnifying glass and study the delicate veins in the leaves, and notice the nuances and shades of color. Turn the leaf slowly and observe its symmetry. And remember: this flower might have gone unnoticed and unappreciated if you had not found and admired it." When the class returned, after carrying out the assignment, the wise old teacher observed: "People are like that. Each one is different, carefully crafted, uniquely endowed. But . . . you have to spend time with them to know this. So many people go unnoticed and unappreciated because no one has ever taken time with them and admired their uniqueness." In a true sense, each one of us is a unique masterpiece of God.

From *The Christian Vision*

*F*or a long time it seemed to me that there was some opposition between love of self and the Christian virtue of humility. My former understanding of humility required a person to deny resolutely anything good about self, and to focus all one's conscious attention on personal faults and failings. I sensed, even while doing this, that it was a course of psychological self-destruction.

So I was delighted to find that one of the Fathers of the Church, St. Ambrose, Bishop of Milan in the late fourth century, had a very different idea of humility. He proposed that the "perfect expression of humility" is found in the Magnificat of Mary, the mother of Jesus.

According to the Gospels, the setting was this: Mary's cousin, Elizabeth, was about to give birth (to John the Baptist). It was a Jewish custom that all women relatives should come to such an expectant mother, at the time of her delivery, to offer their help. I suspect that besides wanting to help, Mary was also anxious to share the secret of her womb with her cousin. At any rate, shortly after the announcement of the angel to her, Mary sets off on the seventy-five-mile journey from Nazareth to Ain Karim, a southwestern suburb of Jerusalem. When Mary arrives, Elizabeth is surprised: "Why should such an honor come to me, that the mother of my Lord should come to visit me?" Mary, we might well imagine, falls into the warm embrace of her cousin and explains:

> "My soul magnifies the Lord, and my spirit rejoices in God, my Savior. For he has smiled upon me, his little servant girl, and now all generations will call me 'blessed' because he, the mighty and holy one, has done such great things in me. Holy is his name." (Luke 1:46–49)

From *The Christian Vision*

*I*t is a fact that we cannot love others if we do not love ourselves. The commandment of the Lord is to love our neighbors as we love ourselves. A psychological version of this commandment might well read: "Love yourself and you will love your neighbor. Refuse to love yourself and you won't be able to love your neighbor." The Jesus I know insistently tells us to put away our pan scales, to stop measuring output versus input, to make love the rule and motive of our lives. "Love one another as I have loved you." Further, Jesus assures us, "If you do this, you will be very happy." (See John 13:17.) However, it is crucial to realize that our attitude toward self regulates our active capacity for loving others. The hard fact is that only to the extent that we love ourselves can we truly love others, God included.

If our attitude toward self is crippling, our capacity to love is proportionately diminished. The pain of a poor self-image is like the noisy strife of a civil war inside us. It magnetizes all our attention to ourselves and leaves us little freedom to go out to others. When we are hurting, even from a simple thing like a toothache, we have only a diminished availability for others. If our attitude toward self leaves us with an ache of emptiness, we have no strength or desire to go out to others. However, as our attitude toward self grows more positive and supportive, our pain is proportionately reduced and we are to that extent more free to read and respond to the needs of others around us. In short, the better the self-image, the larger the capacity for loving. On the contrary, the greater the distraction of pain, the smaller will be our capacity to love and care about others.

From *The Christian Vision*

*W*hen I was young and very zeal-
ous, I once told an older and wiser man that I was going to spend all
my life and all my energies loving others. He gently asked me if I was
going to love myself with equal determination. I protested that loving
others would leave no time for loving myself. It sounded very saintly.
However, my older and wiser friend looked at me long and pensively.
Finally he said, "You are on a suicide course." My facile reply was:
"What a nice way to go, eh?" But of course, he was right. I now know
what he knew all the time: true love of others is premised on a true
love of oneself.

To understand what it means to love oneself, let us first ask what it
means to love another. Love does at least three things:

1. Love esteems and affirms the unconditional and unique value of
   the one loved.
2. Love acknowledges and tries to fulfill the needs of the one loved.
3. Love forgives and forgets the failings of the one loved.

When we are asked to "love our neighbor as ourselves," the clear
implication is that whatever we would do for our neighbor we would
also and first do for ourselves. In other words, it's a package deal.
You have two people you must love: yourself and your neighbor. You
can't really love one without loving the other.

From *The Secret Of Staying In Love*

*S*omehow imagine yourself as another person, whom you most truly love. Stand off at a distance, and ask yourself: Have you really tried to see and affirm your unconditional and unique value? Do you really try to consider and fulfill your needs? Have you really forgiven yourself for your faults and mistakes? Think about it. Do you think of yourself as gently and lovingly as you do those others in your life whom you love most? Do you offer yourself the same kind of warmth and understanding as you offer them?

Let us say that someone else asks you a favor. Now love asks you to try to fulfill your friend's need, but there is also someone else that you must consider with equal attention: yourself. Let us look at your needs. One of your primary needs is to go out in love to others. The only way to be loved is to be loving. The only truly happy people are those who have found someone, some cause to love and belong to. However, you may have other needs to be considered. You may need rest, or you may have another pressing duty. It may be that, all things considered, you will have to refuse your friend's request.

What I am describing is not self-preoccupation or narcissism. It is simply a description of a balanced love, extended with the same concern to self and to neighbor. The balance can shift, so that we give all our concern only to self or attempt to give all our concern only to our neighbor. But neither of these attitudes is humanly viable. Neither is true love.

From *The Secret Of Staying In Love*

*T*here is a growing consensus of opinion that there is one need so fundamental and so essential that if it is met, everything else will almost certainly harmonize in a general sense of well-being. When this need is properly nourished, the whole human organism will be healthy and the person will be happy. This need is a *true and deep love of self, a genuine and joyful self-acceptance, an authentic self-esteem*, which result in *an interior sense of celebration:* "It's good to be me . . . I am very happy to be me!"

Did something in you become immediately uncomfortable and uneasy when you read the previous statement? Conditioned as we are by our culture, we seem to be emotionally allergic to the very vocabulary of love of self. The thought of rejoicing in and celebrating our own unique goodness seems like a very distant and alien thought. Immediate associations of egotism, vanity and selfishness rush like dark clouds into our minds. I suspect that most of us never get through the crust of this difficult vocabulary and these suspicions to find the most important reality of any human life and the beginning of all human love.

From *The Secret Of Staying In Love*

*R*ather than expose a self which we imagine to be inadequate or ugly, we instinctively build walls, contrary to Robert Frost's advice: Do not build a wall until you know what you are walling in and what you are walling out. To the extent that we experience scars of anxiety, guilt, and inferiority feelings, we are tempted to wear masks, to act out roles. We do not trust or accept ourselves. These walls and masks are measures of self-defense, and we will live behind our walls and wear our masks as long as they are needed.

While it may seem to be a safer life behind these facades, it is also a lonely life. We cease to be authentic, and as persons we starve to death. The deepest sadness of the mask is, however, that we have cut ourselves off from all genuine and authentic contact with the real world and with other human beings who hold our potential maturity and fulfillment in their hands. When we resort to acting out roles or wearing masks, there is no possibility of human or personal growth. We are simply not being ourselves, and so we cannot emerge as we should in an atmosphere of growth. We are merely performing on a stage. When the curtain drops after our performance, we will remain the same immature person that we were when the curtain went up at the beginning of the act.

From *Why Am I Afraid To Love?*

*E*ach of us is a unique and individual person. We sometimes facetiously remark to others: "After God made you, he broke the mold." In fact, each of us is fashioned in a unique mold. There never has been and never will be anyone exactly like you or me. However, at the beginning of life this person is, as it were, like the bud of a flower or plant: closed. Only when the bud of the flower receives warmth from the sun and nourishment from the mothering soil will it open and expose all of the beauty that is latent within it. So, too, the human person at the beginning of life must receive the warmth of human love, assurance and the nourishment of parental affection if it is to open and expose the unique beauty that God has placed within every individual.

We know that if the bud of a flower is injured by hostile forces, like an unseasonal frost, it will not open. So, too, a human person who is without the warmth and encouragement of love, and who must endure the chilling absence of praise and affection, will remain closed in on self. The dynamics of personality will be jammed. And, if the dynamics of personality are seriously impeded, the result will be what psychologists call *neurosis*. Although there are many valid descriptions of neurosis, neuroses are commonly recognized in the form of a crippling inability to relate well to others, to go out to them and to accept them as they are without fear of rejection.

From *Why Am I Afraid To Love?*

*D*o you really love yourself? Could I ask you to make a little test with yourself? It has to be done in the bathroom tonight. Be sure to lock the door. Any witnesses will certainly wonder. Go to the mirror and say, "Hey, I love you!" Now that is not the test. I presume that you will do that. The test is: How did you feel when you did that? Can you say those words and really mean them? Or would you rather feel that such an act of loving one's self is silly and ridiculous? Carl Jung, the great psychiatrist, once reflected that we are all familiar with the words of Jesus, "Whatever you do to the least of my brethren, you do unto me." Then Jung asks a very probing question: "What if you discovered that the least of the brethren of Jesus, the one who needs your love the most, the one that you can help the most by loving, the one to whom your love will be most meaningful--what if you discovered that this least of the brethren of Jesus . . . is you?"

From the video program, *Free To Be Me*

*P*eople who go to professionals for help usually go because their negative emotional patterns have become too painful or because their world seems to be falling apart. The first problem encountered in helping such people is the period of disintegration or disorientation experienced in stepping from the old into the new. It is a limbo of uncertainty and chaos. Still, pain is very persuasive. Individuals who have had enough struggling, depression, constant anxiety or smoldering hostility may have hit bottom and be ready to rebound. They may be ready to make the effort, to take risks of thinking and acting in new ways. However, some people have "low bottoms" and have to fall apart pretty badly before they are willing to put pieces together in a new and different pattern. Other people have "high bottoms" and are ready for change. They sense that the course they are on will lead only to a sad nowhere. They are ready for reevaluation, for a new vision.

Then there are the children of the beatitude: Blessed are those who hunger after life in all its fullness! They have no appetite or willingness to settle for mediocrity in any form. These are the pioneer people who write new songs, study new theories, and build better mousetraps. They can be found in offices, schools, factories, or supermarkets, but there is always something of the mountain climber in their blood. They say an expansive "Yes!" to life and "Amen!" to love. They are ready to reexamine their belief systems. They are ready for vision therapy and anything else that promises growth. For them to stop growing is to stop living. And when you're through growing, you're through!

From *Fully Human, Fully Alive*

*T*oday's experiences are tomorrow's memories. I think that the most important memory that children carry out of family life is the memory of their parents loving each other. The only people I know who don't believe in love as a permanent thing, as a reliable thing, are people who have never experienced or observed it.

I often go to the gravesides of my grandparents and my parents and I look at those names. I'm named John Powell after my grandfather. I look at "John Powell and Mary Ellen Hardin Powell," and at "Jennie and William Powell." I look at those names and want to say, "Oh, you are not dead. You are not dead because you are surely with God in heaven. I know that. I know you are living, that life was not ended with death but only changed. But I want to tell you something else: you are very much alive in me. All those stories you told me, all those times you shared with me, all the times you held me on your lap—I remember them all. They are alive in me. And I want to thank you. Thank you for so many beautiful memories."

From the video program, *Families*

W hen the encounter and relationship of true love are missing in a human life, it is usually because the person has either selfishly or timidly kept the doors of his or her heart locked and barricaded. Such persons are either unable or unwilling to risk transparency, to expose the most sensitive areas of their souls to another. Without such willingness to risk, human life can be only a prolonged pain of starvation and the whole world only a bleak prison. Answering the call to love demands much courage and determination because self-exposure always involves a risk of being seriously hurt. But without transparency love is impossible, and without love, human life is seriously incomplete.

Those who are willing to love will eventually find love. And then the mirror will be there, the mirror reflecting back the image of a loving person, and this is the beginning of true self-esteem and self-celebration. This is why Viktor Frankl says that the origin of true self-esteem is in "the reflected appraisal of those whom we have loved."

If love is anything it is a gradual process, the long round curve that must be carefully negotiated, not the sharp right angle turn that is made in an instant, once and for all. A man or woman must set out upon a long journey and walk many miles to find the joys of love. They will have to pass through deep and dark forests and there will be many dangers. They will have to be careful of love as they are of few other things. Love will demand abstinence from all that might prove poisonous to love. Love will demand much courage, perseverance and self-discipline.

But the journey to love is the journey to the fullness of life, for it is only in the experience of love that human beings can know themselves, can love what they are and will become, and find the fullness of life which is the glory of God.

From *The Secret Of Staying In Love*

*T*he fully human person preserves a balance between "interiority" and "exteriority." Both the extreme introvert and the extreme extrovert are off balance. Such introverts are almost exclusively concerned with themselves. They become the center of gravity in their own private universes. Because of their preoccupation with themselves, they are distracted from the vast world outside themselves. The extreme extroverts, on the other hand, pour themselves out, move from one external distraction to another. Their lives are not at all reflective, and consequently there is little interior deepening. As Socrates once said, "The unreflected life isn't worth living." The first condition of human growth is balance.

Balanced "interiority" and "exteriority" is what is meant by integration of personality. We are all of us capable of exaggeration; we can turn too much inward or outward. We can become slaves to our sense pleasures without reflection on our peace of soul or upon our social need to love and give love to others. Or we can exaggerate by becoming prisoners of "intellect," alive only from the neck up.

When we live fully in all our faculties, and harmonize all our powers, human nature will prove constructive and trustworthy.

From *Why Am I Afraid To Tell You Who I Am?*

*I*nteriority" implies that a person has explored self and has experienced the various parts and powers of self. Such persons are aware of the vitality of their senses, emotions, minds and wills. They are neither strangers to, nor afraid of, the activities of their bodies and emotions. Their senses bring them both beauty and pain; and they refuse neither. They are capable of the whole gamut of human emotions: from grief to tenderness. Their minds are alive and searching; their wills reach out for an ever greater possession of all that is good, and at the same time savor all that is already in their possession. They have listened to themselves, and they know that nothing that they hear is evil or frightening.

From *Why Am I Afraid To Tell You Who I Am?*

*H*uman "interiority" implies radical self-acceptance. The desired interiority means that fully functioning, self-actualizing and fully human people are not only aware of their physical, psychological and spiritual hungers and activities, but they accept them as good. They are "at home" with their bodies. They accept their tender as well as their hostile emotions. They do not always understand fully but they do accept fully their impulses, thoughts and desires. Not only are they "at home" with what they have already experienced in themselves, but they are also open to new sensations, new and even deeper emotional reactions, changing thoughts and desires. They accept their inner condition as forever changing. Growth demands change. Their ultimate destiny as human beings, that is, what they will become at the end of life, is delightfully unknown. No human growth patterns can be prestructured for all. So fully alive people don't ambition to turn out like anyone else. They are themselves. Their potential selves, newly actualized every day by new experiences, cannot possibly be defined at any one stage of growth. Their potential is constantly being explored.

Fully human people accept what they are, physically, emotionally and intellectually. They know what they are, and they know that this is good. They know that their potential self is even greater. They are, however, realistic about their limitations. They do not dwell in dreams of what they want to be and spend the rest of life convincing themselves that they are these things. They have listened to, explored and loved what they actually are. They trust their own ability to cope with all the challenges that life will present.

From *Why Am I Afraid To Tell You Who I Am?*

*E*xteriority" implies that we are open not only to ourselves within but also to our environment outside us. Fully human people are in a deep and meaningful contact with the world outside them. They not only listen to themselves, but also to the voices of their world. The breadth of their own individual experiences is infinitely multiplied through a sensitive empathy with others. They suffer with the suffering, rejoice with the joyful. They are born again in every springtime. They feel the impact of the great mysteries of life: birth, growth, love, suffering, death. Their hearts skip along with the "young lovers," and they know something of the exhilaration that is in those young who are "in love." They also know the ghetto's philosophy of despair, the loneliness of suffering without relief. The bell never tolls without tolling in some strange way for them.

"Create in me, O God," the Psalmist prays, "a listening heart."

The opposite of this openness implied in "exteriority" is a kind of "defensiveness," which hears only what it wants to hear. It sees only what it wants to see. Defensive persons cannot be growing persons because their world is no bigger than themselves, and the circle of their horizons is closed forever.

From *Why Am I Afraid To Tell You Who I Am?*

*W*e speak of people as being mature or immature, but the fact is that all of human life should represent an evercontinuing growth towards full maturity. What we have called the dynamics of human personality are very much involved in this process of self-revelation and of self-expansion. Consequently, all the signs of immaturity are somehow characterized by convergence upon self. This self-centeredness betrays itself in many ways; bearing grudges and prejudices, pouting, emotionalized thinking, exaggerated feelings of inferiority, overconcern about the opinions others have of us, worrying, overdependence upon parents or family, rebellious or angry attitudes, bragging or bullying, temper tantrums, the negativism of destructive criticism, procrastination, self-indulgence, "slapstick" humor which is humiliating to another, flirtations, and so forth.

The patterns of maturity are recognized in the ability to go out to others, to get along with them, to exercise a reasonable self-sufficiency, to set realistic goals, to exercise discretion, to differentiate the important and unimportant things in life, flexibility, adaptability, and emotional stability.

From *Why Am I Afraid To Love?*

*T*here is an old Irish ditty: "To live above with the saints we love, ah, that is the purest glory. But to live below with the saints we know, ah, that is another story." In reflecting on how we see other people, I am reminded of a time in my life right after ordination. The oils of ordination were still wet upon my hands when I was asked to give a priests' retreat. Having a lot of mileage on my mouth already, I accepted. However, when I got there and saw my retreatants filing into the chapel for the first conference, I was shocked by a sudden realization. I was going to be the youngest man in that chapel by at least fifteen years. And I was going to be preaching to these considerably older men for a whole week. I saw some of them coming in with stately "Milwaukee tumors," bound in red cummerbunds. I swore that I heard the strains of "Pomp and Circumstance." There were two bishops, also, and this added to my considerable terror. I was standing there watching them enter the chapel with the monsignor who directed the retreat house. With a friendly smile, the monsignor asked, "How do you feel?" I replied, "Scared!" "Scared? Why?" the monsignor asked. And I asked him, "Didn't you see them?" The monsignor then came over to me, put a paternal arm around my shoulder and said, "They just need what everybody else needs: a little love and understanding." And I remember asking him, "Why don't they look like it?" Is this what people really need—a little love and understanding? Of course they do, but you and I often wonder, "Why don't they look like it?"

From the video program, *Free To Be Me*

*A*ll of us to some extent are enduring agonies of loneliness, frustration, emotional and spiritual starvation. Somehow these pains are radically due to failures in love. The essential sadness of such pain is that it magnetizes the focus of our attention; it preoccupies us with ourselves. And self-preoccupation is an absolute obstacle to a life of love.

I once asked a psychiatrist friend of mine, "How can you teach people to love?" His answer was mildly surprising, to say the least. He answered the question by asking one of his own: "Did you ever have a toothache? Of whom were you thinking during the distress of your toothache?" His point was clear. When we are in pain, even if it be only the passing discomforts of an aching tooth, we are thinking about ourselves.

The psychiatrist continued: "This is a pain-filled world in which we are living. And the pains that reside deep in the human hearts around us are not like toothaches. We go to bed with them at night and wake up with them in the morning. This is a pain-filled world, and so, a loveless world that we live in. Most human beings are so turned-in on themselves by their own pain that they cannot easily go out in love to others."

From *Why Am I Afraid To Love?*

*A*lthough it is difficult to accept, the psychological scars that we have acquired during our first seven years remain in some way with us for life. No very deep psychological problems originate after this age, although these scars and scar tissue may be aggravated or inflamed by circumstances occurring later in our lives. The rather common prejudice is that we are personally the masters of our fates and the captains of our souls; the truth of the matter is that we are very largely shaped by others, who, in an almost frightening way, hold our destiny in their hands. We are, each of us, the product of those who have loved us . . . or refused to love us.

From *Why Am I Afraid To Love?*

*W*hatever else can and should be said of love, it is quite evident that true love demands self-forgetfulness. If there are many people who use the word and claim the reality without knowing the meaning of the word or being able to love to any great extent, this is the test: *Can we really forget ourselves?* There are many counterfeit products on the market which are called love, but which are in fact, falsely named. We can sometimes label the gratification of our needs "love"; we can even do things for others without really loving. The acid test is always the probing question of self-forgetfulness.

Can we really locate the focus of our minds on the happiness and fulfillment of others? Can we really ask not what others will do for us, but what we can do for them? If we really want to love, then we must ask ourselves these questions.

From *Why Am I Afraid To Love?*

*T*here is a strong human temptation to judge people in terms of their acts or masks. It is all too rare that we are able to see through the sham and pretense which mask the insecure or wounded heart that is being camouflaged and protected from further injury. Consequently, we lash out with the iron fists of criticism and sarcasm or we try to tear off the masks of our fellow human beings in ferocious anger. We fail to realize that the masks are worn only as long as they are needed. Only the reassurance of an accepting and understanding love will lure the anxious, the guilt-ridden and the supposedly inferior persons out from behind their defenses. It may well be that we ourselves are hiding behind such masks and walls, resulting in very little human encounter and communication . . . only mask facing mask, wall facing wall.

Generally, we can recognize masks. We have a sense that our brother or sister is not authentic, that they are pretentious, and we call them a sham. We do not realize that in the unexposed roots of these exteriors, there is only a cry of pain and the need to be understood and loved into life. Most of the obnoxious qualities that we find in others are the result of some kind of defensive convergence on self, and we openly resent this self-centered posture. It is then that we must remember the psychiatrist's question: "Did you ever have a toothache?" We must learn to look through the sham and pretense of our fellow human beings. We must try to alleviate the pain and lonely voids that have constructed these defense walls. Direct attacks on these defenses will only produce their reinforcement.

From *Why Am I Afraid To Love?*

*T*he surest way to find God is to go out to others: to love them, to accept them wherever they are, to care for them, to be patient with them. God is found both by the person who loves and by the person who is loved.

The thing that keeps us from going out to and loving others in this caring way is a four letter word: pain. Psychological pain, doubts, anxieties, fears. These are the tyrants that imprison us. All obnoxious qualities in us human beings are really cries of pain and calls for help. The liar, the braggart, the deceiver, the arrogant and the self-centered: All these are only poses designed to stifle and conceal the ache inside the hearts of those who cannot love themselves.

If we really believed this, we would no longer see these people as obnoxious. We would see them as hurting. We would see people in need of our love. We would see people who need us to accept them, to clothe them with self-respect, to believe in them. Please think about the people in your life, people who are hurting, people who are not very loving because they just hurt too much inside. They are in fact waiting for a miracle: someone to love them and call them back from the dead.

From the audio program, *My Vision And My Values*

*A*lmost any other apologetic for the Christian faith can be memorized, rehearsed, and delivered without effect except the apologetic of love. Love, which of its essence seeks only the good of others and is willing to pay the high price of self-forgetfulness, is a product which is hard to imitate or counterfeit.

To love, one must have enormous motivation. In a grasping world, in a world which is gouging and clawing for the riches of this world, Christians by their commitment to loving should stand out as breathtaking exceptions. True Christians must seek only the good, the fulfillment and the destiny of their fellow human beings. Love will always be their most eloquent argument and effective means. It is difficult. And yet the Lord Jesus of the Gospels stands with us, and gives us our Christian imperative: "By this shall others know that you are my disciples, that you love one another."

The poet, Archibald MacLeish, has said that we are affected more by symbols than by ideas. The symbol of loneliness, he says, is two lights above the sea; the symbol of grief is a solitary figure standing in a doorway. The symbol of Christ in this world is the Christian. Over the altars of our churches there hangs a large crucifix. Under the crucifix there is the unwritten caption: "Greater love than this no man has . . . love one another as I have loved you." It is a constant reminder of our vocation as witnesses to Christ.

From *Why Am I Afraid To Love?*

*T*he heart of the matter and the crux of the problem is this: Do we get fulfilled by trying to have all the experiences we can? Is it true that the more experiences a person has, the more developed and fulfilled he or she will be as a person? Or is the contrary true, that a person is fulfilled by making a commitment and then choosing experiences according to whether they honor, promote, and reaffirm the commitment?

Making a commitment to permanent, unconditional love will mean for me that certain experiences, which might otherwise have been mine, are now impossible for me. The man who chooses one woman for his wife and life partner by his very choice has eliminated all other women as possible wives and life partners. It is this very elimination that frightens us on the brink of commitment. Every commitment is like every moment of life: there is a birth and a death in every moment. Something is and something else can never be again. There is a choice and a surrender, a "yes" and a "no." To love is indeed costly. To love unconditionally is a life wager. In love we put ourselves on the line and there is no going back. It is at this brink that so many seem to collapse. Within arms' reach of greatness, they faint at the thought of never returning. It is the less-traveled road.

From *Unconditional Love*

*C*hrist our Lord left no doubt about the credential of the Christian. He said, "By this shall others know that you are my disciples, that you love one another . . . love one another as I have loved you . . . this is all I command you that you love one another." St. John reminds us in his First Epistle that it is impossible to love God whom we do not see and not love those around us whom we do see.

All of these things we have read, but perhaps we pay them more lip service than life service. We know that Christ takes as done to himself what we do to others; he accepts as given to himself our concern and kindness for others. In daily battle, however, when our own needs are so throbbing and painful, we forget.

The only attitude worthy of a Christian is that of Christ, who thought of others always, who gave of himself until he had not another drop of blood to give. In his own words, "Greater love than this no one has than that he lay down his life for his friend." This is, of course, what love asks of us, that we lay down our lives for others. Only when we have consented to do this will we find ourselves, our own happiness and fulfillment, and only then will we be true Christians. If we fail to do this, perhaps there will be some justification in the question that the agnostic philosopher, Nietzsche, once asked: "If Christians wish us to believe in their Redeemer, why don't they look a little more redeemed?" It was the same Nietzsche who coined the phrase, so sadly common in our own days: "God is dead."

From *Why Am I Afraid To Love?*

*M*eeting God in other humans is the most costly part of the dialogue between God and us. Our nature requires that we somehow contact God in a bodily or sensibly perceptible way. In the Old Testament God came to us as thunder and lightning over Sinai; his voice emerged from a burning bush. In the New Testament God's goodness to us is even more astonishing. He becomes a man and is raised in agony on a cross for you and me. "This is what I mean when I say I love you." In the Incarnation God brought his gifts to us in the earthen vessel of humanity that he might speak our language and we might know what he is really like.

Just as God expected us to find him under the veil of humanity, even when that humanity was a red mask of blood and agony, so now he expects us to find him under other human veils. It will, indeed, cost us a great deal if we take God seriously on this point:

> . . . For I was hungry, and you gave me to eat; I was thirsty and you gave me to drink; I was a stranger and you took me into your home; I was naked and you covered me; I was sick and you visited me; I was in prison and you came to see me.

> . . . And in explanation the King will say to them: "I will tell you the plain truth, whatever you did to the least of my children you did to me!"   (Matthew 25:35–36, 40)

From *Why Am I Afraid To Love?*

I remember it well. When I was a little boy, my own family had to scrape to get along. But the family next door was "very well off." The little boy in that family was my age, and his daddy had bought him a toy car. It was a real "beauty." It had pedals but you could push it. It must have been worth at least fifty dollars! Bobby and I had a great time with it. We would whiz up and down the street, as fast as our little legs could carry us. It was altogether a magnificent car and a magnificent time of life. Then one day Bobby broke the bad news to me. He was going to give our beautiful car away: to the children at the orphanage. "Why?" I asked, "Is it busted or something?" "No," he replied calmly but confidently, "I wouldn't give it to them if it was busted." So I scratched my head and asked, "Then why are you giving it to them?" Bobby explained, "Well you know, those kids up at the home . . . they don't have mothers or fathers the way we do." So I suggested, "So why are you giving them our car? Why don't you give them a mother or a father?"

Bobby and I took turns pushing each other on our way to the orphanage. Just before we got there, I asked one last time: "Bobby, are you sure you want to do this?" Bobby explained that his Mom and Dad had only asked him to think about it. They left the final decision to him, and it was his decision we carried out. It was a sad day, but I have been glad ever since for that lesson: Values are caught, not taught. I learned something that day about the value of love, of giving to someone else less fortunate, of asking myself the most important of all questions: "What is the loving thing to do?" I learned a lot that day about love.

From the video program, *Families*

*O*ur call to the Kingdom, which each of us must face, is this: I cannot say my "yes" of love to God without saying my "yes" of love to you. Neither can you say your "yes" to him without including me in your act of love. Jesus is very clear about this. If we come to place our gift of love upon his altar, and while there we remember that we are nursing a grudge of unforgiveness, we must turn back. We have to make peace with each other first. Only then can we come to him with a gift of self, the "yes" of love. He does not want my gift of love unless it is also offered to you. He does not want your gift of love unless you have shared that gift with me.

> I have told you this so that my joy may be in you and that your joy may be complete. My commandment is this: love one another, just as I love you . . . . This, then, is what I command you: love one another.   (John 15:11–12, 17; GNB)

In the Kingdom of God I am never less than an individual, but I am never only an individual. I am always a member of a group, called by God to a response of love, which must include the whole group or it is literally unacceptable to God.

The Church is indeed God's family, and the Lord who calls us to a response of love takes as done to himself whatever we do to one another. "Whatever you do to the least of my children you do to me." There can be no relationship of love with God unless we relate to one another in love. Sometimes this seems to be the highest cost of being a Christian. It is so much easier to love the God I don't see than the neighbor I do see.

From *The Christian Vision*

*T*here is a story about the Evangelist St. John, the one who wrote, "God is love . . . , if any man tells me that he loves God whom he does not see, but does not love his brother whom he does see, he is simply a liar." It is of this John that the story is told that in the evening of his long life, he would sit for hours with his younger disciples gathered at his feet. One day, as it is related in this well established tradition, one of his disciples complained, "John, you always talk about love, about God's love for us and about our love for one another. Why don't you tell us about something else besides love?" The disciple who once, as a youth, had laid his head over the heart of God made man, is said to have replied, "Because there is nothing else, just love . . . love . . . love."

Love is the only way to our human destiny and to the feet of God, who is love.

From *Why Am I Afraid To Love?*

*C*onsider the following conversation:

Author: I am writing a booklet, to be called, *Why Am I Afraid To Tell You Who I Am?*

Other: Do you want an answer to your question?

Author: That is the purpose of the booklet, to answer the question.

Other: But do you want *my* answer?

Author: Yes, of course I do.

Other: I am afraid to tell you who I am because, if I tell you who I am, you may not like who I am, and it's all I have.

This short excerpt was taken from an actual conversation, unrehearsed and from life as it really is. It reflects something of the imprisoning fears and self-doubt which cripple most of us and keep us from forward movement on the road to maturity, happiness and true love.

From *Why Am I Afraid To Tell You Who I Am?*

*M*ost of us play games with others in our habitual behavior. We set up others to react to us in the way that we want them to react. For example, we may not ever grow into authentic persons because we have settled for being children, inadequate and in need. We send out our "pity signals" in the sound of our voices and in the expressions on our faces. We condition others to react very gently to us. We sound and look as helpless as any child; most people are obliging enough to follow our stage directions.

Others of us, who are messianic in our assumed role, insist on wanting to save others at all times. We want to be "the helper" and to make everyone else to whom we relate "the helped." Sometimes the perpetual child marries the messiah, and they make a lifelong game of it together. Since these two games mesh, things will go very well, and neither of them will ever have to grow up.

If only our fears and insecurity, which prompt us to assume various ego states and play various ego games, would allow us to be in honest touch with our emotions and able to report them honestly, the patterns of "pity signals" or "messianic mystique" would emerge and become obvious to us.

The perpetual child would find that he or she never relates well to others except when bringing problems or helplessness to them; the self-styled savior would discover that he or she never relates well to others unless the other is troubled and helpless . . . and needy. Being honest with one's self in this way is no easy matter, because it involves letting one's repressed emotions rise to recognition for what they really are; it demands reporting these emotions to others.

From *Why Am I Afraid To Tell You Who I Am?*

*G*ames" in this context are not really fun. They are the patterned reactions to life-situations, programed for us somewhere back in our personal, psychological history. Sometimes these games are extremely grim affairs, because everyone is playing to win . . . to win something. In order to achieve the honest communication of ourself to others, to experience the reality of others, to become integrated and to grow, it helps very much to be aware of our patterned reactions—the games we play. If we become aware of these games, we may give them up.

These games are almost always little maneuvers on our part, which we employ to avoid self-realization and self-communication. They are little shields which we carry in front of us as we enter the battle of life; they are designed to protect us from being hurt and help us to win some little trophy for our egos. Eric Berne calls these little gains "strokes," little victories or successes that bring us protection or recognition. The games are various because psychological histories and programing are always unique, and because there is a variety of ego states in which we may choose to cast ourselves, depending on the needs of the moment and the life-situation.

The one thing that all these games have in common is this: They defeat self-knowledge and destroy all possibility of honest self-communication with others. The price of victory is costly; there is little chance for such a person to experience true interpersonal encounters, which alone can put him or her on the path to human growth and the fullness of human life.

From *Why Am I Afraid To Tell You Who I Am?*

*I*f I really want to "see it like it is. . . and tell it like it is," I must ask myself some difficult questions about the patterns of action and reaction that emerge in my conduct, and I must ask myself what these patterns reveal to me about myself.

What you and I really need is a moment of truth and a habit of truth with ourselves. We have to ask ourselves in the quiet, personal privacy of our own minds and hearts: What games do I play? What is it that I'm trying to hide? What is it that I hope to win?

My willingness to be honest with myself and these questions will be the decisive factor and the essential condition for my growth as a person.

From *Why Am I Afraid To Tell You Who I Am?*

*T*here is a persistent, if uninformed, suspicion in most of us that we can solve our own problems and be the masters of our own ships of life, but the fact of the matter is that by ourselves we can only be consumed by our problems and suffer shipwreck. What I am, at any given moment in the process of my becoming a person, will be determined by my relationships with those who love me or refuse to love me, with those whom I love or refuse to love.

It is certain that a relationship will be *only as good as its communication.* If you and I can honestly tell each other who we are, that is, what we think, judge, feel, value, love, honor and esteem, hate, fear, despise, hope for, believe in and are committed to, then and then only can each of us be what we really are, say what we really think, tell what we really feel, express what we really love. This is the real meaning of authenticity as a person, that my exterior truly reflects my interior. It means I can be honest in the communication of my person to others. And this I cannot do unless you help me. Unless you help me, I cannot grow, or be happy, or really come alive.

I have to be free and able to say my thoughts to you, to tell you about my judgments and values, to expose to you my fears and frustrations, to admit to you my failures and shames, to share my triumphs, before I can really be sure who it is that I am and can become. I must be able to tell you who I am before I can know who I am. And I must know who I am before I can act truly, that is, in accordance with my true self.

From *Why Am I Afraid To Tell You Who I Am?*

*I*f I can communicate with you and you with me only on a "subject-object" level, we will probably both communicate with others, and even with God himself, on this same level. We will remain isolated subjects; others and God will remain merely "objects" in our world, but not experiences. Unless a person has been opened up by a true encounter, he or she will have so-called friendships, and will perhaps retain a so-called religious faith (a kind of relationship with God), mostly because these are the things that are somehow expected. These relationships with others will be social amenities and nothing more. There will be no personal meaning in them.

The world of such a person is a world of objects, things to be manipulated, to serve as distractions and sources of pleasure. The possessions of such a person may be beautiful and expensive or they may be common and cheap, but the person will be lonely. He or she will come to the end of life without ever having lived. The dynamic process of personhood will become a static thing like debris floating on stagnant waters. When the process of personhood is stifled, all of life becomes a terrible bore. If the edges of life for a given person are sharp, life can be very painful. There will be a need for those artificially induced but short-lived stimuli called "kicks." These kicks are little attempts to run away from life, short "trips," in an effort to escape the inexorable intrusion of reality and the essential loneliness of the person without true friends.

From *Why Am I Afraid To Tell You Who I Am?*

*I*f friendship and human love are to mature between any two persons, there must be absolute and honest mutual revelation; this kind of self-revelation can be achieved only through what we have called "gut-level" communication. There is no other way, and all the reasons we adduce to rationalize our cover-ups and dishonesty must be seen as delusion. It would be much better for me to tell you about how I really feel about you than to enter into the stickiness and discomfort of a phony relationship.

Dishonesty always has a way of coming back to haunt and trouble us. Even if I should have to tell you that I do not admire or love you emotionally, it would be much better than trying to deceive you and having to pay the ultimate price of all such deception, your greater hurt and mine. And you will have to tell me things, at times, that will be difficult for you to share. But really you have no choice, and, if I want your friendship, I must be ready to accept you as you are. If either of us comes to the relationship without this determination of mutual honesty and openness, there can be no friendship, no growth; rather there can be only a subject-object kind of thing that is typified by adolescent bickering, pouting, jealousy, anger and accusations.

From *Why Am I Afraid To Tell You Who I Am?*

*I*n spite of our unwillingness and reluctance to tell others who we are, there is in each one of us a deep and driving desire to be understood. It is clear to all of us that we want very badly to be loved, but, when we are not understood by those whose love we need and want, any sort of deep communication becomes a nervous and uncomforting thing. It does not enlarge and enliven us. It becomes clear that no one can really love us effectively unless he or she really understands us. Anyone who feels understood, however, will certainly feel loved.

If there is no one who understands me, and who accepts me for what I am, I will feel "estranged." My talents and possessions will not comfort me at all. Even in the midst of many people, I will always carry within me a feeling of isolation and aloneness. I will experience a kind of "solitary confinement." It is a law, as certain as the law of gravity, that whoever is understood and loved will grow as a person; whoever is estranged will die in a cell of solitary confinement, alone.

From *Why Am I Afraid To Tell You Who I Am?*

*C*ommunication not only is the lifeblood of love and the guarantee of its growth, but is the very essence of love in practice. Love is sharing and sharing is communication. So when we say that communication is the "secret of staying in love" what we are really saying is that the secret of staying in love is to love, to keep sharing, to keep living out of one's commitment. Of course, there is a first "yes," a first commitment made to love, but this first "yes" has an endless number of smaller "yeses" inside it.

One of the most common escapes from the practice of realities like love is the substitution of discussion for doing. We would rather debate, think about, and question these realities than put them into practice. It is much easier to discuss truths than to live them.

It is this way with love. We would rather discuss it than live it. There is no price of admission to the forums of discussion, but the practice of love is a costly discipleship. Dag Hammarskjold writes in his book *Markings*:

The "great" commitment all too easily obscures the "little" one.

From *The Secret of Staying In Love*

*A*nyone who has ever contemplated taking the risk of emotional transparency has asked: Can I trust you? How far can I trust you? Will you understand or will you reject my feelings? Would you laugh at me or pity me? The usual procedure is to play swimmer, testing the temperature of the water, one toe at a time. Unfortunately, most of us decide to wait until we are sure and so never get into the healing waters of dialogue.

Waiting until we have an absolute guarantee of trust reminds me of a story I once heard. It seems that a mother of a young boy told his friends who had invited the boy to go swimming: "I am not going to allow Michael to go into the water until he learns to swim." Obviously, the only way to learn to swim is by getting into the water. Likewise the only way one learns to trust is to trust.

Dialogue can't be delayed. The court can't bring in a verdict until the trial is held. And so dialogue demands an act of the will: I am going to trust you. I can't be sure. Perhaps you will disappoint me. But I am going to risk, to take a chance, to open my most sensitive feelings to you because I want to give you this, my most valuable gift . . . because I love you. Because I love you I am going to give you as my first gift, my trust.

From *The Secret Of Staying In Love*

*O*ne of our strongest needs, which can easily become a neurotic preoccupation, is the need to feel safe. And so most of us like to have a room of our own with selected signs on the door, like: PRIVATE—DO NOT TRESPASS or DO NOT DISTURB. We want a place of safety, barricaded against the invasion of others with their probing questions and inquisitive desire to know all about us. There is no nakedness more painful than psychological nakedness. Out of this need to feel safe and protected from the searching eyes of another grows a myth that everyone needs his own private retreat which no one else can enter. It sounds good; it looks good; most people probably believe it. It is, nevertheless, a myth; something we wish were true, but which is really not true.

Rather than a place reserved exclusively for self, what we really need is to have someone (a total confidante) know us completely and some others (close friends) know us very deeply. The pockets of privacy which we create for a place to run where no one can follow are death to the kind of human intimacy so necessary to the fullness of human life.

It has become a cliché by now, I can know only so much of myself as I have the courage to confide to you. If I can feel totally free with you in a place cleared of "do not trespass" signs, I will no doubt go with the assurance of your companionship into places inside myself I could have never known existed. I will go into places I could never have gone alone. I need your hand in mine and the assurance of your committed and unconditional love even to attempt honesty about myself.

From *The Secret Of Staying In Love*

*C*ommunication between any two human beings is admittedly difficult. When we communicate, we share something. As a result this something becomes a common possession. For example, if I communicate a joke or recipe, this act of sharing will make the joke or recipe our common possession; we will possess something together. Through human relational communication what we gain as a common possession is: *ourselves*. Through our acts of sharing or communication we know and we are known. You share the gift of yourself with me and I share the gift of myself with you.

It seems obvious that human communication is the lifeblood and heartbeat of every relationship. It also seems clear that the gift of self through the sharing of self-disclosure is *the essential gift* of love. All other gifts—the jewelry, colognes, flowers, and neckties—are only tokens and symbols. The real gift of love is the gift of self.

Somehow we too sense that our lives seem to go about as well as our relationships. We are about as happy as our relationships are happy. A "human loner" is a contradiction in terms. The existence of a human in isolation from others is like a plant trying to survive without sunlight or water. No new growth can occur and the life that does exist begins to wither and will slowly die. For us to be is to be with another or with others. The quality of our human existence is grounded in our relationships.

From *Will The Real Me Please Stand Up?*

*I*t seems the more frequently we use exact verbal communication, the less room there is for imagined messages and consequent misunderstanding. It is when we keep our true thoughts and feelings veiled—when we play games, wear masks, and pretend certain postures—that others are left to imagine our meanings. Misunderstanding always results, usually with disastrous consequences.

Clear verbal communication not only spares us this unnecessary suffering of misunderstanding. More positively, it results in deep and lasting relationships. And relationships are the source of growth as persons. We are social beings. We are in this together. For us to be all that we can be, deep and permanent relationships are necessary. And to accomplish such relationships effective communication is absolutely essential.

It is said that a work of art is first and foremost a *work*. Relationships work for those who work at them. Unquestionably, the main work of a real relationship is communication. Communication slowly brings about deep and clearly defined relationships, but only if we keep working at it. Like any other human accomplishment, communication is a matter of continued practice. All the verbal formulas are useless unless practice has made the skills of communication a part of us. There is no formula for success that works unless we do.

Most of us learned to talk in the first year or two of life. And, according to the neonatologists, we began to hear even before birth. Unfortunately, most of us think that because we learn to talk and to hear, we automatically learn to communicate. That is like saying because I can touch the keys of a piano, I will automatically play melodious music. Good communication is not an automatic or easy achievement.

From *Will The Real Me Please Stand Up?*

W hen people begin to communicate effectively, a total change begins which ultimately affects all the areas of life. The senses seem to come alive. Color that was never noticed before is newly appreciated. Music that was not heard before becomes an accompaniment of life. Peace that was never before experienced begins to find its place in the human heart. Of course, the only proof is experiential. To know the truth of all of this, you have to try it. As the old saying goes, "Try it. You might like it."

The suffering of noncommunication in a relationship is a very real and painful suffering. Often in our human relationships the lines of communication are poorly erected, and they fall quickly in the crisis of a storm. The result is loneliness, the scourge of the human spirit. But when these lines are established again, it is like a second springtime of love and joy and all good things. Health and happiness of spirit begin to blossom in this springtime of communication.

From *Will The Real Me Please Stand Up?*

*A*nother very valuable benefit of learning and practicing the skills of good communication is *personal maturity*. If we truly believe the truths and accept the attitudes that underlie honest and open communication, we will come into a healthy contact with reality. Having given up our roles and games, we will soon be dealing more effectively with ourselves as we really are and others as they really are. We will begin to be authentic and true to ourselves and to others. The obvious result of all this is maturity.

No one (including myself) likes to be immature, but in fact we all are. We are beings in process, and have not yet arrived at all we can be. The absolute condition of our human growth is this contact with reality. And honest, open communication is the only street that leads us into the real world. The only alternative is to accept a life that is only an act, a meaningless pretense.

The question of communication may be the most important question you or I have ever considered.

From *Will The Real Me Please Stand Up?*

*T*he beginning of all successful communication is desire—the desire to communicate. This desire cannot be vague and negotiable. It has to be a flint-hard posture of the will, an inner resolution, a firm promise made to ourselves and to others with whom we are trying to relate.

All this may sound as though the commitment to communicate requires a *will* of blue steel. The truth of the matter is that there is no such thing as a strong will. What is strong or weak in us is *motivation*.

If a person really wants to live, the threat of death can be a powerful motivation. We humans can do unbelievable things if we are sufficiently motivated. Almost always a motive takes the form of escape from pain or anticipation of reward. When the presence of pain makes our lives seriously uncomfortable, we are motivated to change. Or when the rewards for accomplishment seem sufficiently great, we are motivated to pay the price and earn those rewards.

And so it is supremely important for you and me to ask: Do I really want to communicate? What are the pains and penalties if I don't? What are the rewards if I do? These may well be among the most important questions we will ever ask ourselves.

From *Will The Real Me Please Stand Up?*

*C*ommitment is clearly a matter of priorities. We all know the importance of priorities from personal experience. If we have five things to get done in one day, we somehow manage to accomplish only those things to which we have given priority. We do those things to which we attach a special sense of importance. So it is important and wise to list, to reflect upon, and to rehearse our personal motives. If we want good communication badly enough, we will give it high priority. And if we give it high priority, we will achieve success.

Once a commitment has been made, the main obstacle to perseverance is *failure*. It is a common human experience that failure obscures and weakens a commitment. It is important to remember that the way to success for us humans is usually paved with failures. Abraham Lincoln lost at least several elections before he was finally elected President. Thomas Edison experimented for two years on many materials from all over the world before he discovered a usable filament for the electric light bulb. When Marconi suggested the possibility of a wireless transmission of sound (the radio), he was committed to a mental institution. But people like Lincoln, Edison, and Marconi were strongly motivated. So they didn't give up. They somehow knew that the only real failure is the one from which we learn nothing. They seemed to go on the assumption that there is no failure greater than the failure of not trying, so they continued to try in the face of repeated failures.

From *Will The Real Me Please Stand Up?*

*S*o it seems that the first thing we must explore in ourselves is our personal understanding of and desire for good communication. We must ask ourselves honestly about our priorities. Is communication important to me? If I were to list the ten top priorities of my life at this time, would communication make my list? Do I really want to know and be known? Are there perhaps bogus fears that communication will end tragically? If I were to share myself honestly with another, what do I fear might happen? If I had to describe my "catastrophic fear" of good communication, the worst thing that could possibly happen, what would it be? What do I see as the the greatest danger in total openness and honesty?

So we leave you to ponder the question at hand: How badly do you want to communicate? If you really want it, and are willing to work at it, success is not far away from you. And the rewards of success are personal growth, effective and good relationships, and in the end the happy life which all of us are seeking.

The only way to know how much you want something is to try it. After you begin to do something, the depth of your desire will be clear.

From *Will The Real Me Please Stand Up?*

*I*t is a very common anticipation that "if I open up to you, I will burden you." Some have said the same thing from a different perspective: "People don't want to hear about me. They have enough problems of their own." Can this be true?

Self-disclosure in and of itself is never a burden. It is more important to realize that in and of myself I am a gift. If I give you this gift as an act of love through honest self-disclosure, it will not be a burden. It will be the unconditional gift of communication. Gifts are never burdens, unless strings are attached. My sharing will ask nothing of you except an empathic listening. My self-disclosure will make no other demands on you but to take my sharing into the gentle and grateful hands of acceptance. In giving you this gift I am truly giving you myself. It is my most precious, perhaps my only true gift.

From *Will The Real Me Please Stand Up?*

*S*ome months ago a sad looking man approached me at a convention. He told me that he had read many of my books, but admitted to having one lingering doubt. "Why should I tell you who I am? What good would it do?" I appealed to the supposed Irish privilege of answering a question by asking one. "Do you think I would be enriched if you were to share your story with me?" "Oh," he shook his head sadly, "I can't imagine that." "Aha!" I responded in my own awkward attempt at shock therapy, "That's where you're wrong!"

Sometimes I fear that most of us are like that dear old man. We think we have to have a star-studded, Fourth of July story to tell. We imagine that a real gift should bear the scent of roses and have gold embroidery at its edges. The truth is that any human story, if shared with another as an act of love, will widen the mind and warm the heart of the listener.

I know that I have learned very much about the human heart and the meaning of a broken human spirit from others. I know that I have become more tolerant, less anxious to judge or label others because some generous souls have shared the gift of their stories with me.

Persons really are gifts, aren't they?

From *Will The Real Me Please Stand Up?*

*A*t first the advice to be honest with myself seems superfluous. I want to ask, How can I lie to myself? And yet the gurus of communication insist that the first obstacle to communication with another is not an obstacle between myself and that other person. The first obstacle is encountered within myself. It is obvious that if I am not telling myself the truth, I certainly cannot tell you the truth. I can't tell you what I am not telling even myself. If I am not in touch with the feelings and attitudes that are within me, it will be impossible for me to share them with you. If I am deceiving myself, I will certainly deceive you.

From *Will The Real Me Please Stand Up?*

*T*he conscious mind rather obviously contains only our present perceptions. The subconscious level of the mind is the storage center for materials that we can bring up into the conscious mind when needed. For example, most of us can recall the multiplication tables if and when needed. But the unconscious is the storehouse for those memories, emotions, and motives that we "just can't live with." It has been called the basement of the mind where "eyesores" are stored. These are buried deep within us. Unfortunately, they are buried alive, not dead. And so they continue to influence us. The burial process is called repression. Repression is not a conscious or deliberate process. We bury our unwanted belongings without even realizing it or remembering them.

Repression into our unconscious minds always tends to throw us off balance. To the extent that we repress we lose contact with ourselves. Fortunately, the realities that we have repressed into the unconscious are always trying to surface for recognition. They are something like wood held under water. Therefore, if we welcome self-knowledge, they will gradually surface.

From *Will The Real Me Please Stand Up?*

*T*he important thing is to want to know what is in us. We must cultivate the desire to be honest with ourselves. Honesty with oneself is a habit of self-awareness that must be practiced daily. And this self-awareness is more a process than a simple fact. We must habitually try to become aware of the highly personal and individual way that we function in processing our *sensations, perceptions, emotions and motives*. We must look more carefully at the way we come to our decisions and ultimately to our actions.

Only in this way will we gain an increased awareness of our personal processes, and a more conscious control over our actions and reactions. We must, of course, all through this process take responsibility for our own decisions and behavior. We know that they are the result of something in us. At the same time we must be listening and looking to find out what that something is. We must be trying to learn who we really are rather than trying to tell ourselves who we should be.

From *Will The Real Me Please Stand Up?*

*B*eing honest with oneself requires giving up our acts and roles. But prior to the surrender must come the recognition. What is my act? It has been said that all of us carry a sign out in front of ourselves. We have composed it ourselves; it announces us. We get treated accordingly. If the sign reads "Dingbat," others do not come to us for serious conversation. And if our sign reads "Doormat," others will tend to roll right over us.

The curious thing about our signs is that others can read them quite clearly, even though we are often unaware of our own self-advertisements. This, I think, is one of our more common fears of intimacy. If I let you get close to me, you will see through my act; you will read my sign back to me. You will expose my charade. It could leave me feeling utterly naked.

From *Will The Real Me Please Stand Up?*

*S*o once more the question boomerangs back to me: Do I really believe that I must be honest with myself in order to be authentic with you? Do I really want to be honest with myself? Do I really want to be honest with you? Do I want to share my true gift with you, or do I want to play it safe and give you only my charade? My act is the price I pay for my safety and my strokes. It is the armor that protects me from getting hurt, but it is also a barrier within myself that stunts my growth. Likewise it is a wall between us that will prevent you from getting to know the real me. Giving up my act will take much courage. I will be taking a real risk, walking out from behind my wall. I will have to rewrite my sign: "This is the real me. What you see is what you get." Be patient with me. This will not be easy. I suspect that old Polonius knew this when he advised Laertes: "To thine own self be true."

However, if I am willing to take this risk, my courage will reap magnificent rewards: the statue will come to life, Sleeping Beauty will awaken. I will get to know who I really am. Maybe for the first time I will realize where the role ends and the real me begins. The real me will emerge from behind the mask, the sham, the pretense. I will begin to thrive in my relationships and grow into the best possible me. The ancient Greeks knew all this when they accepted as the summary of all wisdom: "Know thyself."

The longest journey is the journey inward. *Bon Voyage!*

From *Will The Real Me Please Stand Up?*

*T*he day that Jesus lost all his following is described in the Gospel of St. John. The day starts with Jesus intending to have a private session with his Apostles. But soon a huge crowd gathers around him. So Jesus spends the whole day talking to them. Near the end of the day, Jesus asks his Apostles if these people have had anything to eat. ("Like how could they? You've been talking to them all day.") So one of the Apostles finds a little boy who is offering five loaves and two fish. ("C'mon, Andy, how are we supposed to feed this crowd with five loaves and two fish?") Then the miracle. The multiplication of fish and bread: all over the place. When it registers, the people demand that Jesus be their King. They follow him across the lake with the chanted request: "Be our King!" The Apostles volunteer as cheer leaders.

There he exposes the roots of their request. "It was the fish and the bread, wasn't it? You want a military Messiah of Miracles so that he can multiply swords and shields, and throw off the shackles of Rome. Well, this is not my Kingdom. My Kingdom is one of faith. You enter my Kingdom by believing in me." So the people profess that they are great at believing. They even believe that God fed their ancestors with manna in the desert. Then Jesus confronts them with a great challenge of faith: "Your Fathers ate the manna and they died. But I am the Bread of Life come down from heaven. If you eat this Bread you will never die."

They are not equal to the challenge, and they react angrily. "Who does he think he is? And who does he think we are? Don't we know his mother?" Then they leave him. And Jesus turns sadly to his disappointed Apostles. "Do you want to go with them? Do you want to leave me, too?" he asks. In one of his better moments, Peter replies: "If we leave you, where could we go? You have the words of life."

Our faith in Jesus is our comfort. It is also our challenge. Do I really believe?

From the audio program, *The Growing Edge Of Life*

*S*omeday you will be blind!" An eye-doctor once told me this awesome truth. I have on the wall of my office a picture of a man walking down Park Avenue in New York City with a white cane and a tin cup. He has slung over his shoulders one of those sandwich-type signs. On his back and front, it reads: "Please help me. My days are darker than your nights." I have thought about that a thousand times: "My days are darker . . ."

In the last twenty-five years since the doctor's verdict, my eyes really haven't changed very much. Maybe it is God's will that I will see for the rest of my life. But the verdict of that doctor was nevertheless a very valuable moment in my life. Whether I ever go blind or whether I continue to see, it was and always will be a moment of grace. The possibility of blindness has asked me to say "yes" to God in a depth that has been asked of me in no other way. It has asked me to surrender, to trust. "My whole life is in your hands. Yes. If you want my vision, yes. I know you love me. I trust your love and your will for me." I think that God puts each of us into such a situation. I think of it as the "yes moment." It is very much like the "yes" that Jesus himself said to the Father. It was a "yes" that meant his life. "This is what I mean when I say I love you!" he says with his arms stretched out on a cross. If you and I can say our own "yes" whenever it is asked of us, the epitaph of our lives will read: "And this is what I mean when I say I love you."

From the video program, *Jesus As I Know Him*

*T*he Gospel of Jesus indicts our selfishness and challenges everything that is good and decent in us; it asks us to relocate our center of gravity, to move from the prison of selfishness to a world of others, from egotism to brotherhood, from lust to love. It asks us to believe that the only real power in the world is the power of love. It requires us to love not only our friends but also our enemies. It demands a Copernican revolution, a metanoia or conversion. Once you say the "yes" of faith to Jesus and accept his blueprint for the fullness of life, the whole world can no longer revolve around you, your needs, your gratifications; you'll have to revolve around the world, seeking to bandage its wounds, loving the dead into life, finding the lost, wanting the unwanted, and leaving far behind all the selfish parasitical concerns which drain our time and energies. It is frightening, isn't it? We are called to go out of ourselves, as though we were going out of an old home, a place where we once lived and felt secure, never to return. Once we truly encounter Jesus in faith, we can never be the same again. This is the pilgrimage of faith. What makes it even more frightening is that there are no money-back guarantees, no road maps that mark a certain destiny, no logical processes of verification. Only that voice, the voice of Christ somewhere inside us, asking: "Let go . . . Let go . . . Trust me . . . Believe in me . . . Let go." It would be too much if he did not also gently put his hand into ours, saying: "Fear not. I have overcome the world."

From *A Reason To Live, A Reason To Die*

I heard a story recently—it was fiction, I presume—of a man who had fallen off the edge of a high cliff. He managed to grab onto the root of a tree growing out of the side of the cliff, and was literally hanging on for dear life. He began to pray. Then he heard the voice of God asking him: "Do you really believe in me?" "I do!" protested the poor man whose life hung in the balance. "Do you trust me?" asked the voice of God. "Yes. Yes!" the man answered. Then the voice of God came back: "Then I will see to it that you are saved. Now, do what I tell you to do. Now . . . let go!" If you got the point of the story, you know something of the nature of faith, the surrender of all human certainties and the calculations to which we cling for dear life, as God whispers in our minds and hearts: "Now . . . let go!"

When Jesus rises out of the pages of the Gospel as a living voice, asking us to let go, his request is not something that can be fitted into some unused corner of our lives or confined to a Sunday morning ritual. He simply says: "Let go. . . . Let go of all your little plans for human security. . . . Don't worry about what you will eat or drink or what you will wear. . . . Seek first the Kingdom of God and God will take care of you. . . . Don't try to fit me into your plans, but try to find your place in my plans. . . . Make me your first concern, and I will take care of your concerns." If you feel a little chill of fear running through you as you read the Gospel, or you feel an impulse to look away from the challenge and talk about something else, it may well be a sign that you are beginning to understand the investment and surrender of faith. If it really hits you, you will have a sense of crisis, you will know it by the fear you feel in your heart.

From *A Reason To Live, A Reason To Die*

*F*aith, whether it is in another human being or in God, means taking something on the word of another. It implies new knowledge that can be had only by "taking someone else's word for it." If you explain a problem in mathematics to me, and I understand the explanation, I don't have to take your word that the explanation is correct. I can verify it for myself. I don't have to invest any faith in you. However, if you tell me that you love me and that you will try to make me happy, there is no way you can prove this, and there is no way I can verify it for myself. I must believe in you and your word to me.

In the case of faith in God it is the same. God gives me his word or revelation. If I accept it, if I judge that he has really spoken to me, promising to love me and offering me a reason to live and a reason to die, if I accept him and his message of life, I have in that moment become a believer.

From *A Reason To Live, A Reason To Die*

*P*rejudice is everywhere. There is no shining Camelot that banishes all prejudice or precludes psychological programming. Most human decisions are made in the glands, not by the brain. But something in us wants to shed prejudice, programming, brainwashing. We hate umbilical cords that shackle us to our past, destroying our freedom of choice. We do not want God, with his candles, incense, and stained-glass windows, just because we have been "brought up" that way.

Religion and patriotism are special areas of suspicion. They seem to promote "convenient" truths, the kind that prejudice plays upon, the kind that comfort people in need and control people in conduct.

But not all the tyrants that enslave us are outside us. The parasites of human insecurity have invaded all of us, little termites of terror telling us that it is safer to believe, offering a blanket for Linus. God—if he is really there—is not an aspirin, whatever else he may be.

Prejudice has other forms. It may be that a more angry fiend is raging in my guts: an old, smoldering resentment for the superstitious saints that have tormented me with a sense of guilt—Mommy, Daddy, Maiden-aunt, sanctimonious clergy snarling sermons they didn't really believe, Sister Supernun who threatened to turn anyone into a pillar of salt if you dared look back, the backwash biographies of saints who went to heaven and sinners who went to hell. It may be that I want to reject faith just so all of them will be wrong.

But we can't let prejudice make our decision, either way. There must be some middle ground between the pressures of indoctrination and the prejudice of rebellion.

From *A Reason To Live, A Reason To Die*

*H*ave you ever wondered, as most of us have, if you really believe in God, religion, and the reality of the Church? For many of us, when the question of faith surfaced, at some crisis point in life, it was painful and disconcerting, sometimes weighing heavily within the stomach like undigested food. Maybe for you it came at a time when your back was against the wall, and you wondered about resorting to prayer, when the words of prayer stuck in your throat, and your mind questioned whether prayer is something real or only a shallow superstition.

It may have been on a Sunday morning, when the bells of the nearby church were summoning the faithful to praise and petition God, and you turned over uneasily in your bed before going back to sleep. Or when you were planning your marriage, and you found yourself trying to decide between a candle-lit Church and the offices of the local Justice of the Peace. Or it could have been when someone you had known and loved "passed away," and the thought struck like thunder: What happens after death?

"Do I really believe in God?" You heard the question and it would not sleep.

From *A Reason To Live, A Reason To Die*

*F*or the word *crisis,* the Chinese use a combination of two characters. These two characters are those which designate "danger" and "opportunity." This disjunction seems to be true of every crisis. It is a turning point, and, depending on how we make the turn, we can find danger or opportunity. The forks in the road of human life that demand decisions of us are always crossroads of danger and opportunity. As in the medical usage of this term when a patient is pronounced "critical," the implication is that he or she can either move towards life or death.

In the process of faith, doubts and crises must occur. Paul Tillich points out that only through crises can faith mature. Doubt eats away the old relationship with God, but only so that a new one may be born. The same thing is true of our human, interpersonal relationships. They grow from initial fragility into permanence only through the tests of doubt and crisis. So Kahlil Gibran says that we can "forget those we have laughed with, but we can never forget those we have cried with."

There is something in old people that feels uneasy with, or even resents, crises of faith in the young. We lose sight of the fact that faith can mature only because of these crises. We forget that none of us can say a meaningful "yes" of commitment until we have faced the alternate possiblility of saying "no." The most destructive thing we can do to those passing through periods of crisis is to attempt to silence these legitimate doubts and encourage their repression. Repressed doubts have a high rate of resurrection, and doubts that are plowed under will only grow new roots. One thing is certain, that passage through the darkness of doubts and crises, however painful they may be, is essential to growth in the process of faith.

From *A Reason To Live, A Reason To Die*

*M*ost of us, in our desire for meaningful faith, seem to be saying to God: "Show me, and I'll believe!" This approach never works. God has made it very clear to us, in the life and teaching of his Son Jesus, that the process must be reversed. He is saying to us: "Believe in me, and I'll show you." Faith in him is an absolute prerequisite for the religious experience of God's power in and over our lives. Notice how many times in the New Testament Jesus tells the people who have received his favors that it was their *faith* that released his power. The Roman centurion is told that his son is cured "because of your faith" (Matthew 8:13). On the other hand, when the disciples come to Jesus to ask why they had been unable to cast the devil out of a certain young man, Jesus tells them very simply and bluntly:

> "Your faith is too weak. I tell you this: if you have faith no bigger than even a mustard-seed, you will say to this mountain, 'Move from here to there!' and it will move; nothing will prove impossible for you." (Matthew 17:20)

From *A Reason To Live, A Reason To Die*

*T*he soldiers who crucified Jesus had their own version of the futile formula "Show me and I will believe." While Jesus was dying on the cross, they called out to him: "If you are really the King of the Jews, save yourself. . . . If we see you come down from the cross, we will believe." There was, of course, no answer to such a demand, only the silent echo of his own earlier prayer: "Father, forgive them, for they do not know what they are doing." I personally believe that this is the apropos theme that pervades the whole life and teaching of Jesus: *Believe first* and you shall certainly see the power of God! Do not come to me, asking to see signs and wonders so that you might believe. Believe in me *first* and I shall show you more signs and wonders than you could ever have expected. In fact, you will find yourself doing far greater things than I have done myself.

At this point there is room for an honest question and an honest answer. If we find ourselves with only a very weak faith, if we experience more doubt than certainty within ourselves, what should we do? The answer I would give might seem simplistic or even repulsive to some, but here it is. One should read the New Testament slowly and prayerfully, trying to keep an open mind and an open heart. If it is true that God really takes and keeps the initiative in this matter of faith, it is up to him to act in us. Our only responsibility, since we cannot produce faith, is to be open to God. We must open our hearts to his gentle attraction and our minds to his illumination.

Jesus urges us to ask and to keep asking. The rest is up to God.

From *A Reason To Live, A Reason To Die*

*T*here is no scientific proof for the claims and contents of faith, nor is there any possibility of objectifying and substantiating any of the stages in the process of faith. The experience of coming into faith is simply not open to this kind of scientific investigation. No natural science could possibly establish as fact the supernatural entrance of God into human history or into an individual human life. These events lie outside the scope of the natural sciences. There is, however, what we might call an "existential" or experiential verification of faith. It is something like the experiential proof for the delight of chocolate ice cream or the beauty of a day in Autumn when the leaves are changing and the air is crisp. There are, in fact, many realitities that can be known only through personal experience.

In the movie, *A Patch of Blue*, the blind girl asks her grandfather: "Old Paw, what's green like?" The irritated grandfather answers: "Green is green, Stupid. Now stop asking questions." There follows a pathetic scene in which the young girl paws the grass with her hand and rubs a leaf against her cheek, vainly trying to experience the reality of greenness.

The playwright, William Alfred, author of *Hogan's Goat,* once said: "People who tell me that there is no God are like a six-year-old saying that there is no such thing as passionate love. They just haven't experienced Him yet." The evangelist, Billy Graham, says: "I know that God exists because of my personal experience. I know that I know him. I have talked with him, and I have walked with him. He cares about me, and he acts in my everyday life." The experience of God must somehow be generally available because a recent Lou Harris poll revealed that 97% of the American people believe in some sort of a personal God. Statistics are not, and never could be, the last word. Faith remains a matter of personal experience, like chocolate ice cream, a day in Autumn, and greenness.

From *A Reason To Live, A Reason To Die*

*I*n the act of faith, the motive or moving force is God himself who has spoken both his external word to all and his internal word inside the will and mind of the believer. In almost all of the other judgments of truth that we make, the motive is our perception of available evidence. We gather in evidence, evaluate it, and gradually come to our conclusion. The process of faith is quite different. There simply is no conclusive evidence available to our minds. We cannot reason our way into faith as we reason our way to other conclusions. It is simply a conclusion that results from God's attraction in the will and his enlightment of the intellect.

To make an act of faith we have to trust our own experience of God, whom we have experienced in our minds and hearts. However, while we must ultimately make some kind of "blind leap," we do not act against reason. The blindness of faith does not imply irrationality. In crossing the chasm into the world of faith, we do surpass the limits of our own reasoning powers, but only through an utter reliance on the God who has already acted within us. Reason does not possess a road map to the destiny of faith, but we are confident that another hand is really in ours, and that we are not throwing ourselves into a black void but rather into the arms of Someone who loves us. God has spoken a living, loving word within us, and we have responded with our own "yes," the response of faith.

From *A Reason To Live, A Reason To Die*

*I*t is obvious that, if faith must be defined as an act, it must also be seen as an act that inaugurates a new relationship between God and the believer. In his external and internal words God has invited a believer-to-be into a relationship. In the act of faith, the believer responds to God: "I accept your invitation. I will be yours, and I want you to be mine." Two things should be said of the relationship that begins at this moment.

The first is that, as in all relationships, there are three distinct possibilities for its future. We can either grow in our relationship with God, or we can maintain a distant and superficial connection with God, or we can discontinue the relationship. The relationship of faith is subject to moments of crisis, turning points at which the believer can take the road either to danger or to opportunity, to a great depth or even to ultimate loss of faith. There are many different things that bring an influence to bear in this matter. The most important of these is the psychological balance of the believer and the environment in which he or she lives. However, more than anything else the destiny of this relationship will be determined by the amount of communication and interaction between God and his believer. There can be no doubt that all interpersonal relationships thrive on and are as good as the communication between the partners of the relationship. The communication between the inviting God and the accepting believer is the heart and meaning of faith, its life nourishment.

From *A Reason To Live, A Reason To Die*

*W*hat is generally true of human relationships is also true of the relationship of faith; if it does not deepen, it will gradually die. Like the roots of a plant, faith must seek greater depth or be subject to the law of death. Interpersonal relationships are living things; their growth depends upon a dynamic evolution, new discoveries in the beloved and new self-revelations to the beloved. A relationship of love, St. Ignatius Loyola writes, consists in an exchange of gifts. Without these, a person cannot maintain interpersonal union. In the faith relationship, this interaction, this mutual self-revelation, this exchange of gifts is largely dependent on what is called a life of prayer. If we do not find God in prayer, we will not long retain a meaningful faith.

Secondly, crises in all relationships are inevitable and valuable when they are handled well. It is only through crises that the bonds of faith and love pass from an original fragility to a tested permanence. Through the growth that is possible in the successful handling of crises, faith becomes more and more marked by faithfulness and depth. It becomes the continued, personal response, the "yes" of mine to the initiatives of God. But there are so many "yeses" inside the original "yes" of faith. Michel Quoist, in his book *Prayers,* writes:

> I am afraid of saying "Yes," Lord.
> Where will you take me?
> I am afraid of drawing the longer straw,
> I am afraid of signing my name to an unread agreement,
> I am afraid of the "yes" that entails other "yeses."

Father Quoist says that "Only those who have experienced this 'wrestling' with God can really understand this prayer."

From *A Reason To Live, A Reason To Die*

*S*omeone has said that what we are is God's gift to us, and that what we become is our gift to God. It is true that God gives you and me the lumber of our lives, and offers to help us build from it a cathedral of love and praise. In this matter I have to face my own obvious responsibility. I will either use this lumber I have been given as a stepping stone, or it will become for me a stumbling block. To use another analogy, day by day God gives me new pieces to fit into this gigantic jigsaw puzzle of my life. Some of these pieces are sharp and painful. Others are drab and colorless. Only God, who has planned and previewed the picture of my life, knows the beauty that is possible when all the pieces have been faithfully put into place. I will know that beauty only after I have put into place the very last piece, the piece of my dying.

No satisfying theological understanding of suffering can be achieved if one considers only this life and this world which we know. The context of an endless, eternal life must be in the background of any Christian exploration of suffering. What happens in this life, in this world, can never make sense to the inquiring mind. There is no apparent fairness or equal distribution of blessings. But Christians have always believed that this life is a mere dot on the endless line of our human existence which reaches from now into forever.

Like Job, I do not have all the answers. After all, where was I when God made the world? But I do have some understanding of trust. And I do trust the God of love who is my Father. I'm sure you yourself must have been in such a situation, when you had to ask another to trust you. Do you remember that you couldn't really explain? You had to ask for an act of trust. Somehow, I think, in this matter of suffering God puts himself in that very position with regard to us. The great and infinite God asks a very limited and finite you and me: "Can you—will you—trust me?"

From *The Christian Vision*

*I*n the long history of Christian spirituality there have been various emphases. It is true that some of the saints so stressed the detachment of open hands that there is little in their writings of the joyful experience of God's creation. Fortunately other saints have described what has been called an "incarnational spirituality." In his Incarnation, in becoming a man and living in our world with us, Jesus underlined and validated the goodness of creation. Like us in all things, sin alone accepted, the incarnate Word of God was repeating the spoken word of God at the dawn of creation: "It is very good!"

St. Ignatius Loyola (1491–1556), in his Jesuit rule, instructs his followers to "seek and find God in all things." Consequently, it is no surprise that this incarnational approach is beautifully developed in the writings of contemporary Jesuits like Karl Rahner, Bernard Lonergan, and Pierre Teilhard de Chardin. It is also reflected in the beautiful poetry of Gerard Manley Hopkins, the Jesuit poet.

Incarnational spirituality seeks and finds God present in all things. Jesus has come among us that we might through him have the fullness of life. Commenting on this, St. Irenaeus insists that "the glory of God is a person who is fully alive!" We give glory to God by using all the gifts that he has given us and using them to our fullest capacity. A part of this fullness is being fully alive in our senses, in our emotions, in our minds, and in our hearts. If the unexamined life isn't worth living, as Socrates once observed, then the unexperienced universe isn't worth living in. Most of all, our Christian faith encourages us to be alive in our hearts. As Antoine de Saint-Exupéry says, "It is only with the heart that one can see rightly; what is essential is invisible to the eye." It would be an unbearably cold world if we passed through it without loving.

From The Christian Vision

I am reminded of what Dorothy Thompson, a journalist, once wrote. She was interviewing a survivor of a Nazi concentration camp. During the interview, she asked the survivor if any in those camps had remained human. His immediate reply was: "No, none remained human." Then he caught himself and remembered: "No, there was one group of people who did remain human. They were the religious people." The survivor said that all the others, even those who had great knowledge and skill, seemed to be using their abilities only selfishly for survival. The very architects of those camps had used their great knowledge and skill only to destroy. The knowledge and skills of a technological age without the compassion and wisdom of faith proved in Nazi Germany to be gruesomely dangerous and destructive. In her summary, Dorothy Thompson wrote: "I am beginning to think that when God goes, all goes." Her line was somewhat reminiscent of what George Washington wrote in his Farewell Address: "Morality cannot be maintained withouth faith and religion."

From *The Christian Vision*

*S*ometimes some frightening questions surface in me: Is all this a dream, a lovely little fairy tale? Is this community of love which we call the Church a fact or a fiction? Did God really make us in his image and likeness, or have we made up a God of love? Oh, I do believe. I have believed with enough depth and with enough strength to wager my life on the reality of the Church. In fact, I resonate deeply to the words of Jean Anouilh's Becket when he says, "I have rolled up my sleeves and have taken this whole Church upon my back. Nothing will ever persuade me to put it down."

Still, there are parts of me that faith has not yet claimed. "Lord," I pray, "I do believe but please help me with my unbelief." I try to love my unbelieving questions until I can live the believing answers. One thing, however, seems certain: Every life must be based on some act of faith. Faith is basically a judgment, a judgment about whether the Word of God is true or not. If faith is a judgment about something for which there is no logical or scientific proof, then sooner or later all of us must make our decision, some act of faith in this matter. We must gamble our lives on something. Not to decide in this matter is really not a clever way to escape error. Not deciding is in itself a decision.

For myself I have made a decision and a life commitment. I have also reflected that if the love of God, the call of the Kingdom, and the reality of the Church are only a dream, then the opposite would be a nightmare. The opposite judgment or act of faith would see us all as mere animals in search of prey. The strong would then devour the weak. The rich would buy and sell the poor. The handicapped would be destroyed as defective and unproductive. In the end, our only destiny would be to turn into dust and become food for worms.

From *The Christian Vision*

*O*nce I made a retreat high up in the Alpine Mountains in Bad Schönbrun, Switzerland. My first night there, I went to the chapel for the evening prayer service. Directly from behind me came one of the most beautiful tenor voices I have ever heard. When I put the hymnal back in the pew I turned to look at the owner of the voice I had been admiring. On the way out of chapel, I complimented him (in German). I was going to tell him that he had such a naturally good voice that he really should have it trained. Only I couldn't think of the German word for "trained." As I was searching for it, he offered me his card. It read: "Walter Hegge, Lead-tenor, the Zurich Opera Company." (Color me "red.") After a few German exchanges he asked: "Do you speak English?" I told him I spoke something close, "American." Later, he told me of his own origins in South Africa. And he invited me to take a stroll after dinner. On the way up the mountain path, I asked him: "Walter, what are you doing here? Are you making a retreat?" His response was beautiful. "No," he replied. "I'm going to be baptized on Sunday, and am spending the week in prayer, getting ready for the biggest moment in my life." Then he shared with me the story of his life and the loving pursuit of God, who would claim him on Sunday. When we came to a log, I sat down and requested a solo. So the lead-tenor sang a Puccini aria for me. My mind and heart were overflowing. The story of God's love for this man . . . his baptism on Sunday . . . the beauty of the Swiss Alps . . . this breathtaking voice and Puccini . . . I felt I could touch the face of God. I wanted to stop all the clocks and calendars, and never go down from the mountain. I knew what Peter must have felt on the Mountain of the Transfiguration.

From the audio program, *My Vision And My Values*

*T*he first point in my own spiritual synthesis or faith overview is this: *"God is Love"* (1 John 4:16). St. John defines God as being love. It means that all God ever does is love. His love, like all real love, is self-diffusive; it asks only to give, to share. Dietrich Bonhoeffer, in his *Ethics,* suggests that, in trying to understand John's definition of God, we must not take the word "love" as our starting point, but we must begin with the word "God." As St. John says, only the person who knows God can really know what love is. "It is not," Bonhoeffer adds, "that we first of all by nature know what love is and therefore know also what God is." None of us can know what God is, and therefore understand the meaning of love, unless God reveals himself to us. We first know God through the experience of faith.

St. John says that love originates in God (1 John 4:10) and that we perceive God's love in Jesus, especially in his act of dying for us (1 John 3:16). It is an "utterly unique event," according to Bonhoeffer, that God laid down his very life for us in Jesus. "God was in Christ," St. Paul writes, "reconciling the world to himself, not holding our faults against us" (2 Corinthians 5:19). Jesus is, therefore, the living definition of love, and, as Bonhoeffer says, "the only definition of love." Love is what God unchangeably is, and Jesus is the revelation of what God is.

From *A Reason To Live, A Reason To Die*

*T*he second point of my own spiritual synthesis is this: *God loves us as we are.* The kind of love that brings us into the fullness of life is not the love which regards what we have been or what we might become, but the love which takes us as we are. This is precisely the way God loves us. Of course we are imperfect, but God sees us as beings in process. He takes us, at whatever point we may be in our development, as we are. The deadliest of all delusions about God is the notion that he can be *angry.* It is simply a figure of speech when Scripture refers to the "wrath of God." That there is actually wrath or anger in God is a deception and misunderstanding that we must bury beyond all possibility of resurrection. We must prayerfully meditate on God's unchanging nature. Theologians call it his "immutability." God is always the same. He can neither hurt nor be hurt. He is not subject to heat and coldness, the ups and downs, the mercurial emotions that affect us. We must not make God to our own human image and likeness. This would be the death of all authentic faith. We might consider an analogy with the sun. The sun only shines, just as God only loves. It is the nature of the sun to shine, to offer its warmth and light. It is the nature of God to love, to offer the warmth and the light of his love to us.

We have all hidden, in large ways and small, from his light and warmth. We have taken refuge in a series of distractions, concealed ourselves under the cover of pretext and delusion, but the sun of God continues to shine. He contiues to love us, to offer the gifts that will bring our total fulfillment. There is no time in the history of human life that one cannot go back into the light and warmth of God's love. No matter what obstacles sin and selfishness have erected, God is always there for us, always offering himself in warmth and light. It is important that we understand this during life. The only alternative would be to discover in death what we never knew in life, and with St. Augustine lament, "Too late, too late, O Lord, have I loved you. . . . Memory is indeed a sad privilege."

From *A Reason To Live, A Reason To Die*

*T*he third point in my own spiritual synthesis: *God's providence rules our lives.* Strictly speaking, there is no such thing as time, as "before" or "after," in God. However, we are creatures of time, and in our limited way of understanding God, we must conceive his actions as temporal. And so we might say that, before God created this world, he knew all the possible worlds he could have created. In some of the possible worlds that God could have created, you and I existed, in others we did not. In some of the other worlds that God could have created, you and I would have had very different types of existence, different circumstances of life, different talents, different joys and sufferings.

However, in God's act of creation, he was saying that he did not want these other worlds. He wanted this world. In his own eternal decree of creation, he wanted this blade of grass to spring through the earth at precisely the moment it did, and that leaf on the distant tree to fall at the precise moment when it will fall on a day in Autumn. He wanted you and me to be born of the parents who gave us life, at the precise moment he chose. He knew what we would look like, how we would sound, what we would be able to do and what we would not be able to do. He knew the agonies and ecstasies that life would ask of us and confer upon us. It was to this world that God said his "yes" of creation. Having seen the whole of our lives from all eternity, in the mystery of time God gives us these lives piece by piece, something like the pieces of a jigsaw puzzle which we must fit together. In putting together the pieces of this puzzle we must believe that he who has given us the pieces knows the beauty that will result when the final piece, the act of our dying, is put into place.

From *A Reason To Live, A Reason To Die*

*T*he fourth point in my own spiritual synthesis: *Our response to God—love one another.* It is a theological truism that we cannot give God anything. He already has everything. However, in the revelation of Jesus, we are clearly directed to place our response of love to God's love in the form of charity towards our neighbor. In fact, Jesus calls this love which we have for one another the badge of his discipleship: "A new commandment I give you; love one another. As I have loved you, so you must love one another, then all will know that you are my disciples" (John 13:34–35). All this is perhaps obvious to anyone who has read the New Testament carefully. What is not obvious, perhaps, is that the ability to love one another is God's gift to us. We do not win the favor of God by loving one another, but rather it is the favor of God that enables us to love one another.

St. John says: "We know that we have passed from death to life because we love one another. Whoever does not love abides in death" (1 John 3:14). The whole first letter of St. John is a beautiful treatise on this marvelous but mysterious fact. In writing to the Corinthians, St. Paul tells them of the many gifts of God, and in the famous thirteenth chapter of *First Corinthians,* he describes the most excellent gift of God: charity. Finally, there is the description of the Last Judgment by Jesus. He portrays the saved coming into the blessedness of heaven:

> Then the King will say to the people on his right, "You that are blessed by my father: come! come and receive the kingdom which has been prepared for you ever since the creation of the world. I was hungry and you fed me, thirsty and you gave me drink; I was a stranger and you received me into your homes, naked and you clothed me; I was sick and you took care of me, in prison and you visited me. . . . I tell you, indeed, whenever you did this for one of the least important of these brothers and sisters of mine, you did it for me!" (Matthew 25:34–40)

From *A Reason To Live, A Reason To Die*

*T*he fifth and final point in my own spiritual synthesis: *God is our destiny.* Some years ago, after failing by several hundred yards to complete her swim across the English Channel, a woman named Florence Chadwick said that the reason for her failure was the morning fog that hung heavily above the Channel. She said: "If I could have seen the shore, I would have made it." The whole Christian view of life sees God as both the Alpha and Omega of human existence. We are, in this life and in this world, a pilgrim people on our way home. No synthesis of life, provided by the vision of faith, would be complete without a vision of the shore. In the mystery of the Tranfiguration of Jesus, when the beauty of God momentarily flashed out of the person of Jesus, the reaction of Peter was typically human. He wanted to build three tents, to stay on that mountain forever.

It is typically human because all of us want to do this; we want to crystallize our moments of extreme happiness and remain within them forever. But our clocks and calendars continue their counting, and we must come down from these mountains of supreme happiness. However, if life and death are to have a meaning for us, it is critical to remember that someday we shall ascend the mountain of God, and behold his beauty forever and ever. There will be a moment when the clocks and calendars have finished their work for each of us. This is the Christian's sense of destiny. St. Paul writes to the Romans: "I consider that what we suffer at the present time cannot be compared at all with the glory that is going to be revealed to us" (Romans 8:18).

From *A Reason To Live, A Reason To Die*

*T*his synthesis or overview of faith puts life into a meaningful perspective. It enables us to find a personalizing relationship with God in all dimensions of human reality. Only the eyes of faith can see beneath the surface of things, and only the hope of faith gives a coherence to the disparate aspects of human existence. It deepens us not only in our unity with God but in our unity with one another. The first thing we see is a body, an external appearance. But under the surface beauty or ugliness, in a deeper mode of existence, is a person, a person with broken dreams and newborn hopes, a person of loneliness and love. And somehow, in an even deeper mode of existence, in the center of that person is God. The deepest mode of existence in all creation is the presence of God, whose being is shared by and mirrored in all creation. He is in the light in the sky, the suddenness of the storm, the first cry of the newborn baby, and in the last breath of the dying man. His pulse is the heartbeat of the universe.

In the vision of faith, God is found in joy, love, pain, and loneliness. There is nothing in all creation that is not touched by his presence. All the movements with which creation stirs reveal the life of a transcendent God deeply immanent in all things. He is present in the darkness of despair and in the light of hope. He is in laughter and in the cry of pain. He is in the high-noon and in the dead of night. There is no distant star, no drop of water at the bottom of the deepest ocean, no mountain or rock or fragile blade of grass that does not somehow share his life, and reveal his person.

From *A Reason To Live, A Reason To Die*

*J*esus holds out to each one of us the same love he extended to the people of his own time. There are many stories of his goodness. We must remember these because Jesus is the same today, tomorrow and yesterday. *Dismas, the Good Thief* (Luke 23:39–43): St. Luke tells us that one of the two criminals crucified with Jesus began to challenge him: "Aren't you supposed to be the Christ? Save yourself and us, too!" The other thief tried to silence him: "Have you no fear of God at all? We are getting a punishment that we deserve. We are paying for what we did. But this man has done nothing wrong." Then, perhaps raising his eyes to the plaque above the head of Jesus, which indicated the "crime" for which he was dying, Dismas read: "This is Jesus of Nazareth, the King of the Jews." The plaque was part of the ceremonial of crucifixion, so that bystanders and passersby would know the reason for the punishment. Death by crucifixion was usually a lingering form of dying, usually lasting two or three days. We remember that Pontius Pilate was surprised that Jesus had died in a matter of two or three hours.

Then the man we call Dismas said his prayer, perhaps the only sincere prayer he had ever said in his entire life:

> "Jesus . . . when you come into your kingdom, will you please remember me?" And Jesus, turning to him, replied: "You can be sure of this. Today you will be with me in paradise."

Jesus, as always, even in the agony of his own dying, was the "man for others." His words to the dying Dismas were the last that he said to anyone before his own death. But his mercy is the same, yesterday, today and always. There can be no question that this gift of mercy and love has been repeated uncountable times down the long course of human history and of human weakness.

From *A Reason To Live, A Reason To Die*

*T*he Twelve Apostles: Like any other rabbi and itinerant preacher of his times, Jesus chose a small group of twelve men, whom he invited to be his constant companions and preachers of his gospel (Mark 3:14). All of these men, except Judas Iscariot, are now canonized for our admiration and imitation. But, in all honesty, they were not "born saints." In fact, when Jesus called them they were a rather strange assortment of human misery. They are classic examples of men who were loved into greatness by the patience of Jesus. All greatness, it would seem, is somehow born out of the patience of love; and these men were no exceptions. They were all rather slow learners. They found an egocentric prudence the better part of valor, when their own safety was threatened; they were cowards. Their number included a loudmouth, two mama's boys, a bullhead, and an apparent bird-brain. They were just as weak as you or I can be.

From *A Reason To Live, A Reason To Die*

Spring

*T*he central figure among the Apostles was Simon, son of Jonah, known as the Rock. In fact, this man wasn't very much of a rock at all; he was more like a sandpile of human weakness. His first question, upon being invited into the discipleship of Jesus, was "What's in it for me?" And after three years in the service of Jesus, when the Lord told the Apostles of his coming passion and death, it was the loudmouth Peter who protested that this wasn't a very good idea. Jesus had to tell him the plain truth: "The way you think is not God's way of thinking, but man's" (Matthew 16:21–23).

At the Last Supper this same Peter arrogantly denied the prediction of Jesus that Peter would disown him. He suggested that maybe one of the others might be so weak, but never the Rock. Of course, he did disown Jesus. While Jesus was being tried for his life before the Jewish court of Sanhedrin, Peter waited anonymously in the courtyard outside, posing as a disinterested bystander. When he was recognized as a companion of Jesus, the Rock not only denied any knowledge of Jesus, but even swore an oath before God that he did not know Jesus at all. As Jesus was being led out of the palace of the High Priest on his way to prison and death, Peter was there in the courtyard bellowing his frightened denials of Jesus.

> . . . and the Lord turned and looked straight at Peter, and Peter remembered what the Lord had said to him, "Before the cock crows today, you will have disowned me three times." And Peter went off in the darkness and cried his heart out.   (Luke 22:61–62)

From *A Reason To Live, A Reason To Die*

*A*s he hung dying on the cross, the eyes of Jesus must have searched the jeering crowd below for the faces of his beloved friends, the Apostles. He had given his trust and love to these men. He was now giving his very life for them. However, as the arms of Jesus were stretched out as if to embrace the whole sinful world in the act of his dying, the Apostles were huddled and hiding in the upper room, with the doors barred and bolted. They were very visible public figures on Palm Sunday, but they faded fast into a safe obscurity on Good Friday. Jesus would have to die alone. The old way of seeing things, characterized by self-centeredness and self-protectiveness, was still the fixed mind-sct of the Apostles. They seemed to be what we might call "fair-weather friends." But Jesus is committed to loving them into human wholeness and the fullness of life.

And so Jesus comes to the Apostles on Easter Sunday morning to share with them his triumph over death. He tries to put them at ease with kindness and patient understanding. "Shalom!" he says. "Be at peace." The frightened Apostles were apoplectic. "We are seeing a ghost! We must be suffering from mass hallucination." The predictions of his resurrection, which Jesus had made previously, had been lost on them. So Jesus graciously offers to eat their fish and honeycomb, which ghosts don't ordinarily do. He patiently lets them touch him by way of reassurance.

The Apostles must been deeply moved by this faithful act of love on the part of Jesus. They had been walking out on him and here he was, walking after them. It may well have been this act of kindness that broke down the barriers of their resistance. The old vision was finally beginning to give way to the new, life-giving, joyful vision. It seems that making the vision of Jesus one's own is never really a completed process.

From *The Christian Vision*

*S*halom. . . . Be at peace. . . . I understand," is the constant word of Jesus to his Apostles and to us. Peace in all the storms of life. Peace when your heart is sinking at failure. Peace when your world seems to be falling in on you. Peace in the monotony and endlessness of small things. Peace in the watching and waiting, when your heart is anxious and your hands are useless to do anything. But most of all, peace with your human weakness, when you can't seem to do anything right. "Shalom. I understand."

'Do not let your hearts be troubled. Trust in God always, and trust in me. . . . Peace I leave you, my own peace I give you, a peace that the world cannot give. This is my gift to you, my peace.' (John 14:1, 27)

From *A Reason To Live, A Reason To Die*

*I*f we were made by God to be fully alive, why do we so often find ourselves reduced to making the best of a bad thing? Obviously, in our lives and in the lives of so many others something needed for the fullness of life is missing or at least is not being recognized and enjoyed. Somehow, somewhere, something has gone wrong. Somewhere along the way the light has failed many of us. In his verse "Out of Order," Andre Auw describes his reactions when he comes upon the scene of a young mother trying to explain to her four-year-old boy that the popcorn machine cannot give out its contents:

"You can't get any popcorn, Child. The
    machine is out of order. See, there
    is a sign on the machine."

But he didn't understand. After all, he had the
    desire, and he had the money, and he
    could see the popcorn in the machine.
    And yet somehow, somewhere, something
    was wrong because he couldn't get the
    popcorn.

The boy walked back with his mother, and he
    wanted to cry.

And Lord, I too felt like weeping, weeping for
    people who have become locked-in,
    jammed, broken machines filled with
    goodness that other people need and
    want and yet will never come to enjoy,
    because somehow, somewhere
    something has gone wrong inside.

From *The Secret Of Staying In Love*

A healthy and growing person accepts the human condition of weakness. "People are mistake-makers and I am one of them. That's why there are erasers on pencils, you know." Healthy and growing persons are also good communicators because they are ready to share openly and honestly. They share not only the light and bright, but also the weak and wounded side of themselves.

Defenses of our wounded egos lead us into endless and sticky games of phoniness. Fortunately, there is a positive, creative, and health-producing antidote. It is simply to accept ourselves in the human condition of weakness and to admit the facts of our limitations. Such honesty and openness counteract our unhealthy tendencies. Honesty and openness, willingness to share ourselves, warts and all, make us real. It puts us into the kind of contact with reality that enables us to grow up and become all that we can become.

From *Will The Real Me Please Stand Up?*

*Y*ou and I can profit by asking ourselves: What do I see when I look through the lens of my attitude toward myself? Am I more a critic than a friend? Do I look beyond the surface blemishes to find the truly beautiful and unique person that I am? Or do I play the destructive "comparison game"? What verdict does the juror of my mind pass on me: "good at heart" or "guilty on all counts"?

A healthy Christian attitude toward self acknowledges and accepts the human condition of fragility. But we always see ourselves walking through life hand in hand with the Lord, feeling glad to be who we are, knowing that he accepts and loves us as we are. Our Father who is mighty has indeed done great and beautiful things in us and for us, and holy is his name. Only through the lenses of this vision can we find the peace and joy which are the legacy of Jesus. Only if we see ourselves in this way can we experience the fullness of life which he came to bring us.

From *The Christian Vision*

*L*ife itself is a process and we are all "beings in process." None of us has yet come to full maturity; none of us has arrived at completion. We are all fractions on our way to becoming whole numbers. I remember once seeing this sign on a button a woman was wearing: "Please be patient. God is not finished with me yet." God is not finished with any of us yet. We are all en route to our full personal growth and potential. And certainly we need a lot of patience during the process—patience from ourselves and patience from others.

The process of human development and growth is much like the process of accepting death. We humans have to move at our own pace, and all during the process we need to be accepted wherever we are. We know, for example, that we cannot insist on consistently mature behavior from small children. We must let them be children and we must accept them as such. We also know that we cannot demand a rigid conformity from adolescents who are trying to learn how to think for themselves and become their own independent persons. In a similar way we must learn to be patient with ourselves in the passages of the human process.

From *Will The Real Me Please Stand Up?*

*A*ctually, from conception to death each of us is involved in a continually spiraling process of change and growth: birth-death-new birth in all the phases of our personhood. Every stage of life has in it certain developmental tasks. To accomplish each task and so to further our personal development we must constantly be involved in changing. Obviously, changing always involves giving up the old and comfortable behaviors in order to embrace new and more mature behaviors.

There is a death and a birth in every change. And each death, however small or great, seems to require that we go through the five stages of dying: denial—anger—bargaining—depression—acceptance. It seems that we have to go through these same five stages before we can accept and experience new life. If those who love us will only accept us "in process," that will be the greatest gift of their love to us.

The journey through life has many valleys that we just can't skip over, and also many mountains to climb that we just can't jump over. It is also true that we need the space and the freedom to make our own mistakes. Trial and error seem to be the only way we can learn and grow. Life is first and foremost a process. And this process is a zig-zag process at that.

From *Will The Real Me Please Stand Up?*

*T*he person who is trying not merely to get by during a difficult period but to get out of a rutted existence and find the fullness of life will have to revise his or her basic vision. With or without professional help this is reconstructive psychotherapy. As we have been repeating: Our participation in the fullness of life is always proportionate to our vision. Whoever is not living fully is not seeing rightly. However, to give up an old vision in favor of a radically different perspective always involves the limbo of the in-between, the temporary experience of chaos. This is why there is always an initial period of disorientation or disintegration. It is a necessary part of the growth process.

Have you ever tried to cross a stream stepping from one rock to another? While perched on any one rock there is a sense of security. It is safe. Of course, there is no forward movement, no progress, no satisfaction beyond safety. The challenge to move on—to step out to the next rock—is precarious and frightening precisely because of that moment when one is firmly footed on neither rock. The precarious and frightened feeling is comparable to what we feel at the moment an insight beckons and we are tempted to step out of our rigidity into a new vision and into a new life. Just as it is foolish to want a dentist or doctor who can always cure us instantly without any discomfort, it is likewise foolish to think that human growth can be accomplished instantly and without pain. There is no painless entrance into a new and fully human life.

From *Fully Human, Fully Alive*

*A*t all times in every life there is at least a tentative vision. It is a necessary result of the dynamism of the human mind. The senses pick up phenomenological data—sights, smells, tastes, sounds, and sensations of touch. These are transmitted to the mind, which immediately begins to process and evaluate this material. Like a computer, the mind interprets all the different impulses, first grasped by the senses, and organizes reality into intelligible perceptual patterns.

It is something like receiving one by one the pieces of a mosaic or a jigsaw puzzle. The mosaic is "reality." It does not come all at once in a neat box. It comes piece by piece in packages marked "days." Each day brings new pieces. Every new piece adds its own contribution of deeper understanding to the total picture of reality. We put the pieces together differently because each of us perceives reality in his or her own way. The qualities most needed for the construction of an adequate and accurate vision are *openness* and *flexibility*. The trap to be avoided is *rigidity*.

Rigid people are like detectives who take the first scraps of evidence discovered and immediately come to a definite and unshakable conclusion about the mystery they are trying to solve. If any new evidence is uncovered they insist on bending it to fit their original, premature conclusions. Flexible and open people are contented with tentative judgments, which they keep revising as new evidence comes in. Instead of bending the facts to fit their conclusions, they keep revising their conclusions to accommodate all the known facts.

From *Fully Human, Fully Alive*

*P*ain in itself is not an evil to be avoided at all costs. Pain is rather a teacher from whom we can learn much. Pain is instructing us, telling us to change, to stop doing one thing or to begin doing another, to stop thinking one way and begin thinking differently. When we refuse to listen to pain and its lessons, all we have left is to become an escapist. In effect we have said: I will not listen. I will not learn. I will not change.

When applied to human beings almost all labels are meaningless. However, I do think there is one really meaningful distinction, and that is between "growing" and "static-escapist" people. It is a distinction between those who are "open" to growth and those who are "closed." Open and growing people do not begrudge the pedagogy of pain, and are willing to try change. They will initiate appropriate responses and adjustments. Others, for reasons we do not know, simply will not address themselves to the lessons of pain. They rather seek a narcotized and tranquilized existence, a peace without profit. They are willing to settle for 10% of their potential. They are willing to die without having really lived.

Through true and lasting love relationships, we can recover acceptance of self, a realization of our worth. When these are present, everything else will somehow move in the direction of growth on the paths of peace. When love and a sense of personal worth are missing, there is left only a partial existence. We can achieve only a fraction of what might have been. We will die without having really lived. The glory of God—a person fully alive—will forever be diminished.

From *The Secret Of Staying In Love*

*D*id you ever ask yourself the surprisingly difficult question: How does one choose evil? How do we commit sin? The will can choose, by its very nature, only that which is good. I am personally convinced that the exercise or use of free will in a given situation of guilt is that the will, desirous of some evil which has good aspects (if I steal your money, I will be rich), forces the intellect to concentrate on the good to be acquired in the evil act, and to turn away from the recognition of evil. This need urges the intellect to rationalize that which was originally recognized as evil. While I am doing something wrong (in the act of doing it), I cannot be squarely facing its evil aspect; I must be thinking of it as good and right. Consequently, free will is probably exercised primarily in the act of coercing the intellect to rationalize rather than in the execution of the act itself.

From *Why Am I Afraid To Tell You Who I Am?*

*A*ccording to Ernest Becker in his book *The Denial of Death,* one part of the reality which we commonly refuse to confront is death. Most of us have no idea how we would react to impending death because we just don't want to think about it. And just as we fear the end of our finite existence, death, Becker maintains that we also fear the full experience of life. One integral part of a human life is the experience of pain—our own and that of others. However, when someone cries, the most common response is a plea: "Don't cry." It is probably good for people to cry, but most of us don't know how to handle tears.

When we cut off the experience of pain, we also separate ourselves from the full experience of the pleasures and the beauty of life. There is so much excitement and stimulation in the world of reality that surrounds us—the sights and the sounds, the light and the darkness, the agonies and the ecstasies of God's world. There is so much, in fact, that we are afraid of it. We are sure that we cannot handle it. We sense that we cannot cope with the charge of such high voltage; we are sure that we would suffer a short circuit. So we shut out much of reality and build a little house by the side of the road, laid back from the heavier traffic and surrounded by a hedge of small bushes. There we live a low-risk existence, with the sedations and distractions we need in order to cope with the limited part of the reality we are willing to confront.

It is obvious that you and I do have a limited capacity. We cannot take in all the suffering or all the beauty of our world. No one could rightly ask us to do this. It is rather a question here of using more of the capacity that we do have. It would be a waste of our human potential if we were to paint ourselves into a small corner of life and stay huddled there, frozen by the fear of a larger world and a fuller life.

From *The Christian Vision*

*A*s a great psychiatrist said, "Children are excellent observers but poor interpreters." They observe everything that others do but they are poor interpreters of these actions; they know exactly what you are doing but they don't know exactly what it means.

I know a lady who once told me that when her father died she was only a child. She observed that her mother didn't cry over her father's death. The mother told me later, "I was trying to keep that traditional stiff upper lip for the sake of the children. I wanted them to know that their father was in heaven and that death isn't a tragedy. I didn't want to show my own grief, not to the children." So she kept the stiff upper lip, and her little girl concluded, "You didn't love my father, did you? You didn't love him at all. I loved my father and you didn't!" And so, the little girl hated her mother for years. She really did. And it was all based on a child's excellent observation and faulty interpretation.

From the video program, *Free To Be Me*

*I*n my book *Fully Human, Fully Alive*, I told the story of the sudden death of a car which I was driving on a busy Chicago expressway. Standing on the shoulder of the expressway, alongside the unresponsive automobile, I glanced down into the ravine on one side of the expressway, noting the high fence and dense foliage at the bottom. Looking out across the expressway, I was faced in that direction with six lanes of whizzing traffic. The result in me was instant panic. I did not know what to do. What I did not reveal about this episode in that other book was that several months later a woman who works with me (Loretta Brady) came late for a meeting. "Sorry," she said, "my car broke down." I made sympathetic enquiries only to find out that her car broke down at the very same place where my own tragedy had occurred. (Shades of the "Bermuda Triangle!") I know it sounds a bit contrived, but it is actually true.

"What did you do?" I asked. "I climbed down the hill on the west side of the expressway!" she chirped with a slightly triumphal smile. "Then I went under the overpass, found a phone, and called for help." (Long and painful pause) "Could I ask you a personal question: How did you feel when you were doing all this?" I asked wearing my "Father Confessor" look. (So help me God:) "Exhilarated!" she squealed. (So help me God:) Under my breath I whispered, "Oh, I hate you."

The old Roman philosopher, Epictetus, was right: "It's not your problem that bothers you. It's all in the way you look at it." Next time, I'm going down that hill!

From *The Christian Vision*

*I*t is very important that all of us confront the question of self-understanding and self-forgiveness. An insight about this has been very helpful to me. Just as I must make an effort to be gentle and forgiving in my dealing with others, so must I extend this same gentleness and forgiveness to myself. I am so complex that I cannot accurately judge myself or be sure about the extent of my responsibility. I am not suggesting that we cop out with some projection like: "The devil made me do it." I have to be willing to accept responsibility for my actions and the effects of those actions. Still it is difficult to be certain about my subjective intentions. I am a fraction and the roots of my motivation are all entangled.

However, I can face the fact that my actions have been disordered and may have inflicted some harm on others. How responsible I was subjectively for those actions will always remain something of a mystery, even to me. Therefore, even though I must accept my responsibility, at the same time I must continue the effort to understand and forgive myself. In any case, an apology to those whom I have hurt, by commission or omission, remains very much in order.

At the same time, I acknowledge that I am a being in process, that "God is not finished with me yet." I am not about to dissolve in a sea of regret that I am not perfect. I have to be gentle with myself, to withhold all harsh judgments.

From *Will The Real Me Please Stand Up?*

A few years ago I was giving a retreat at a girls' high school in Chicago. One of the girls who came in to talk to me asked: "Father, do you remember the terrible fire at Our Lady of Angels Grammar School?"

"Oh, yes. Yes, I do." I replied.

"Well, I was in that fire," she said. "And I want to tell you about something. They told us that we couldn't go out into the hall because flames were raging in the corridors. We were told to jump out of the windows of our classroom. But I was so small that I couldn't get up on the windowsill. All the other kids in my grade got out. I was the last one, still trying to get up on the windowsill, when a larger girl who was just about to jump looked back and saw me. She came over to me and lifted me up on the windowsill. Then she pushed me out. As I landed in the schoolyard and looked up, I saw only flames coming from the window. She didn't make it. I will always remember that. It's a memory in me that will never sleep. She died but I have lived. She gave her life for me."

Memories are made of our past experiences. Like recordings, they keep playing in us. The things that have happened keep coming back like a refrain or a piece of music. I think it is really important for a family to know this and to think about it. The *experiences* of today will be tomorrow's *memories*. And memories are forever.

From the video program, *Families*

*T*heoretically, most of us would accept the fact that emotions are neither meritorious nor sinful. Feeling frustrated, or being annoyed, or experiencing fears and anger do not make one a good or bad person. Practically, however, most of us do not accept in our day to day living what we would accept in theory. We exercise a rather strict censorship of our emotions. If our censoring consciences do not approve certain emotions, we repress these emotions into our unconscious minds. Experts in psychosomatic medicine say that the most common cause of fatigue and actual sickness is this repression of emotions. The fact is that we have emotions which we do not want to admit. We are ashamed of our fears, or we feel guilty because of our anger. We are reluctant to admit our emotional and physical desires.

Before anyone of us can be liberated enough to practice "gut-level communication," in which we will be emotionally open and honest, we must feel convinced that emotions are *not moral* but simply *factual*. My jealousies, my anger, my sexual desires, my fears, and so forth do not make me a good or bad person. Of course, these emotional reactions must be integrated by my mind and will. However, before I can integrate them, and before I can decide whether to act on them or not, I must allow them to arise; I must clearly hear what they are saying to me. I must be able to say, without any sense of moral reprehension, that I am afraid or angry or sexually aroused.

Before I will be free enough to do this, however, I must be convinced that emotions are not moral, neither good nor bad in themselves. I must be convinced, too, that the experience of the whole gamut of emotions is a part of the human condition, the inheritance of every person.

From *Why Am I Afraid To Tell You Who I Am?*

*I*t is extremely important to understand this point. The non-repression of our emotions means that we must experience, recognize, and accept our emotions fully. It does not in any way imply that we will always *act on* those emotions. This would be tragic and the worst form of immaturity, if a person were to allow his or her feelings or emotions to control life. We can't let our emotions make our decisions. It is one thing to feel and to admit to myself and to others that I am afraid, but it is another thing to allow this fear to overwhelm me. It is one thing for me to feel and to admit that I am angry and another to punch you in the nose.

In the integrated person, emotions are neither repressed nor do they assume control of the whole person. They are recognized (What is it that I am feeling?) and integrated (Do I want to act on this feeling or not?).

From *Why Am I Afraid To Tell You Who I Am?*

I can understand myself only after I have communicated myself adequately to another. As a result of this growth in self-understanding I will find my patterns of immaturity changing into patterns of maturity. I will gradually change! Anyone of us who sees the *patterns* of his or her reactions, and is willing to examine them, will soon discover which ones are crippling and stifling. We may come to the realization, for example, that there are repeated patterns of hypersensitivity or paranoia in our habitual reactions. At the moment this realization penetrates, we will find the patterns changing. We must not believe that emotional patterns are purely biological or inevitable. *I can and will change my emotional patterns*, that is, I will move from one emotional reaction to another, if I have honestly allowed my emotions to arise for recognition and, having honestly reported them, judge them to be immature and undesirable.

In summary the dynamic is this: We allow our emotions to arise so that they can be identified. We observe the patterns in our emotional reactions, report them and judge them. Having done these things, we instinctively and immediately make the necessary adjustments in the light of our own ideals and hopes for growth. We change. Try this and see for yourself.

If all this is true, and you have only to experience it to know its truth, it is obvious that the little phrase we have used so conveniently, "I'm sorry, but that's the way I am . . . I was like this in the beginning, am now, and ever shall be . . ." is nothing more than a refuge and delusion. It is a handy explanation if we don't want to grow up. But if we do want to grow up, we must try to rise above this fallacy.

From *Why Am I Afraid To Tell You Who I Am?*

*F*ully human beings do not repress their emotions, as far as this is under their control, but allow them to rise to the surface of recognition. They experience the fullness of their emotional lives. They are "in touch with," attuned to their emotions, aware of what these emotions are saying about their human needs and their relationships with others. On the other hand, we have also said that this does not imply surrender to the emotions. In the fully human person, there is a balance of senses, emotions, intellect and will. The emotions have to be integrated. Though it is necessary to "report" our emotions, it is not at all necessary that we "act on" them. Above all, we don't allow them to make our decisions.

The critical importance of all this will be clear to you if you will reflect for just a moment that (1) almost all the pleasures and pains of life are deeply involved with the emotions. (2) Most human conduct is the result of emotional forces (even though we are all tempted to pose as pure intellects, and to explain on rational, objective grounds all of our preferences and actions). (3) Most interpersonal conflicts result from emotional stresses (e.g. anger, jealousy, frustration, and so forth), and most interpersonal encounters are achieved through some kind of emotional communion (e.g. empathy, tenderness, feelings of affection and attraction). In other words, your emotions and how you deal with them will probably make you or break you in the adventure of life.

From *Why Am I Afraid To Tell You Who I Am?*

*T*here is something already in us that explains our emotional reactions, but this doesn't mean that what is in us is bad or regrettable. The fear I have that there is a discrepancy between the word level and the commitment of my life is not bad or regrettable. It is me. Likewise I may become angry at seeing a bully picking on a defenseless victim, and find that the source of my anger, the thing which is inside me, is a healthy sense of justice and an active compassion for the underdogs of this world.

The important thing is the realization that every emotional reaction is trying to tell us something about ourselves. We must learn not to assign these reactions to others, preferring to blame them rather than to learn something about ourselves. When I do react emotionally, I know that not everyone would react as I have. Everyone does not have the same stored-up emotions which I have. In dealing simultaneously with many people, there is a great variety of emotional reactions. They are different people, have different needs; they come out of a different past and are seeking different goals. Consequently, their emotional reactions are different because of something inside each of them. The most I ever do is to stimulate these emotions. Similarly, if I want to know something about myself, my needs, my self-image, my sensitivity, my psychological programing and my values, then I must listen very sensitively to my own emotions.

From *The Secret Of Staying In Love*

*T*here are three general motives for emotional repression. We bury undesirable emotions because: 1) *We have been programed to do this.* Our so-called "parent-tapes" are constantly replaying their messages in us. Our deepest instincts have been educated in the first five years of our lives by our parents and others who have influenced us. 2) *We "moralize" emotions.* Depending on our background, we tend to label certain emotions "good" or "bad." For example, it is good to feel grateful but bad to feel angry or jealous. 3) The final consideration that prompts us to deny certain valid human feelings is a *"value conflict."* For example, if "being a man" has become an important part of my identity and self-image, a value upon which I place high premium, certain emotions will almost certainly be considered damaging to this image. I will have to edit my emotions carefully to preserve my masculinity.

I am not sure that all three of these motives cannot be reduced to one simple motive. What I need in order to go on living is self-acceptance-esteem-appreciation-a sense of celebration. I have tried to build up some kind of structure that will allow me this needed self-acceptance. I admit that it is like a house of match sticks. I must protect it from all threats: those that come from within as well as those which come from the outside. Emotions arising from within, if they are judged incompatible with self-acceptance, might endanger the precarious leaning tower of my self-image. I cannot have that. So I have headaches, allergies, ulcers, virus colds and spastic parts. Buried emotions are like rejected people; they make us pay a high price for having rejected them. Hell hath no fury like that of a scorned emotion.

From *The Secret of Staying In Love*

A friend invited me to make a week-long communications workshop and gave me a brochure which promised that this workshop would "put the participants in touch with their emotions." I remember my reaction. What? I smugly reassured myself that I was definitely in touch with my feelings and by a vote of one to nothing I agreed that I had no need of such a workshop. Finally, after further insistence from my friend, I agreed to go "just to see what they're doing at these things." The result was a Copernican revolution that turned me inside out and upside down.

Somehow, in sifting out the effects of that week, I became painfully aware that I had been lying to myself about me, about my feelings, my motives and goals. I had been so busy telling my feelings what they should be that I refused to let them tell me what they actually were. And I was so preoccupied socially with being a good and holy priest that I denied people my own authenticity. I had been playing the role of priest, spinning out like a phonograph record the messages that had been recorded and drilled into me by those who trained me. I never told people how I really felt. I never even told myself.

From *He Touched Me*

*I*n learning to understand ourselves we must learn to become very open to and accepting of all our emotional reactions. Being in touch with our emotions is the key to personal understanding. Consequently, we must learn to listen to our own emotions if we are to become growing persons. The basic belief in which I must repose absolute faith in order to understand myself by listening to my emotions is this: No one else can cause or be responsible for my emotions. Of course, we feel better assigning our emotions to other people. "You made me angry . . . You frightened me . . . You made me jealous," and so forth. The fact is that you can't make me anything. You can only *stimulate* the emotions that are already in me, waiting to be activated. The distinction between *causing* and *stimulating* emotions is not just a play on words. The acceptance of the truth involved is critical. If I think you can make me angry, then when I become angry I simply lay the blame and pin the problem on you. I can then walk away from our encounter learning nothing, concluding only that you were at fault because you made me angry. Then I need to ask no further questions of myself because I have laid all the responsibility at your feet.

If you and I can really believe this we will begin dealing with our emotions in a profitable way. We will no longer allow ourselves the easy escape into judgment and condemnation of others. We will become growing persons, more and more in touch with ourselves. Growing always begins where blaming ends.

From *The Secret Of Staying In Love*

*O*ur feelings in a sense are the summary expressions of our whole personal history. They are not simply our own highly personalized reaction to a given person or situation. They grow out of our earliest human experiences and our so-called "parent tapes" (messages received from parents and other significant persons early in life). Also, we model our emotional reactions on those of our parents, our brothers and sisters. But our emotional reactions are never exact copies because they are also an expression of our own unique human experiences. In fact, they summarize and express all the roots of our highly individualized human existence.

Viewed only in a here-and-now context, our emotions are the psychophysical reactions to our perceptions. If I perceive you to be my friend, I will feel secure when I am with you. The perception comes first. The emotion results from the perception. Historically, our perceptions, the way we see or perceive a given object, have been largely shaped by other significant persons and events in our lives. These persons and events are like recorded messages that have been left on our mind-machines.

Consequently, in telling you my feelings I am somehow sharing with you the whole of my life: the people who have influenced me and the experiences that have shaped me. It is true that my feelings can be tilted in one direction or another by recent amounts of sleep or food, by what has gone right or wrong during my day. Still the sharing of my feelings is my ultimate self-revelation. In confiding my feelings to you, I may be saying that a person who has had my parents and experiences reacts thus and so when he is tired or hungry. I am always telling you where I have been and who I am when I am sharing my feelings with you.

From *Will The Real Me Please Stand Up?*

*H*ave you ever watched a tight-rope walker? Maybe you noticed that the performer carried a "balance bar." Ever so carefully he moved the bar from side to side in order to keep his balance. Now life is something like this for us. You and I are negotiating the difficult, if different, courses of our lives. Life means action and action means other people. Other people mean that there will be some friction, and friction often results in stress. Some of this stress is helpful and positive. Some of it is negative and harmful. We badly need our balance bars.

Some have suggested that the management of tension should be holistic, should affect all our parts. Therefore it should be approached:

Physically—by getting physical exercise and eating a balanced diet.

Emotionally—by expressing all our significant feelings at the time we are having them.

Socially—by phoning a friend, having a party, getting together with people we like.

Intellectually—by feeding the mind with reading, doing a crossword puzzle, attending a lecture.

Spiritually—by admiring the beauty of the world, listening to music; by spending ten minutes a day meditating or praying.

From *Will The Real Me Please Stand Up?*

*T*he practice of emotional openness will eventually result in two very valuable abilities: We will learn to *identify* our negative stressors and we will be able to *reevaluate* them. As mentioned earlier, stress of itself can be either a positive or negative force. It's like the tension in a violin or guitar string. If it is too tight, it will snap. If there is no tension, there is no music either. And so, stress in itself is neutral. However, our reactions to it, based on our personal beliefs and values, are what give a stressor either a positive or negative power over us. The biological computer of the body often helps us differentiate. However, if I examine my daily life by listening to and learning from an open expression of my emotional reactions, I will slowly locate and learn to identify the negative stressors in my life.

In other words, under every emotion lies an attitude: toward success, conflict, expectations, time, perfection, pleasing others, and so forth. However, I can uncover and explore these attitudes only if I am willing to experience and to express my feelings. I've got to welcome, acknowledge, and express these feelings before I can learn from them.

So have your feelings, own them and express them. And above all, learn from them.

From *Will The Real Me Please Stand Up?*

*I*t is obvious to me that each new day—along with all the persons and events of that day—does in fact question us, if we will submit to the test. The needy, unattractive person asks me how much I can love. The death of a dear one asks me what I really believe about death and how profitably I can confront loss and loneliness. A beautiful day or a beautiful person asks me how capable I am of enjoyment. Solitude asks me if I really like myself and enjoy my own company. A good joke asks me if I have a sense of humor. A very different type of person from a background dissimilar to my own asks me if I am capable of empathy and understanding. Success and failure ask me to define my ideas of success and failure. Suffering asks me if I really believe I can grow through adversity. Negative criticism directed to me asks me about my sensitivities and self-confidence. The devotion and commitment of another to me asks me if I will let myself be loved.

Yes, every day does, in fact, question us. However, most answers do not pop out automatically, because we have quarantined them out of sight. Selective inattention has buried so many of my memories, thoughts, and emotions in graves of obscurity. My illusory self has served as a self-appointed censor, allowing me contact only with thoughts and emotions that are judged to be acceptable, but not permitting me those thoughts and emotions which would threaten my fictitious identity.

From *Fully Human, Fully Alive*

A sense of his or her own worth is no doubt the greatest gift we can offer to another, the greatest contribution we can make to any life. We can give this gift and make this contribution only through love. However, it is essential that our love be liberating, not possessive. We must at all times give those we love the freedom to be themselves. Love affirms the other *as other*. It does not possess and manipulate another *as mine*. Pertinent here is the quotation of Frederick Perls: "You did not come into this world to live up to my expectations. And I did not come into the world to live up to yours. If we meet it will be beautiful. If we don't, it can't be helped."

To love is to liberate. Love and friendship must empower those we love to become their best selves, according to their own lights and visions. This means that wanting what is best for you and trying to be what you need me to be can be done only in a way that preserves your freedom to have your own feelings, think your own thoughts and make your own decisions. If your personhood is as dear to me as my own, which is the implication of love, I must respect it carefully and sensitively. When I affirm you, my affirmation is based on your unconditional value as a unique, unrepeatable and even sacred mystery of humanity.

In evaluating my love for you, I must then address myself to the question of whether my love is in fact possessive and manipulative or really affirming and freeing. It will help, in this evaluation, to ask myself these questions: Is it more important to me that you be pleased with yourself or that I be pleased with you? Is it more important that you attain the goals you have set for yourself, or that you attain the goals I want for you?

From *The Secret of Staying In Love*

*T*he vocation of putting people straight, of tearing off their masks, of forcing them to face the repressed truth, is a highly dangerous and destructive calling. Eric Berne warns against disillusioning people about their "games." It may be that others just can't take this. They sought out some role, began playing some game, took to wearing some mask, precisely because this would make life more liveable and tolerable.

So we must be careful, extremely careful in fact, that we do not assume the vocation of acquainting others with their delusions. We are all tempted to unmask others, to smash their defenses, to leave them naked and blinking in the light of the illumination provided by our exposé. It could be tragic in its results. If the psychological pieces come unglued, who will pick them up and put poor Humpty Dumpty Human Being together again? Will you? Can you?

From *Why Am I Afraid To Tell You Who I Am?*

*W*e must become aware that we are capable of using people for our own advantage, for the satisfaction of our deep and throbbing human needs. And we can be deluded into thinking that this is really love. The young man who professes to love a young woman may often be deceived into thinking that the gratification of his own egotistical urges really constitutes love. The young woman who finds the voids of her own loneliness filled by the companionship and attention of a young man may well mistake this emotional satisfaction for love. Likewise, the mother and father who anxiously try to promote the success of their children can easily rationalize their desire for the vicarious experience of success and convince themselves that they are loving parents. The critical question always remains that of self-forgetfulness. Does the young man or woman, the mother or father really forget self and their own convenience and emotional satisfaction, to seek only the happiness and fulfillment of the beloved? These are not merely theoretical questions. The fact of the matter is that, for most of us, our own needs are so palpable and real to us, that it is enormously difficult for the seed to fall into the ground and die to itself before it can live a life of love.

From *Why Am I Afraid To Love?*

I feel pretty sure that most people I know identify love with a feeling or emotion. They "fall in love" and "fall out of love," in uneven rhythms. The flame of love is extinguished in their lives only until a new match can be struck.

Now everyone knows that feelings are like yo-yos, up and down, depending on such fickle things as the barometer, amounts of sunshine, digestion, the time of the month and the side of the bed out of which we crawl on a given morning. Feelings are fickle, and people who identify love with feelings become fickle lovers.

It is obvious that feelings *are related to love*. The first attraction of love is usually experienced in terms of very strong feelings. And I cannot—unless I am some kind of a hero or masochist—put your satisfaction, security and development on par with my own if I do not for the most part have supportive, loving feelings towards you. However, in the course of a love-relationship, we will have to go through an occasional winter of emotional discontent to find a newness of our love in the springtime. As the tinsel of young love is burnished by time into the more valuable gold of mature love, there will be times when emotional satisfaction will be absent, and there will be other times when negative feelings will cloud the skies of our world; but certainly growth in love supposes and needs generally good emotional weather.

It would be fatal to identify love with a feeling, because of the fickleness of feelings. However, it would be equally lethal to a relationship of love if there were no warm and loving feelings to support the intentions of love.

From *The Secret Of Staying In Love*

We have said that any suggestion of competition undermines a love-relationship and the practice of dialogue. The opposite and appropriate spirit is that of collaboration. It is a spirit that takes for granted that we are committed to each other in love, that we are willing to bear each other's burdens and share each other's joys. We have lost two I's to become one We. We will work at life's challenges together. We will succeed sometimes and sometimes we will fail, but we will be together. This sense of "togetherness" may well be the nicest and most sustaining awareness we will have. It is the joy of achieving together, of collaboration, of unity.

If self-appreciation and celebration are really the beginning of love and the fullness of life, we will achieve it together. You will look into my eyes and see there the great cause you have for self-celebration and I shall see my beauty, my value in your eyes. I want to be the first of the invited guests at your celebration-of-self party. And I want you to come to my party, because without you there never could have been such a party. Where there is unity like this, the butterfly of happiness cannot be far away.

From *The Secret Of Staying In Love*

*L*oving you does not mean that I cease to love myself. On the contrary, the idea that I cannot love you unless I love myself is universally accepted by psychologists. Those who do not love themselves are sad, plagued by a constant sense of emptiness which they are always trying to fill. Like a person with a painful toothache, they can think only of themselves and are constantly in search of a dentist, someone to make them feel better. If I do not love myself, I can only *use* others; I cannot love them.

My loving you can never be an abdication of my own self. I could possibly give my life for you out of love, but I could never deny my identity as a person. I will try to be what you need me to be, to do what you need done, to say whatever you need to hear. At the same time I am committed to an honest and open relationship. As a part of my gift of love, I will always offer my thoughts, preferences, and all my feelings, even when I think they may be unpleasant or even hurtful to your feelings. If we are committed to total honesty and total openness, our relationship will never become a sticky one, marked by hidden agendas, repressed resentments, displaced emotions, acting out in adolescent ways what we do not have the courage to speak out. Unless we agree to honor honesty and openness, we will never be sure of each other. Out relationship will seem more like a charade than a real life drama.

From *Unconditional Love*

*A*ll of us experience at some time or another a feeling of loneliness or isolation, a very painful void inside of ourselves that becomes an unbearable prison. We have all felt at some time alienated from others, separate from the group, alone and lonely. By its very nature this loneliness, like all of our toothaches, centers the focus of attention on ourselves. We seek to fill this void, to satisfy this hunger . . . we go out to find others who will love us.

We may do things for them in an obvious attempt to gain their love. We may come to them with hands stretched out like pan scales. On the one hand is our donation to them, the other hand being extended to receive their donation to us. We may even be deceived into thinking that this is loving.

We know that our loneliness can be filled only by the love of others. We know that we must feel loved. The paradox is this: if we seek to fill the void of our own loneliness in seeking love from others, we will inevitably find no consolation but only deeper desolation. It is true that "You're Nobody Till Somebody Loves You." Only the person who has experienced love is capable of growing. It is a frightening but true reality of human life that, by loving me or refusing to love me, others hold the potential of my maturity in their hands. Most of us, driven by our own aching needs and voids, address life and other people in the stance of seekers. We try to seek the love that we need from others. But the paradox remains uncompromised; if we *seek* the love which we need, we will *never find it*. We are lost.

From *Why Am I Afraid To Love?*

*L*ove can effect the solution of our problems, but we must face the fact that to be loved, we must become lovable. When we orient our lives toward the satisfaction of our own needs and when we go out to seek for ourselves that love we need, no matter how others may try to soften their judgments of us, we are in fact self-centered. We are not lovable, even if we do deserve compassion. We are concentrating on ourselves, and so our ability to love will always remain stunted, and we will remain perennial infants.

If however, we seek not to gain love for ourselves directly, but rather seek to give it, we will become lovable and we will most certainly be loved in return. This is the immutable law under which we live: concern for ourself and convergence upon self can only isolate self and induce an even deeper and more torturous loneliness. It is a vicious and terrible cycle that closes in on us when loneliness, seeking to be relieved through the love of others, only increases.

The only way we can break this cycle formed by our lusting egos is *to stop being concerned with ourselves* and *to begin to be concerned with others*. This, of course, is not easy. To relocate the focus of one's mind from self to others can, in fact, mean a lifetime of effort and work. It is made more difficult because we must put others in the forefront, in place of ourselves. We must learn to respond to the needs of others without seeking the satisfaction of our own needs.

From *Why Am I Afraid To Love?*

*T*he problem is that we are all clutching to our own life-rafts. Each of us must make a decision about how we intend to spend our lives. If we decide to spend our lives in the pursuit of our own happiness and fulfillment, we are destined to failure and desolation. If we decide to spend our lives seeking the fulfillment and happiness of others, and this is what is implied in love, we shall certainly attain our own happiness and fulfillment.

People who want only their own fulfillment, or who decide to love in order that they might be fulfilled, will find that their efforts are in vain because the focus of attention remains on themselves. Persons can grow only as much as their horizon allows, and those who decide to love in order to be fulfilled and happy will be disappointed and will not grow because their horizon is still themselves. Consequently, we cannot conceive of love in any way as a means of self-fulfillment, because if we do we will still be within the treacherous vicious circle, traveling always from our own needs through others and back into ourselves. We cannot ever use others as means. They must always be the end-object of love. We will attain maturity only in proportion to the shifting of the focus of our minds away from ourselves and our own needs and away from the self-centered desire to satisfy those needs.

From *Why Am I Afraid To Love?*

*L*oving others can be truly accomplished only when the focus of our minds and the object of our desires is another, when all the activity results from concern for another and not from concern for ourselves. If we truly love in this way, we will be loved and we should accept the love of others. However, the delusion to be avoided at all costs is to love in order to receive this return. I must, as Christ suggests, lose my life before I can gain it. I must find out that the only real receiving is in giving. I have to lose my life and I cannot lose it if I always have it clearly before my own mind.

In other words, love means a concern for, acceptance of, and an interest in the others around me whom I am trying to love. It is a self-donation which may prove to be an altar of sacrifice. I can love others only to the extent they are truly the focus of my mind, heart, and life; and I can find myself only by forgetting myself. Love is indeed costly and demanding. Because of the inward pains that all of us bear, the scar tissues that are part of our human inheritance, because of the competition and example of a self-grasping world, it will be difficult for us to make the sacrifice of ourselves that is involved in loving. Loving always means at least this sacrifice, the orientation of my thoughts and desires towards others and the abandonment of my own self and self-interest. Needless to say, such abandonment always involves a high cost to self.

From *Why Am I Afraid To Love?*

A life of love is difficult, but it is not a bleak or unrewarding life. In fact, it is the only truly human and happy life for it is filled with concerns that are as deep as life, as wide as the whole world, and as far reaching as eternity. It is only when we have consented to love, and have agreed to forget ourselves, that we can find our fulfillment. This fulfillment will come unperceived and mysterious like the grace of God, but we will recognize it and it will be recognized in us. We will have made the Copernican revolution that relocates the focus of our minds and hearts on the good and fulfillment of others; and although this conversion has sought nothing for itself, it has received everything. The lovable person is, in the last analysis, the one who has made the consent to love.

So often we demand that others love us without being willing to make the sacrifice and abandonment of self that is necessary to become lovable. However, if anyone has mastered the delicate and profound paradox that love involves, and has been willing to dedicate him or herself without reservation or demand for return, he or she will certainly be loved and fulfilled.

From *Why Am I Afraid To Love?*

*B*ut how can we love if we have never been loved? Between black and white there is always an area of gray. All of us have some capacity to love, some ability to move the focus of our minds out from ourselves to the needs, happiness and fulfillment of others. To the extent that we do this, to the extent that we actualize this potential that is latent within us, we will be loved. Even if at the beginning we can love only a little, we shall be loved a little; and the love that we receive will empower us to grow more and more out of ourselves in the direction that love leads. This, then, is the challenge that lies before each of us: we must utilize whatever capacity, be it small or great, we have for loving. To the extent that we are willing to make the effort and dedication that is involved, we will be nourished and strengthened by the love that we shall receive in return; but we must remember that, in making this self-donation, the focus of our minds must always be away from self and this precludes thinking of or asking for a return. When we ask that question: "What have you done for me?" we have ceased to love.

From *Why Am I Afraid To Love?*

*T*he biblical formula for a good life is this: "Love persons/Use things." When God made the world he saw that it was very good. The world is charged, indeed, with the grandeur of God. And he calls upon us to join him in that pronouncement: "It is very good!" We are invited to use and to enjoy all God's good things. But we are warned: Don't ever let your heart be owned by things. If you *love* things, you will soon begin *using* persons to get, or get more of, the things you love. Save your heart for love, and save your love for persons.

The biblical imperative is illustrated by an example from the life of Martin Buber, the "I–Thou" philosopher. Buber directed his philosophical speculation toward "I–Thou" matters, toward the primacy of persons, after a very sad incident. A young man came to Buber's office one day, asking for some time. "I need to see you." Buber declined on the grounds that he was preparing a paper for delivery at a convention at a later date. That night the young man killed himself. His suicide touched Buber very deeply. In a renewed and painful way, he learned the importance of loving persons and using things.

This "Love persons/Use things" is a delicate equilibrium that is easily unbalanced. The moment that we start loving things we begin to use people to get the things we love. Consequently, the Bible does not say that "money is the root of all evil." It says that "*love* of money is the root of all evil." Where your treasure is there your heart will be. When we get hooked, for example, on praise and adulation, we allow entrance into our world only those who bring with them the necessary price of admission. When we get hooked on our own pleasures and satisfactions, we refuse to allow a place in our world for those who might be a burden or an inconvenience. We will not accept the challenge of love.

From *The Silent Holocaust*

*I*n the Gospels (Luke 1:26–38), we read of an angel coming to a young girl with a question she could not have anticipated: "Will you be the mother of the Messiah?" Gathering her startled wits together, the young girl asks the only important question: "Is this really the will of God? Does God really want this of me?" This had always been her heart's desire: to do God's will in all things. The angel assures her that it is the will of God, and the young girl, Mary, bows her head with an immediate "yes!" "I am the Lord's servant. Let it happen to me as you have said!" (Luke 1:38). And so, in this moment the Word was made flesh. The Son of God took his humanity from her body and from the power of God, took up his residence within her, under her immaculate heart.

When Mary said, "Let it be done!" she did not understand all the other "yeses" that would be inside her first "yes." Scripture scholars do not think she knew that the Messiah whom she had consented to mother would in fact be the Son of God. I am also sure that when she became visibly pregnant, she did not know how to explain her motherhood to Joseph, who was "making plans to divorce her." I think she wondered often about the future of the little baby she held in her arms that night in Bethlehem. Afterward, she did not understand that faraway look in the eyes of her little boy. It was a look that seemed to stare far into the future. It was almost as though he knew it was his destiny to do something that would change the whole course of human history. Likewise, I think that Mary was puzzled by his response to her worried question when he was lost in the temple: "Son, why did you do this to us? Your father and I have been terribly worried trying to find you." He answered only, "Didn't you know that I had to be about my Father's business?" I am sure that Mary did not understand.

From *The Christian Vision*

*M*ary was not with Jesus on Palm Sunday. She did not hear the "Hosannas!" or experience the tingling excitement of his public acclamation and triumphant entry into Jerusalem. The final gospel portrait of Mary is the terrifying scene on Calvary. She stands there bravely at the foot of his cross, watching her son die slowly and painfully. And as the sky darkens, she holds the dead body of her son in her trembling arms.

Michelangelo has carved out of marble a beautiful tribute to this young woman. It is likewise a tribute to her "yes" to God's will. In the statue, Mary is holding Jesus in her arms, looking upon his torn body with a mother's tender and loving compassion. Michelangelo calls his statue the "Pietà." *Pietà* is an Italian word which means "faithfulness." Mary is the woman who with all her heart wanted only the will of God, who said her "yes" but did not understand all that it would involve. But she trusted God, trusted that he loved her, trusted his wisdom and his ways, even when she did not understand. Michelangelo's summary of her incredible achievement is the one word: PIETÀ.

She said her "yes" to God's will, and she was faithful to the end.

The Christian who has really put on the mind of Christ knows that the Lord never really spoke of success, but only of "faithfulness," of *pietà.* When we see our Christian lives in the perspective of the gospels, faithfulness to God's will is the only real, eternal crown of success.

May an angel write on our tombstones, yours and mine, the appropriate epitaph to summarize our lives upon this earth: PIETÀ.

From *The Christian Vision*

I am fairly sure that when you or I confide our *feelings* to another, we have a sense that we are really sharing our *true selves*. We don't have many completely original thoughts. At least I can't remember having one. And we haven't made many original choices. But no one in all of human history has had your precise feelings. No one has ever felt as I do. Our feelings are as unique and original as our fingerprints. For example, a person might summarize himself or herself by saying: "I am a Christian and a lawyer, and my family is my life." Nice and neat, eh? But you don't really get to know the individual person from such summary statements. The majority of Americans identify with Christianity, and there is a lawyer for every seven thousand of us. Devotees of the family are also fairly common.

People who are willing to share only their thoughts and choices with us in this manner might as well be sharing the last book they have read. But if a person confides and describes his or her feelings—the loneliness and the struggling, the fears and the joys, the peace of certainty and the pain of doubt—then we will have a sense that we are getting to know who the person really is. Tell me what you think and I can possibly put you in a category; tell me what you feel and I will get to know you.

From *Will The Real Me Please Stand Up?*

*D*ialogue must precede discussion because the static of unresolved and unexpressed emotions will block all attempts at the open, free-flowing exchange that leads to plans, decisions, and so forth. The presumption has been that these emotions are negative. In the case of positive emotions, there is an even more compelling motive to practice dialogue before discussion. I become a transparent, knowable individual to you only when I tell you my feelings. My ideas, convictions, values, persuasions are really not original with me. I have got them from reading, by inhaling traditions, by listening to and imitating others, by the inevitable osmosis of human contagion. My ideas and the stances I take can locate me in a category, like "Irish," "Catholic," or Democrat," but they can never make me transparent and knowable, so that you can experience me, share my person. Only my feelings, positive-negative-neutral, do this. My feelings are like my fingerprints, the color of my eyes, and the sound of my voice: unique to me and unrepeatable in anyone else. To know me you must know my feelings. And only when you know *me* through dialogue, at any moment of my life, will you be able to understand my ideas, preferences, and intentions, shared in discussion.

I have watched this truth proved again and again in public forums, in classrooms, in living room conversation, and in one-to-one communication. My emotions are the key to me. When I give you this key, you can come into me, and share with me the most precious gift I have to offer you: myself.

From *The Secret Of Staying In Love*

I think that we fail not so much in the great commitment of love, but rather in the daily work of love which is comunication. We can share anything else with a person and still not be close to that person. We can share food and money. We can even share sexual intimacy and not be close to the other person. But there is one thing, I would suggest, that we cannot share with another person and not be close. The honest and open sharing of all *feelings* has to result in personal closeness and intimacy.

Your feelings reveal, as nothing else can, the real you. For example, I can stand up here and say to you, "I am a priest!" And you would reply, "Oh, come on, the woods are full of them." And I reply, "That's the essential commitment of my life!" And you say, "Yeah, but you haven't told us very much about yourself. How does it feel to be a priest? Are you lonely? What is Saturday night for you? When you walk down the street and there is a young, loving couple walking in front of you, holding hands, do you wish you had a hand you could hold? Do you sing in your heart, 'Hello, Young Lovers Wherever You Are'? How do you feel about these things?" If I tell you how I feel about these things, then you will get to know me. You can talk on the level of clichés or about other people, and have all the news at your fingertips, or you can be the humorous person who keeps everyone laughing, but you don't really share yourself until you share your feelings. We call it "gut-level" communication. It is this, I think, that is the secret of love.

From the video program, *Free To Be Me*

*S*omeone has aptly distinguished five levels of communication on which persons can relate to one another. Perhaps it will help our understanding of these levels to visualize a person locked inside a prison. It is the human being, urged by an inner insistence to go out to others and yet afraid to do so. The five levels of communication represent five degrees of willingness to go outside of ourselves, to communicate ourselves to others.

The man in the prison—and he is Everyman—has been there for years, although ironically the grated iron doors are not locked. He can go out of his prison, but in his long detention he has learned to fear the possible dangers that he might encounter. He has come to feel some sort of safety and protection behind the walls of his prison, where he is a voluntary captive. The darkness of his prison even shields him from a clear view of himself, and he is not sure what he would look like in broad daylight. Above all, he is not sure how the world, which he sees from behind his bars, and the people whom he sees moving about in that world, would receive him. He is fragmented by an almost desperate need for that world and for those people, and, at the same time, by an almost desperate fear of the risks of rejection he would be taking if he ended his isolation.

From *Why Am I Afraid To Tell You Who I Am?*

*T*he person locked inside self is reminiscent of what Viktor Frankl writes in his book, *Man's Search For Meaning,* about his fellow prisoners in the Nazi concentration camp at Dachau. Some of these prisoners, who yearned so desperately for their freedom, had been held captive so long that, when they were eventually released, they walked out into the sunlight, blinked nervously and then silently walked back into the familiar darkness of the prisons, to which they had been accustomed for such a long time.

This is the visualized, if somewhat dramatic, dilemma that all of us experience at some time in our lives and in the process of becoming persons. Most of us make only a weak response to the invitation of encounter with others and our world because we feel uncomfortable in exposing our nakedness as persons. Some of us are willing only to pretend this exodus, while others somehow find the courage to go all the way out to freedom.

From *Why Am I Afraid To Tell You Who I Am?*

*C*ommunication on level five, cliché conversation, represents the weakest response to the human dilemma and the lowest level of self-communication. In fact, there is no communication here at all, unless by accident. On this level, we talk in clichés, such as: "How are you? . . . How is your family? . . . Where have you been?" We say things like: "I like your dress very much." "I hope we can get together again real soon." "It's really good to see you." In fact, we really mean almost nothing of what we are asking or saying. If the other party were to begin answering our question, "How are you?" in detail, we would be astounded. Usually and fortunately the other party senses the superficiality and convention-ality of our concern and question, and obliges us by simply giving the standard answer, "Just fine, thank you."

This is the conversation, the non-communication, of the cocktail party, the club meeting, the neighborhood laundromat, and so forth. There is no sharing of persons at all. Everyone remains safely in the isolation of pretense, sham, and sophistication. The whole group seems to gather to be lonely together. It is well summarized in the lyrics of Paul Simon in *Sounds of Silence* used so effectivly in the movie, *The Graduate:*

> And in the naked light I saw
> Ten thousand people, maybe more,
> People talking without speaking,
> People hearing without listening,
> People writing songs that voices never shared.
> No one dared
> Disturb the sounds of silence.

From *Why Am I Afraid To Tell You Who I Am?*

*C*ommunication on level four, reporting the facts about others, keeps us from stepping very far outside the prison of our loneliness into real communication because we expose almost nothing of ourselves. We remain contented to tell others what so-and-so has said or done. We offer no personal, self-revelatory commentary on these facts, but simply report them. Just as most of us, at times, hide behind clichés, so we also seek shelter in gossip items, conversation pieces, and little narrations about others. We give nothing of ourselves and invite nothing from others in return.

From *Why Am I Afraid To Tell You Who I Am?*

*C*ommunication of level three, my ideas and judgments, offers some communication of my person. I am willing to take this step out of my solitary confinement. I will take the risk of telling you some of my ideas and reveal some of my judgments and decisions. My communication usually remains under a strict censorship, however. As I communicate my ideas, and so forth, I will be watching you carefully. I want to test the temperature of the water before I leap in. I want to be sure that you will accept me with my ideas, judgments and decisions. If you raise your eyebrow or narrow your eyes, if you yawn or look at your watch, I will probably retreat to safer ground. I will run for the cover of silence, or change the subject of conversation, or worse, I will start to say things I suspect that you want me to say. I will try to be what pleases you.

Someday, perhaps, when I develop the courage and the intensity of desire to grow as a person, I will spill all of the contents of my mind and heart before you. It will be my moment of truth.

From *Why Am I Afraid To Tell You Who I Am?*

*C*ommunication on level two involves the sharing of my feelings (emotions). "Gut-level." It might not occur to many of us that, once we have revealed our ideas, judgments, and decisions, there is really much more of our persons to share. Actually, the things that most clearly differentiate and individuate me from others, that make the communication of my person a unique knowledge, are my *feelings* or *emotions.*

If I really want you to know who I am, I must tell you about my stomach (gut-level) as well as my head. My ideas, judgments, and decisions are quite conventional. If I am Republican or Democrat by persuasion, I have a lot of company. If I am for or against space exploration, there will be others who will support me in my conviction. But the *feelings* that lie under my ideas, judgments, and convictions are uniquely mine. No one supports a politcal party, or has a religious conviction, or is committed to a cause with my exact feelings of fervor or apathy. No one experiences my precise sense of frustration, labors under my fears, feels my passions. Nobody opposes war with my particular indignation or supports patriotism with my unique sense of loyalty.

It is these feelings, on this level of communication, which I must share with you, if I am to tell you who I really am.

From *Why Am I Aftraid To Tell You Who I Am?*

*M*ost of us feel that others will not tolerate emotional honesty in communication. We would rather defend dishonesty on the grounds that our honesty might hurt others, and, having rationalized our phoniness into nobility, we settle for superficial relationships. This occurs not only in the case of casual acquaintances, but even with members of our own families; it destroys authentic communion within marriages. Consequently, we ourselves do not grow, nor do we help anyone else to grow. Meanwhile, we have to live with repressed emotions—a dangerous, self-destructive path to follow. Any relationship, which is to have the nature of true personal encounter, must be based on this honest, open, gut-level communication. The alternative is to remain in my prison, to endure inch-by-inch death as a person.

From *Why Am I Afraid To Tell You Who I Am?*

*C*ommunication on level one: peak communication. All deep and authentic friendships, and especially the union of those who are married, must be based on absolute openness and honesty. At times, gut-level communication will be most difficult, but it is at these precise times that it is most necessary. Among close friends, or between partners in marriage there will come from time to time a complete emotional and personal communion.

In our human condition this can never be a permanent experience. There should and will be, however, moments when encounter attains perfect communication. At these times the two persons will feel an almost perfect and mutual empathy. I know that my own reactions are shared completely with my friend; my happiness or grief is perfectly reduplicated in him or her. We are like two musical instruments playing exactly the same note, filled with and giving forth precisely the same sound. This is what is meant by level one, peak communication.

From *Why Am I Afraid To Tell You Who I Am?*

*T*o understand the effects of peak communication let us imagine a man who stays in his apartment alone all day. While there he has a feeling of safety. There is no necessity to interact with other people who may threaten or actually hurt him. He knows where everything is, the night lamp, the bathroom, the Pepto Bismol. He is at least secure from harm in his stagnation. The whole world outside his little apartment is lost on him. He is alive but not very. He is breathing but not really living. Then one day he looks out his window and sees another person who is experiencing a moment of emotional intensity. It is so interesting, so captivating that he forgets about all his fears. He unlocks the door, he goes out to the other and for that lovely, liberating moment he experiences another world. He breathes a new and fresh air. The light and warmth of the sun fall on him for the first time. And then he knows something. The life in him has been expanded. He can never go back, never be the same again, or live the same narrow, cramped existence. He wouldn't fit in that world anymore, and all because he has been drawn out of himself to someone else in a profound way. All the dimensions of his world, the anticipations and prejudices in which he has been imprisoned to some extent fall away.

In the wake of peak experiences, both partners are permanently, even if not always dramatically, altered because the whole relationship acquires a new depth and intensity. There will be a new perspective in which each will see the other.

From *The Secret Of Staying In Love*

*L*et me try to explain what I mean by peak experience in communication. First of all, I presume that in such a peak experience one of the persons opens up in such a way that the other is called out of him or herself and out of all the old and fixed positions, out of old calculations, into a new experience. This new experience is not only a deeper knowledge of the reality of one's partner, but also by later refraction and assimilation it will be a new experience of one's own capacity and reality. Such an experience will leave that reality forever changed, more open, more loving, more alive.

Since my emotions are what define and reveal the essential me, I will necessarily be revealing my *feelings* in the moment of transparency. It is the sharing of my feelings that will provide you with the opportunity to know me in a new way, to know yourself in a new way, and to be changed by that knowledge. Perhaps it will be in the context of relating an incident or expressing my love, but it will be the feeling or emotional content that will carry the charge and offer the experience of my person. Unless I open my feelings, you will simply "project" into me your own emotions. For example, if I tell you that I have failed in some way without describing vividly my exact emotional reaction to the failure, you will anticipate that my reaction was what yours would be in a similar situation; and it never, never is. You will, if I deny you my emotional depths, never get to know me, or be enriched by the kind of peak experience described here.

From *The Secret Of Staying In Love*

*A*nother person or circumstance may stimulate a reaction in me. But the specific way that I react will be determined by my own attitudes and personal perspective. These in turn have been shaped by the messages recorded on my mind-tapes and the experiences of my life. Attitudes are as highly personal as fingerprints. Consequently, no two people ever see anything in exactly the same way. You may laugh off something that I will take seriously. You may react compassionately to a person with whom I would become angry. Let us both suppose that the very same thing happens to both of us. It is very possible that you will be exhilarated by the challenge while I am devastated by the catastrophe.

A blamer who projects the responsibility for his or her reactions never really grows up. The life of such a person is a perpetual exercise in projection and rationalization. It is a life of pretense that is never really penetrated by reality. Blamers insist that someone else is pulling their strings. So they never really get to know the inner reality of themselves. "The fault, Dear Brutus, is not with our stars but within ourselves that we are underlings." (*Julius Caesar,* Act 1, Scene 2)

If we really sit and soak in the truth of all this, it will be immediately apparent in our communication. We will make "I statements" rather than "You statements." The significance of this will be far greater than a mere choice of words.

From *Will The Real Me Please Stand Up?*

*I*f I make an "I statement"—"I felt angry"—I am assuming responsibility for my own reaction. I am acknowledging that another person in my position might well have reacted differently. I may not easily or readily understand all the attitudes and the perspective that have shaped my reaction. However, I do know that my reaction has been the result of something in me. When I make an "I statement," I admit this to myself and to you.

In fact, I notice that I get angry at some people while others only feel sorry for them. I get upset by certain circumstances while others take them in stride. I perceive some situations as "absolutely awful," but I am aware that others see these exact situations as "a chance to be creative."

The important personal effect of all this is that if I do own my own reactions and accept responsibility for them, I will discover my true self. I will gradually realize that I do have some crippling, distorted attitudes that must be revised. And this kind of honesty will prove to be an irresistible initiation into maturity.

From *Will The Real Me Please Stand Up?*

*L*et us suppose that I have reacted angrily to something you have done or said. In this case I can tell you of my anger in one of two ways: (1) "You made me angry!" (This is a "You statement.") (2) or I can say, "When you said what you did, I felt angry." (This is a "I statement.") The first expression, the "You statement," directly denies the truth of all that we have said about personal responsibility for our own reactions. But more than this, it lays a guilt trip on you. It is an attempted but thinly disguised manipulation. I am maneuvering you into the positon of the "bad guy." Right? Such a remark, if you are the combative type, will invite you into a heated, win-lose argument. It will certainly generate more heat than light.

From *Will The Real Me Please Stand Up?*

*M*ost of us are tempted to generalize our personal experience. We forget that others are really "other," different from us. We often make the false presumption that everyone reacts exactly as we do. This temptation to generalize is an indication that I have discovered "otherness" only imperfectly. I have not yet fully realized how unique and individual each of us is. Because of this I am persistently tempted to project my reactions into others. If something hurts or bothers me, I presume that it will hurt or bother everyone. If a given situation stimulates a worried reaction in me, I presume that anyone would worry in such a situation. Such a habit of thinking and speaking makes me the norm of all human reality and reaction. The discovery of "otherness" is essential to a good communicator.

No human being on the face of this earth possesses the whole truth. Each of us has only a small part; but if we are willing to share our small parts, our pieces of the truth, we will all possess a much fuller reality, a much larger share of the total truth. The picture comes to mind of two people on opposite sides of a solid fence. One side of the fence is painted brown and the other green. If the person on the green side keeps insisting, "This fence definitely is green," he will invite contradiction from the person standing on the other side of the fence. "No, it's not. It's clearly brown." Obviously each has a part of the truth, just as we all do in most of our disagreements. It's hard to imagine that a person could be totally wrong about any complex issue. Everyone has some part of the truth to share.

From *Will The Real Me Please Stand Up?*

*T*he classic temptation in this matter, and it would seem to be the most destructive of all delusions in this area of human relations, is this: we are tempted to think that communication of an unfavorable emotional reaction will tend to be divisive. If I tell you that it bothers me when you do something you are accustomed to do, I may be tempted to believe that it would be better not to mention it. Our relationship will be more peaceful. You wouldn't understand, anyway.

So I keep it inside myself, and each time you do your thing my stomach keeps score 2 . . . 3 . . . 4 . . . 5 . . . 6 . . . 7 . . . 8 . . . until one day you do the same thing that you have always done and all hell breaks loose. All the while you were annoying me, I was keeping it inside and somewhere, secretly, learning to hate you. My good thoughts were turning to gall.

When it finally erupted in one great avalanche, you didn't understand. You thought that this kind of reaction was totally uncalled for. The bonds of our love seemed fragile and about to break. And it all started when I said: "I don't like what she's doing, but it would be better not to say anything. The relationship would be more peaceful." That was all a delusion, and I should have told you from the beginning. Now there has been an emotional divorce, all because I wanted to keep the peace between us.

From *Why Am I Afraid To Tell You Who I Am?*

I am simply not mature enough to enter into true friendship unless I realize that I cannot judge the intention or motivation of another. I must be humble and sane enough to bow before the complexity and mystery of a human being. If I judge you, I have only revealed my own immaturity and ineptness for friendship.

Emotional candor does not ever imply a judgment of you. In fact, it even abstains from any judgment of myself. For example, if I were to say to you, "I am ill at ease with you," I have been emotionally honest and at the same time have not implied in the least that it is your fault that I am ill at ease with you. I am not saying that it is anyone's fault, but simply giving a report of my emotional reaction to you at this time. I have not judged you. Perhaps it is my own egotism that has made me so sensitive. I am not sure, and, in most cases, I can never be sure. To be sure would imply a judgment. I can only say for sure that this has been and is my emotional reaction.

If I were to tell you that something you do annoys me, again I would not be so arrogant as to think that your action would annoy anyone. I don't even mean that your action is in any way wrong or offensive. I simply mean that here and now I experience annoyance. All that I know is this, that I am trying to tell you that I am experiencing annoyance at this moment. It would probably be most helpful in most cases to preface our gut-level communication with some kind of a disclaimer to assure the other that there is no judgment implied.

From *Why Am I Afraid To Tell You Who I Am?*

*O*f all the threats to successful dialogue, the one to be most carefully avoided is the intrusion of judgments, either about oneself or about one's partner in dialogue. We have said that no one can cause our emotions, but can only stimulate emotions that are already in us. The most common way that judgments enter into and ruin dialogue is through the door of believing that you have caused my emotions, or at least that there is such an obvious connection between your action and my emotion that "anyone would have reacted as I did." Both reactions are based on judgments and both judgments have to be false.

For example, we agreed to meet at a certain time and in a certain place. You arrive one half hour late. I am angry. I should tell you this as a simple fact, implying only that there is something in me that reacts angrily when I am left waiting. But think of all the possible judgmental accusations that could enter into my words, voice inflections or facial expressions.

> "You could have been on time." . . . "You're always late!" . . . "You're very selfish." . . . "You did this to hurt me or to get even with me." . . . "This is why you have no friends." . . . "You don't think ahead." . . . "Anyone else would have left on time to get here."

Judgments are death to true dialogue. Furthermore, the kind of judgments we are tempted to make usually involve a kind of indirect, destructive criticism that is fatal to self-acceptance, self-appreciation, and self-celebration. And when these are gone, love has been lost.

From *The Secret Of Staying In Love*

*I*f I am to tell you who I really am, I must tell you about my feelings, whether I will act upon them or not. I may tell you that I am angry, explaining the fact of my anger without inferring any judgment of you, and not intending to act upon this anger. I may tell you that I am afraid, explaining the fact of my fear without accusing you of being its cause, and at the same time not succumbing to the fear. But I must, if I am to open myself to you, allow you to experience (encounter) my person. I must tell you about my anger and my fear.

It has been truly said that we either *speak out* (report) our feelings or we will *act them out*. Feelings are like steam that is gathering inside of a kettle. Kept inside and gathering strength, feelings can blow the human lid off, just as the steam inside of the kettle will blow off the lid of a kettle.

We do not bury our emotions *dead*; they remain *alive* in our subconscious minds and intestines, to hurt and trouble us. It is not only much more conducive to an authentic relationship to report our true feelings, but it is equally essential to our integrity and health.

From *Why Am I Afraid To Tell You Who I Am?*

*T*here is a real need in all of us to be loved. It is consequently very important that we can take it in and savor the realization when someone offers us love unconditionally. Love is unconditional when it is offered as a simple gift with no strings attached. It is expressed when someone says (and means): "I just love you. You don't have to pay any price of admission for my love. All you have to do is accept it. I love you." When love is offered in this way, we must know how to take it in! To do this we must realize that we are lovable.

On the other hand, it is equally necessary to be totally honest in the communication of oneself. We have to say who we really are and refuse to play any roles that might be suggested to us. If I decide to be just myself I may wonder if it will cost me your love. "Do you think I'm sweet and patient? Well, what if I got angry and impatient? Would you still love me?" I can't let you paint me into a corner or put me up on a pedestal where I will be uncomfortable and unable to move. I must insist on my right and necessity to tell you who I really am. If you are going to love me unconditionally, you must offer me an atmosphere of freedom so that I can tell you who I really am.

From the video program, *Free To Be Me*

*M*any years ago I read a book on public speaking. The first chapter was entitled: "Never Try To Be A Better Speaker Than You Are A Person Because Your Audience Will Know." It was reminiscent of Quintilian's definition of a good speaker: "a good person who speaks well." The obvious implication is that our motives usually show through in spite of our attempts to camouflage them. We have all felt and been misunderstood at times, but over the long haul, the intuitions of others about our motivations are usually accurate if incomplete. People attempting dialogue should listen sensitively, therefore, to their motives. I suggest that there are three possibilities to be given special consideration.

Ventilation: When we ventilate a room, we air it out. We rid it of stale air or odors. Emotions, too, can accumulate inside us to the extent that we feel a need to ventilate them, to get them "off our chest." There may be occasional moments when this is necessary, but the fewer they are, the better the dialogue and relationship will be.

Ventilation is essentially egocentric. I want to feel better, so I am using you as a garbage dump for my emotional refuse. The occasional necessity for such ventilation is understandable, but nobody wants to be a habitual garbage dump or crying towel. Pouring out my emotional troubles to you so that I can feel better is self-centered. If it becomes a habit, a self-centered person develops and such a person has little capacity for dialogue or love.

From *The Secret Of Staying In Love*

*M*anipulation: the second possible motive for sharing my feelings is "manipulation." Love, we have said, is essentially freeing. Love asks only: "What can I do for you? What do you need me to be?" The unexpressed question in manipulation is exactly the opposite: "What can you do for me?" Manipulation is a sleight-of-hand way of pressuring another into fulfilling my needs. Now, obviously there are going to be times when I need you to help me, to stay with me, to listen to me. I should feel free to ask you without fear of rejection.

Manipulation, however, as a motive for dialogue implies that one person reports and describes his or her feelings to the other so that the other will do something about them. The manipulator makes the other feel responsible for his or her emotions. For example, I can tell you that I am lonely. It is simply a fact that I am going through a period of loneliness, and I want you to know because I want you to know me. Or I can tell you in such a way that I clearly imply your responsibility to fill the void of my loneliness. By subtle innuendos of voice, facial expression, and so forth, I make you feel the necessity to fulfill my needs. I am, by indirection and suggestion, using emotional leverage on you to get you to solve my problem.

From *The Secret Of Staying In Love*

*C*ommunication: The only motive from which true dialogue can result is the desire for communication. We have said that communication means sharing. And that we share our real selves when we share our feelings. Consequently, the only valid motive for dialogue is this desire to give another the most precious thing I can give: myself in self-disclosure, in the transparency achieved in dialogue.

Note. I'm sure you have felt at times, as I have, that others are not really interested in you. Not even those who supposedly love us and whom we supposedly love seem interested in listening to us. I have certainly known many wives who feel this way about their husbands and many husbands who feel this way about their wives. The same thing is often reported to me by young people whose parents supposedly aren't interested in them. I really think that many or most of these cases can be explained by the fact that the "put off" party was using one of the first two motives for self-disclosure: either ventilation or manipulation. I know from my own experience that I get uncomfortable when I feel that I am being used or manipulated by another. I begin looking at the clock, looking for a way out. Human nature is essentially gregarious. The law of togetherness is written upon our hearts. However, this desire to know and to be known does not include the wish to be a garbage dump or a problem solver.

From *The Secret Of Staying In Love*

*D*uring my childhood a sense of God's nearness stirred in me whenever I was in sacred places. Tinged as it might have been with some superstition or a child's imagination, I knew in some vague way that this or that church was God's house, and I thought it was good that God had colored windows (stained glass) and a special fragrance (possibly lingering incense or altar flowers). It was all very vague, and perhaps some psychologist with nothing better to do would analyze it in terms of religious programing. Somehow I knew that it was not just this. God had touched me, and the first inklings of my own faith and the first desires for God were being formed in me.

I remember that, when the day of my First Holy Communion was approaching, I wrote the date on the back of my hand in indelible ink. Perhaps it was only a child's memo to himself, but I rather think that, even in those first days of faith, meeting God at one or other of his points of rendezvous was something special to me.

From *He Touched Me*

*S*aying "Yes!" to God's gift to love and life primarily and above all means *choosing love as a life principle*. However, saying "Yes!" to God is not a simple matter because making our lives into lives of love is not a simple or easy thing. To choose love as a life principle means that my basic mind-set or question must be: What is the loving thing to be, to do, to say? My consistent response to each of life's events, to each person who enters and touches my life, to each demand on my time and nerves and heart, must somehow be transformed into an act of love. However, in the last analysis, it is this "Yes!" that opens me to God. Choosing love as a life principle widens the chalice of my soul, so that God can pour into me his gifts and graces and powers.

From *Unconditional Love*

I have to be honest in asking myself: Do I really want to know and do God's will? Or is it rather that I want God to do my will? Do I go to God with the assurance that I want only to know and do his will? Or do I rather first make my own plans and then insist that God make my dreams come true?

It seems to me that I will not seek and do God's will unless I am convinced of two other things: (1) that God wants my happiness even more than I want it; (2) that God knows much better than I what will make me truly happy.

I must ask the marrow of my bones if I really believe these two truths. Really wanting God's will as my only delight will depend on my belief in these two truths.

From the audio program, *The Growing Edge Of Life*

*I*n the head of the book it is written of me, that to do your will, O God, is all my delight. Behold, I come." (Psalm 140)

Everyday we pray in the Lord's prayer, "Thy will be done on earth as it is in heaven." It is all there, isn't it? For me there is no doubt that the wanting and the doing of the will of God is the measure of a person's holiness. It is the measure of faith. It is the measure of our love. Holiness is not measured by the intensity or devotion with which we pray. It is not measured by the graces we have received or the union with God that we have enjoyed. The only measure of holiness or nearness to God is our wanting and doing his will. "Thy will be done."

In the seventh chapter of Matthew's Gospel, Jesus is quoted as saying: "Not everyone who calls out 'Lord, Lord!' will enter the Kingdom of God. The one who does my Father's will: this person will enter the Kingdom."

From the audio program, *The Growing Edge of Life*

*I*t was customary in the forties for seminaries to accept young men after high school. One day in my senior year I found myself across the desk from my spiritual counselor, and I heard myself telling him that I wanted to be a priest. Had you asked me then, as he did, why I wanted to become a priest, I would certainly have come up with some precocious reasons and motives. In fact, they would have been only convenient if articulate explanations of a deeper experience, the touch of God, the same current of grace that has moved me slowly but surely all the days of my life. Somehow entering the service of God as a priest seemed like the "right thing" to do. Everything else was mere verbiage (I was pretty good at that, too).

No one in my family or among my friends believed that I was serious about my intention to become a priest. Even my father, who was sure that I was destined to become a great lawyer, registered disbelief as the days dwindled down before my actual departure. I think I rather liked the idea that people wouldn't believe me. I didn't want to seem a pious, "destined-for-the-ministry-from-early-youth" type. I was the "Battler," debater, the jazz-pianist, the jitterbug dancer. But the irresistible force of God's love and the current of his grace was moving me to do a far better thing and taking me to a far better place.

From *He Touched Me*

*A*s a Jesuit "Novice," I experienced a prolonged period of painful doubts about faith. One summer's night during this period of trial, I was sitting at my desk studying when a moth came thumping at the screen of my window, trying to reach the light that burned on my desk. Again and again he would streak for the light and thump into the screen, drop down and circle around and try again. It struck me that he and his frustration symbolized my pursuit of God. For me there was some kind of mysterious veil over the face and heart of God. All the old warmth and comfort of his presence were gone. Was I unfaithful, or was he asking my faith to grow deeper roots? There is an admitted tendency in all of us to seek the consolations of God rather than the God of consolations. Perhaps this was the laboratory of life and love in which I was being asked to mature and be purified.

Paul Tillich once wrote that the death-resurrection cycle of Christianity is characteristic of growth in faith also. The old faith must die, eaten away by doubts, but only so that a new and deeper faith may be born.

From *He Touched Me*

I came to the altar of my ordination as a priest, with my ambivalent habits and my ambiguous identity. On the day of ordination, I gave God a fraction of myself—how large or small I do not know. I did not feel very deeply the shame of my condition because I had never faced it honestly. The coping devices of human nature are ingenious. Vision and memory are very selective. We tend to see and hear only what we want to see and hear. Having made a public holocaust of myself for God, I could not face the private fact that I was poking in the embers for unburned pieces. My lip-service was not my life-style. I talked a much better game than I was able to live.

The sun was bright and hot on the day of my ordination. The families and friends of the ordinands were crowded into our humid chapel, and we priests-to-be prostrated before the high altar at the beginning of the ceremony. This prostration is a gesture by which the priest-to-be signifies his dying, his dying to himself and to his own self-interest and advantage. He arises at the call of the Bishop, and his rising symbolizes that he is alive only to Christ and his Kingdom. His priesthood is interpreted theologically as a deeper identity with Christ. He is called, in fact, an *alter Christus*, an "other Christ." I have since agonized over the discrepancy between the word and gesture level of my life and the bone-marrow of my commitment; but I did not do so then. The sun shone brightly; the ceremony was solemn and impressive, and I became a priest. My mother cried and hugged me proudly.

From *He Touched Me*

I have always believed that, when God touches a human being, the experience will survive three tests: (1) *The Time Test*: The person touched by God will never be the same again. Even if the change is not dramatic, the experience of God will leave a permanent mark. Overheated emotions or subconscious suggestions come and go. God's hour has a definitely observable perdurance. (2)*The Reality Test*: The soul which has been touched by God will not be drawn up into an otherworldly posture or into the bowered ivory towers of private ecstasy, but will be deepened in a personal awareness of the world. Such people will see with new eyes the beauty of the world; as never before, they will hear its music and poetry and know that it is a beautiful world. But they will also find a deeper contact with the sadness of human hearts. Those who experience God will notice a new awareness of the reality of their total environment, a new aliveness. As old St. Irenaeus, in the second century, once said: "The glory of God is a person who is fully alive." The true touch of God results in a new and vital "Yes!" to life. (3) *The Charity Test*: Those human beings who have opened to God's touch will be made more Godlike by reason of that contact. They will become more loving. St. John says that God is love and that anyone who fails to love cannot have known God. He who abides in God abides in love. The grandest, most glowing of all God's miraculous interventions will always be the production of a loving person, the transformation of a go-getter into a go-giver. Essentially, this is what the hours or touches of God are all about. This is what God is doing in us. The gift of love is the highest gift of the Spirit of God.

From *He Touched Me*

*S*ometimes I think we try to dictate to God the manner of our witness and discipleship, instead of putting ourselves at his disposal. Maybe the experience of God, his power and presence are obstructed by our own incorrigible selfishness. Maybe we didn't hear Jesus say that the person who is always seeking his or her own life will never find it, but that those who are willing to lose their lives will find them. I personally think that there are many situations in my own life, situations in which I might have felt God's presence but didn't because my own presence was so preoccupying. I didn't hear God's requests of me because I was too busy forcing my requests on God. I got no answers because I was asking the wrong questions.

Somehow I feel sure that the most direct route to religious experience is to ask for the grace to give, to share, to console another, to bandage a hurting wound, to lift a fallen human spirit, to mend a quarrel, to search out a forgotten friend, to dismiss a suspicion and replace it with trust, to encourage someone who has lost faith, to let someone who feels helpless do a favor for me, to keep a promise, to bury an old grudge, to reduce my demands on others, to fight for a principle, to express gratitude, to overcome a fear, to appreciate the beauty of nature, to tell others I love them, and then to tell them again.

There is a haunting possibility that I have not heard the voice of God speaking to me in all the circumstances and persons in my life because I have been asking the wrong questions, making the wrong requests. I may have been too busy speaking to listen.

From *A Reason To Live, A Reason To Die*

*A*n authentic experience of God is possible for us. We can, if we seek it, experience his light when we are in darkness, his strength when we are weak, his presence when we are lonely, his healing when we have been hurt. In fact, the eyes of faith will seek and find God in all things. This was the specific religious genius of St. Ignatius Loyola, who gave his followers this rule: "Let them seek and find God in all things."

We must seek and find God in the joys of human love, in the exhilaration of a sunset, starlight, a heavy snow bending the branches of evergreens in winter, in a fireplace at the end of a perfect day. All reality is a reflection of God, and God dwells in a deeper mode of existence, in all things. There are many modes or strata of existence in all reality. The danger for us is the danger of superficiality. We might look at a beautiful bank of trees and see only lumber. We might look at a page of profound poetry and see only words. The deepest and ultimate level of all existence is God himself, because all reality is a participation in his existence and in his beauty. Consequently, for the believer all reality becomes sacramental, a visible sign of the power and presence of God. The Jesuit poet, Gerard Manley Hopkins, writes in his poem "The Wreck of the Deutschland:"

> I kiss my hand
> To the stars, lovely-asunder
> Starlight, wafting him out of it; and
> Glow, glory in thunder
> Kiss my hand to the dappled-with-damson west:
> Since, tho' he is under the world's splendour and wonder,
> His mystery must be instressed, stressed;
> For I greet him the days I meet him,
> and bless when I understand.

From *He Touched Me*

*G*od has always been big on what is called "petitionary prayer." St. Augustine once called petitionary prayer "our greatest strength and God's greatest weakness." The Lord assures us: "Ask and you shall receive; knock and it will be opened to you. Whatever you ask in my name will be granted to you."

In fact, I have often thought about God as being like an electrical outlet. Behind every outlet is the mysterious power of electricity. It can light a room, heat a home, show a movie, and so forth. However, the outlet is literally useless unless we get plugged in, connected to the source of power. The power of God, we are assured, is ready to enlighten our darkness, mend our brokenness, fill our emptiness, brace our courage, straighten our twistedness, and create in us hearts of love. The connection to all this power is prayer. The psalmist assures us: "The Lord is near to all who call upon him." (Psalm 145:18)

From *Will The Real Me Please Stand Up?*

*W*e do not need a theologically accurate portrait of God to begin the dialogue of prayer. If this were the case, none of us could ever begin to pray. Getting to know God is a dialogical process. We begin with mistaken impressions, distorted ideas, unfounded fears and personal prejudices. But gradually, as we unfold ourselves to him and he unfolds himself to us, we correct old erroneous impressions, gain new insights, experience new facets of the mysterious, tender God who cannot forget us even if a mother should forget the child of her womb. Having been wrong about God doesn't mean that we haven't been talking to him. It is only by perseverance in this type of prayer that we will come to be less and less wrong about him until that day when we shall know him even as we are known.

What I needed most, in arriving at this moment in my life, was the knowledge that God really wanted to be intimately close to me. I needed to be rid of the deistic concept of God as distant, uninterested, inoperative in me and in my human powers. But most of all, I needed some success in this method of prayer. I needed to feel the touch of God, to experience his thoughts stretching my mind, to feel the firmness of his strength and desires in my will, to hear his voice and experience his light in the darkness of my nights, to feel his calm in the moments of my distress. Only then, in these meanderings into the mercy of this tender, present, and available God did I know that he really wanted me to be his and wanted himself to be the portion of my heart forever. Only then, with this success, did I know that God could never seem the same and I could never be the same again.

From *He Touched Me*

I now understand and approach prayer as *communication in a relationship of love*, a *speaking* and a *listening* in truth and in trust. Speaking to God honestly is the beginning of prayer; it locates a person before God. I believe that the primary "giving" of love is the giving of oneself through self-disclosure. Without such self-disclosure there is no real giving, for it is only in that moment when we are willing to put our true selves on the line, to be taken for better or for worse, to be accepted or rejected, that true interpersonal encounter begins. We do not begin to offer ourselves until we offer ourselves in this way, for love demands presence, not presents. All my gifts (presents) are mere motion until I have given my true self (presence) in honest self-revelation. As in all interpersonal relationships, so in the relationship with God, I do not put myself into his hands or confront his freedom of choice to accept me or reject me, to love me or to loathe me, until I have told him who I am. Only then can I ask him: Will you have me? Will you let me be yours? Will you be mine? Martin Luther's first law of successful prayer is: *Don't lie to God!* In speaking to God in the dialogue of prayer, we must reveal our true and naked selves. We must tell him the truth of our thoughts, desires and feelings, whatever they may be. They may not be what I would like them to be, but they are not right or wrong, true or false. They are me.

I have told him where I really live, in belief and unbelief. I have told him of my weariness in answering his call, of my emotional resentment at being a public utility, a servant to be taken for granted. I have been like Job of the Old Testament, cursing the day he made me, and like the prophet Jeremiah, accusing him of making not a prophet but a fool of me. I have been a King David singing of his mercy and forgiveness. I have always needed this mercy and forgiveness along the way of my pilgrimage.

From *He Touched Me*

*I*f speaking to God is no simple matter, my experience has convinced me that listening to God in the dialogue of prayer is even more difficult. How does God communicate himself to me? How does he disclose who he is after I have revealed myself to him? Do I have to wait hours, days, weeks or even years to see what God will do with and about my openness to him? Or is there a more immediate and direct response? I think that there is.

I ask myself questions like these: Can God put a new idea directly and immediately into my *mind*? Can he give me a new perspective in which to view my life with its successes and failures, agonies and ecstasies? Can God put new desires into my *heart*, new strength into my *will*? Can he touch and calm my turbulent *emotions*? Can he actually whisper words to the listening ears of my soul through the inner faculty of my *imagination*? Can God stimulate certain *memories* stored within the human brain at the time these memories are needed? I feel sure that God can and does reach us in these ways.

I pray by telling God who I am and by listening to him as he reveals to me not only who he is, but also who I am, and what my life and this world mean to him. My listening to him is the silent turning over to him the five faculties or powers of perception through which I truly believe that he comes to me.

From *He Touched Me*

*H*ow does God speak to us? We have said that there are five antennae through which God can and does communicate with us. The first of these antennae is the mind.

God acts on my mind. After putting myself before the Lord, he comes to me to help me see the person and the problems I have described, through his eyes and in his eternal perspective. He puts his ideas into my mind, and especially his perspectives. He widens my vision, helps me to see what is really important in life and to distinguish the really important from the unimportant. I have always wanted to define *delusion* as the confusion of what is important in life with the unimportant. I personally get uptight, blow things up out of all proportion, especially when the lightning strikes close to the home of my ego. I enter the wrong arenas to do battle, focus on the wrong issues of contention. And I tell him all about it, when I pray to him. Then he comes, and, in his own gentle way, fills my mind with his thoughts and his vision. He rescues me from my delusions.

From *He Touched Me*

*G*od also acts on my will. The one thing I have learned about myself in the last forty years of life is that I am weak. No pretense or sham. No mock humility. I am truly a weak person, badly in need of redemption. In the days of my early fervor in the service of God after entering the seminary, I used to offer God my day upon awakening. I promised him a "perfect" day, a day of perfect love and service. In my night prayers I could only offer him my remorse. It has taken me a long time to sincerely distrust my own strength and to turn my life over to him.

Only when I was willing to admit my nothingness did God begin to make something of me. In my weakness his strength is made manifest. But more than simply steeling my will to the challenge of costly discipleship, he has come to me in prayer and put into my will new desires. Psychologically as well as spiritually, it seems so important that we be persons of desire. I am sure that every great accomplishment in all of human history began with the birth of a desire in some human heart.

So he comes to me, in the listening, receptive moments of prayer, and he transfuses his power into me; he rekindles my desires to be his man, to be a public utility, a town pump for the Kingdom of God, just as his Son was during his life among us.

From *He Touched Me*

*G*od acts on my emotions. When I am emotionally embittered or discouraged, when I experience that dull ache of loneliness, or I am saddened in the trough of some criticism or failure, he comes to comfort me. It is as though his healing power is extended to my neurotic feelings. If he can make a leper clean, he can make a neurotic normal. I often ask Jesus to raise the hand which calmed the winds and waves of Gennesareth over my turbulent soul. Make me calm and tranquil, too. However, I firmly believe that God comes not only to comfort the afflicted, but also to afflict the comfortable.

There are times when he comes not to trouble me, but only to rearrange my values or make me aware of someone in need; and always to challenge me to grow. I have never asked him for a problemless life or a plastic tranquility. I ask only for that peace which knows what is important and what is unimportant, only for that serenity which knows that I have been loved and that I am called to love.

From *He Touched Me*

*G*od acts on my imagination. Somehow the same people who believe that God can enter the mind with ideas and perspectives, the will with his strength and desires, or the emotions with his peace, balk at the thought that God can stimulate our imaginations to hear inwardly actual words or see actual visions. My own mother once told me, in a hushed and confidential way, that God had often spoken to her, giving her rather specific directives for her life. She said, "I wouldn't tell anyone else because others would certainly think that I am a little crazy." I remember reassuring her that it runs in the family. For I, too, have heard God and perceived inwardly a gentle loving look of Jesus, and I believe that this was really the touch of God stimulating my imagination.

This, of course, was the problem with Joan of Arc and her voices. The following is a short excerpt from George Bernard Shaw's play, *St. Joan*:

> *Robert*: How do you mean? voices?
> *Joan*: I hear voices telling me what to do. They come from God.
> *Robert*: They come from your imagination.
> *Joan*: Of course. That is how the messages of God come to us.

Granted that it might be difficult to distinguish words coming from the stimulus of God's grace from those which might proceed simply from self-stimulation or autosuggestion, the reality must not be denied simply because God's grace in us can be simulated. God has access to us through this power of imagination. I once discussed this avenue of God into us with a prayerful psychologist, and it was her opinion that there would always be "something surprising, distinctive and lasting" in the communication of God. I think she is right.

From *He Touched Me*

I remember once asking God what he might wish to say to me, or ask of me. It was a moment of white-heat fervor, when I felt ready to hear anything. In the quiet moments of listening, inwardly I heard the words: "I love you." I felt disappointed. Oh, I knew this. But he came back to me, this time through the channel of my mind. Suddenly it became very clear to me that I had never really accepted and interiorized the love of God for me. In the flash of this graced intuition I saw that I had always known that God had been patient with me and forgiving; but it struck me that I had never really opened to the reality of his love. He was right, I slowly realized. I had never really heard the message of his love. When God speaks, there will always be "something surprising, distinctive and lasting."

From *He Touched Me*

*G*od acts on my memory. The final channel or antenna of human reception to the communication of God is the memory. It is said that love consists in equal parts of memory and intuition. We have also remarked that the only real mistakes we make are the ones from which we have learned nothing. When God communicates to us through the stimulation of some stored memory, he can stir up our love by reminding us of his tenderness and goodness in the past, thus fortifying us to meet the present moment and have hope for the future. He can also prevent us from repeating an old mistake by reminding us of the past. For me, at least, the bedrock of my faith and gratitude is the *remembered goodness* of God in the history of my life: his hours, his touches. "All I ask of you is forever to remember me as loving you."

From *He Touched Me*

*I*n the last years of my dear mother's life, she suffered from a seriously immobilizing arthritis. There were times when I would carry her up and down the stairs of our family home in Chicago. The routine was predictably regular. We would descend several steps, and then mother would extend her hand and firmly grasp the bannister. The dialogue that followed always went like this:

"Mama, you have to let go. We can't move unless you let go."
"I am afraid you'll drop me."
"If you don't let go, I am going to count to three and drop you.
    One . . . Two . . ."

Mother always let go after the count of two, and then we would descend several more steps. However, after we had progressed several more steps, we rehearsed the same procedure and dialogue. Mama would grab the bannister and I would warn her of her impending doom if she didn't let go.

On one such occasion, I reflected that the exchange between my mother and myself must be something like the exchange between myself and the Lord. Of course, he's got the whole world in his hands, including me, and he's moving me along to my desired destiny. However, I keep grabbing and holding onto the "security bannisters" that help me feel safe. Jesus reminds me that we can't move as long as I hold on so tightly to the little gifts, possessions, and achievements that are part of my security operation. I hear him clearly asking me to "let go . . . ," but out of my ever-honest stomach comes the painful whimper: "I am afraid you will drop me." I am frightened by the prospect of open hands. What if I do say the "yes" of surrender? What will happen to me?

From *The Christian Vision*

*S*ecurity is such a deep need in us, isn't it? We have all those trembling and disquieting questions pulsing through our nerves and muscles: What will happen to me if I let go? Will I have enough—enough time, enough money, enough provisions for old age, enough people to care for me, enough intelligence, enough health . . . ? And so I hold on tightly to my security bannisters. They make me feel safe but they keep me stationary. They are an obstacle to grace.

The Lord must smile upon me as I once smiled upon my dear little mother, who was afraid I might drop her. He must want to meet my nervous, tremulous questions about "enough" with a comforting but challenging, "Trust me. I WILL BE YOUR ENOUGH!"

When we love another person, our love sometimes takes the form of comfort and sometimes the form of challenge. Jesus, who loves us, is both of these for us: a comfort and a challenge. There is an inestimable comfort in his presence and the reassurances of his unconditional love. There is also an endless challenge in his request for trust: "Let go. I will be your enough!" It is the challenge of love, asking for our open hands. There will be so many moments in your life and mine, like the stations along my mother's stairway, when we will let go and experience the freedom of being able to move. There will also be times of white knuckles, trembling fears about personal security, and not enough trust to "let go and let God."

From *The Christian Vision*

Summer

I remember it well: my entrance into the Jesuit Novitiate. When I tell my students of today about the conditions of life in a Jesuit Novitiate of the forties, there is a definite credibility gap. I won't invite you to the test, but I assure you that in many ways, from the 5 a.m. rising, to the furniture that was early American orange-crate, the conversation of daily business in Latin, the long silences, and the four hours of prayer each day—it was a clear case of trauma for most of us.

When the novelty of the challenge wore off and the cost of this kind of discipleship became obvious, doubt struck me like a sudden crack of thunder on a summer's night, and the storm of uncertainty that followed darkened every area of my soul and life. Was there really a God? Was Jesus Christ really the Son of God? Is the Gospel fact or fiction? I ran in panic to prayer, but no one was there to meet me. The experience of God was for me one of a vast aloneness and barren silence: the death of all that had been with no vision or promise of a new birth. It was then that my old neighbor's words came back to me, with a new urgency and insistence. He had seemed so sure when he said, "You see, there is no God . . . there is no God . . . there is no God!"

From *He Touched Me*

I looked out at the stark surroundings and went through the motions of this spartan novitiate life sadly. In fact there was a constant funeral going on in my heart. God had left me—alone and here in this lonely place. I thought I had lost my very faith. The Master of Novices, who was supposed to guide us through this wilderness, did not seem too alarmed at my sudden atheism. He counseled patience, with myself and with God. I thought he had not really gotten the full impact of my problem; he had not felt my whole world shaking.

This "dark night" of disbelief lasted four bleak and barren months. Then it happened. It was the beginning of the rest of my life, the pivotal religious experience of my own personal history. In the evenings, we novices had a fifteen minute examination of conscience, during which we knelt on wooden blocks, our hands resting on our desks, our minds combing through the day for failures of commission and omission in thought, word, and deed. The only thing I did well, or at least so it seemed to me, was to get that wooden block in the right place. A well adjusted kneeler, I used to say humorously to myself, was half the battle.

On that night, without a doubt, God touched me.

From *He Touched Me*

*I*t happened on a definite Friday evening in the early spring, while I was kicking my wooden kneeler into place for the evening examination of conscience. With all the suddenness and jolt of a heart attack, I was filled with an experiential awareness of the presence of God within me. It has been said that no one can convey an experience to another, but can only offer his reflections on the experience. I am sure that this is true. I can only say, in trying to share my experience with you, that I felt like a balloon being blown up with the pure pleasure of God's loving presence, even to the point of discomfort and doubt that I could hold any more of this sudden ecstasy. I think of the song "He Touched Me!" as the most apt way to describe the experience of that night. I am convinced that all human experiences but especially the experience of an infinite God, are fundamentally incommunicable. Somehow God will always exceed the peripheries of our human understanding. Precisely because he is infinite, he can never be brought into the focus of a finite human mind. Somehow our brushes with his infinity cannot be fitted into finite concepts or words. I can only tell you that "He Touched Me (and nothing seemed the same)." If there is a "honeymoon" period in one's relationship with God, mine was the following year. There were repeated "touches," always at an unexpected time, always startling, and always incredibly warming. During this year I read for the first time Gerard Manley Hopkins' poem, "The Wreck of the Deutschland." I found in it a poet's words to say what I was experiencing:

> Thou mastering me
> God! giver of breath and bread;
> World's strand, sway of the sea;
> Lord of living and dead;
> Thou has bound bones and veins in
> me, fastened me flesh,
> And after it almost unmade, what with
> dread,
> Thy doing: and dost thou touch me
> afresh?
> Over again I feel thy finger
> and find thee.

From *He Touched Me*

*I*n Thornton Wilder's play, "Our Town," a young woman dies, but Emily discovers that she is allowed to relive any one day of her life over again. She chooses to relive the day of her twelfth birthday. When she comes back, she is really eager to savor every moment of this wonderful day in her life. She regrets that she just can't seem to look hard enough at everything. Then she notices that everyone around her isn't sharing her joy in living. She pleads with her mother, "Come on, let's really look at one another!" When she realizes, with great sadness, that no one else understands, she says, "Oh, earth, oh life, you're too wonderful for anyone to realize you. Do any human beings ever realize the meaning of life while they are still living?"

I have often asked myself why we don't live more fully. Why don't we savor every moment of this great opportunity called life? The average person uses only ten percent of his or her potential during the course of life. What happens to the other ninety percent? I have a theory I would like to propose to you. In my theory there is a vision of reality that controls everything else about us and our lives. Each of us perceives reality differently. Our vision includes the way we look at ourselves, the way we look at other people, the way we look at life, the way we look at the world around us, and the way we look at God. Such a vision is inside you and there is likewise one inside me, but it is a different and distinctive vision in each of us. It is this vision that controls and regulates our ability to live and to enjoy. I would like to suggest that the quality of every human life is determined by such a vision. The ability of every human being to participate in life, to join the dance of life, and to sing the songs of life is controlled by this vision.

From the video program, *Free To Be Me*

*M*ay I ask you to run a short homemade movie on the screen of your imagination? Imagine that you come home some dark night and, to your horror, you see a thirty-five foot snake on your front lawn. Your heart begins to pound wildly and adrenalin starts pumping in your blood-stream. You quickly grab a garden hoe and in your frenzy you hack the writhing snake into small pieces. Satisfied that it is dead, you go inside and try to settle your nerves with a warm drink. Later, lying in bed, even with your eyes closed, you can still see the wriggling form on the front lawn.

The next morning you return to the scene of the snake slaying and find, again to your horror, that there had never been a snake on your front lawn. That which lies in pieces before your eyes was simply the garden hose which had been left out on the lawn. It was always a hose, of course; but last night for you it was a snake. What you saw last night was a snake, and all your actions and reactions followed from what you saw. The fear, the hoe, the struggle, the effort to calm down—all followed from the vision of a thirty-five foot snake. (The end of our homemade movie. Please turn on the house lights.)

What this exercise of imagination was meant to illustrate is that all our emotional and behavioral actions and reactions follow from our perceptions. In the snake drama, we were talking about the perceptions of an ocular vision, about a vision seen with the eyes of the body. But we also have an inner vision of reality, a highly personal and unique way that each one of us perceives reality—a vision seen with the eyes of the mind. We look at the various parts of reality through the eyes of our minds, and no two people ever see those parts of reality in exactly the same way. You have your vision. I have mine.

From *The Christian Vision*

*W*e all have a vision because of the very nature of the mind and its instinct to interpret reality. There is also a special need for this vision because it gives life consistency and predictability. A vision enables us to know how to act. Without some kind of vision we would be psychologically blind, stumbling and groping through completely uncharted territory. We would soon be confused and fragmented.

This vision serves as an inner resource by which we can gauge appropriate responses to persons, places, and things. It also becomes the source of our emotional responses. As we have said, all our emotional patterns and reactions are based on our perceptions. It doesn't matter whether the perception is accurate or not, the emotional response will inevitably be proportionate to our perception. For example, let us imagine that a child leaves a toy tiger in the backyard. If I perceive it as a real tiger, it doesn't matter whether it is real or not. My emotional reaction will follow my perception.

Emotions are always the result of a given perception and interpretation. However, emotional reactions to a given perception can have a profound effect on further perceptions and interpretations. Have you ever been alone in a large, remotely situated house? You hear a noise in the night which you cannot locate or explain. It may have been a shutter blown closed by the wind. From that point on, every creak and shadow becomes suspicious. It is a kind of vicious circle. A perception causes emotional reactions, and the emotional reactions color and distort future perceptions.

From *Fully Human, Fully Alive*

*T*he Christian vision of reality would call us out of isolation and gently usher us back into the larger world, into the drama of human existence. The Christian vision does not easily tolerate the "comfort zones" of cowardice and escape. The Christian clenched fists take into their grasp the full spectrum of human experience. We are challenged to come alive in all our senses to the sights and sounds, the heat and the coldness, the heights and the depths, the noise and the silence of God's vast world. The Christian vision challenges us to emotional openness, to a willingness to feel both pain and pleasure, the consolations of love and the desolations of loneliness, the agonies of failure and the ecstasies of success. The Christian mind does not wear blinders, does not construct barricades or plant high bushes around its estate. It knows that somewhere a newborn baby is nestling in its mother's arms, and at the same time somewhere else a human being is sweating and writhing in pain with no hope of immediate relief. Finally, the Christian heart, that alone can see rightly, reaches out to love this world into life.

I must choose this Christian vision. It is the most important choice I will ever make in my life. It is the choice that will truly set me free, but I still must choose it. The beatitudes of Jesus are formulas for happiness, but I must appropriate them, make them my own, if I am to have a singing heart and a celebrating spirit.

From *The Christian Vision*

*B*eginning his career as a rabbi or teacher at the customary age of thirty, Jesus began to recruit disciples. All rabbis of the time did this. However, twelve of those chosen by Jesus were called to special roles and invited into a special intimacy.

Jesus would spend the greater part of his life during the next three years preparing these twelve men. The master vision would be gradually laid out before them in the person and teaching of Jesus. In his teaching the Lord often used a literary form that began "Blessed (happy) are they who . . ." We call them *beatitudes* because the Latin word *beatus* means "happy." These beatitudes were and are the Jesus-formula for true happiness and a full life. They call for a profound surrender of faith. "Blessed (happy) is the person who puts his faith in me!" (See Luke 7:23.)

Many of the old attitudes of these twelve were challenged by these new beatitudes. In fact, its seems that Jesus was telling them that their life-wagers had been misplaced. The things that they thought would make them happy, Jesus seems to be saying, were empty illusions that could only disappoint them. Often, his teaching seemed to make almost impossible demands.

Once I thought that the Twelve Apostles were a bit slow, that they were missing the candlepower or intelligence to learn the lessons of their Master. I had counted seventeen places in the Gospels where Jesus asks them, "Are you yet without understanding?" In our present-day jargon, we would probably translate this, "You don't get it yet, do you?" I once thought these things, but not now. I now think that the real challenge of Jesus was not a matter of intelligence, but ultimately a challenge to give up an old vision and to accept a new one. It was a matter of radical faith and profound trust.

From *The Christian Vision*

A life principle is a generalized, accepted intention of purpose that is applied to specific choices and circumstances. For example, "Good must be done and evil avoided." If this is one of my life principles, whenever I come to a specific choice involving good and evil, my principle directs me to choose that which is good and to avoid that which is evil.

I would like to suggest that everyone has one dominant life principle. It may be difficult to lure it out of the dark, subconscious regions to face examination in the light, but it is there. There is in each of us a set of needs, goals, or values with which we are psychologically preoccupied. There is something, in all the zigs and zags of daily living, which dominates all our other desires. This life principle runs through the fabric of our choices like the dominant theme in a piece of music: it keeps recurring and it is heard in different settings. Of course, only you can answer for yourself, just as only I can answer for myself: What is my life principle?

For example, some people are above and before all else seeking *safety*. They avoid all places where danger might lurk, even if opportunity could be waiting in the same place. They will take no risks, make no gambles. They stay at home at night and reveal their deepest selves to no one. It is better to be safe than sorry, they say. The same kind of thumbnail sketch could be made of a person whose primary concern and life principle is *duty, recognition, money, fame, need, success, fun, relationships, approval of others,* or *power.*

From *Unconditional Love*

*I*t is very important to realize that we are creatures of habit. Every time we think a certain way, seek a certain good, use a given motive, a habit is forming and deepening in us. Like a groove that is being furrowed, each repetition adds a new depth to the habit. (Have you ever tried to break a habit? Then you know what I am trying to say.)

And so it is with a life principle, whatever it be. With each use it becomes a deeper and more permanent habit. And in the twilight of life our habits rule us. They define and dictate our actions and reactions. We will, as the saying goes, die as we have lived. People who in old age prove quite self-centered and demanding, as well as those who are "mellow" and tolerant, did not become so only in their last years of life. Old cranks have practiced all their lives, just as old saints have likewise practiced all their lives. They just practiced different life principles. What you and I will become in the end will be just more and more of what we are deciding and trying to be right now. There is a fundamental choice, a life principle, which one day will possess us in the marrow of our bones and by the blood in our veins. It is a certainty that we will die as we have lived.

From *Unconditional Love*

I am convinced: There can be no change in any human life, in the quality of a life and in a person's participation in life, until there is a change in that person's vision of reality. I remember thinking deeply about this when I was a seminarian many years ago. I had a head cold and went up to the infirmary in the late evening to get some medicine. While I was waiting in the corridor of the infirmary, I watched the Brother Infirmarian as he was tucking in two old, bedridden priests for the night. As he tucked the blanket of the first man under his chin, the old fellow snarled, "Oh, get your face out of mine. What do you think this is?" But when the Brother went into the next room, and did the very same thing for the second old priest, the old man said, "Oh Brother, you are so good to us. Before I fall asleep tonight, I'm going to say a very special prayer just for you." As I was standing out there in the corridor, the thought struck me like a thunderclap: Some day I am going to be one of those two old men. Which one? Even then it seemed quite clear to me that I wouldn't make that decision in old age. You just don't make decisions like that when you are old. I know that I am making that decision right now. I am choosing and rehearsing and practicing a definite vision right now. Every time we perceive ourselves, others, life, the world and God in a certain way, we are deepening the habits that will take over in old age. Every time I act on the insights that I am getting now I am deciding my future and choosing to be a kindly or cynical old man. Our yesterdays lie heavily upon our todays and our todays will lie heavily upon our tomorrows.

From the video program, *Free To Be Me*

*O*ne of the most startling lines I have ever read in any book was in *The Diary of A Young Girl* by Anne Frank. Anne wrote the book while she was being hunted down by the Nazis. While she was literally running for her life, Anne Frank wrote this in her diary, "I do believe that deep within his heart, every person is good." When I read that line and considered the circumstances under which it was written, I kept asking: "Do you really believe that, Anne Frank, do you? With all the malice that you are experiencing, in the midst of all the hatred directed towards you because you have Jewish blood in your veins, while you are in hiding and frightened by every noise, can you really believe that? Is it true that every person, deep within his heart, is good?"

I also recall encountering a very healthy view of others at the Illinois State Penitentiary. I was visiting a prisoner there. While being admitted with the other visitors I found myself walking next to an elderly black lady who was exuding love and greeting everyone around her. Anyway, this dear lady was doing her best to make the dismal atmosphere of the prison seem cheerful. I finally said to her, "I think that you must spread a great amount of cheer in this world. You really like people, don't you?" She replied, "Oh, thank you. You know, there are no strangers in my world. There are just brothers and sisters, some of whom I haven't yet met." I kept looking at her. She really meant that. In her deepest self she really meant that. No wonder she was happy and loving.

From the video program, *Free To Be Me*

*T*he most important part of my vision of reality is the vision of myself. If I see myself as a worthless person, I can certainly anticipate many painful and persistent emotions—discouragement, depression, sadness, and maybe even suicidal feelings. But if I can be brought to realize, by the affirming and unconditional love of another, that I am really a decent and lovable person of considerable worth, this whole pattern of emotional reaction will be radically changed. As the distortion in my perception of myself is eliminated, I will be gradually transformed into a self-confident, assured, and happy person.

If I think of you as a friend and collaborator, my emotions on meeting you will be warm and positive. If I see you as an enemy and competitor, my emotions will be just the opposite. You remember the little verse:

> Two men looked out from prison bars.
> One saw mud, one saw stars.

In the pursuit of the fullness of human life, everything depends on this frame of reference, this habitual outlook, this basic vision which I have of myself, others, life, the world, and God. What we see is what we get.

Consequently, if you or I are to change, to grow into persons who are more fully human and more fully alive, we shall certainly have to become aware of our vision and patiently work at redressing its imbalances and eliminating its distortions. All real and permanent growth must begin here. A shy person can be coaxed into assuming an air of confidence, but it will only be a mask—one mask replacing another. There can be no real change, no real growth in any of us until and unless our basic perception of reality, our vision, is changed.

From *Fully Human, Fully Alive*

*A*s best I can understand Jesus and his good news, it seems that Christian spirituality involves both a spirit of possession and a spirit of dispossession. To be able to integrate and harmonize these two spirits is the genius of Christian spirituality. The spirit of possession reaches out to embrace life and all the parts of life. The glory of God is a person who is fully alive. The Christian spirit of possession sees a unique beauty in each of the seasons of the year, hears the music and poetry of the universe, smells the fragrance of a day in spring, and touches the soft petals of a flower. The spirit of possession tends to make me fully alive in my senses, emotions, mind, and will. It helps me to become fully functioning in all the parts of my unique giftedness.

The genius of Christian spirituality is to integrate this spirit of possession with the spirit of dispossession. The spirit of dispossession implies that all the good and delightful things of this world are never allowed to own, possess or shackle me. Dispossession implies that I am always free, my own person, liberated from the tyranny that possession can easily exercise over us.

There is an old adage, "We are all born with clenched fists, but we must all die with open hands." I like this symbolism of clenched fists and open hands. These two expressions aptly symbolize the spirits of possession and dispossession in incarnational Christian spirituality. I reach out to take into my hands the fullness of life and creation. But nothing is ever so fastened into my grasp that I cannot give it up.

From *The Christian Vision*

*T*he crucial insight and realization, which opens up a whole new dimension of personal growth, is this: Something in me—my attitudes, my vision of reality—determines all my actions and reactions, both emotional and behavioral. Something in me is writing the story of my life, making it sad and sorrowful or glad and peaceful. Something in me will ultimately make the venture of my life a success or a failure. The sooner I acknowledge this, taking responsibility for my actions and reactions, the faster I will move toward my destiny: the fullness of life and peace. This fullness of life and peace is our legacy from the Lord.

I must not let this remain a matter of words, a lip-service admission. I must ask myself if in fact I really believe this. Am I really convinced that my inner attitudes evaluate the persons, events, situations of my life and regulate all my reactions? If so, I must press on and ask: Do I truly believe that it is in my power to change these attitudes, wherever necessary, in order to have a full and meaningful life? If I find that I am convinced on both scores, then I must close all the escape-from-reality doors and walk bravely down the corridor of personal responsibility. I must resist the ever-present temptation to blame other people, to complain about the past and present circumstances of my life, including the weather and the position of the stars. In a true sense, I must become "the master of my fate," and under God, take the responsibility for my own happiness.

Consequently, the key and profitable question is not: Will this day bring me my desires? It is not: Will I get the breaks? Nor is it: How can I change all these people who surround me and shackle me and carry me along in the stream of their movement? The only key and profitable question is this: What is in me? It is not what happens *to* me but rather what happens *in* me that will shape, color, and write the story of my life

From *The Christian Vision*

*I*t is extremely important that we do not run away from our discomfort, but rather enter into it and examine it. Discomfort is a signal, a teacher offering us a valuable lesson. The way we enter into our discomfort profitably and find the source of our difficulty is usually by asking: What is in me? I must ask myself: How am I looking at myself, at this other person, at this situation? My physical, emotional, and behavioral reactions are ultimately a result of my outlook. They are an outgrowth of my attitudes. In most moments of discomfort, I am feeling the effect of my attitudes in my body, in my feelings, in my actions and reactions. It is very important that I trace this discomfort to its cause: What is in me? How am I perceiving myself, another, this circumstance? The honest answering of these questions will explain my bodily, emotional, and behavioral reactions.

After I have located the attitude in question, then I must ask another question: Is there a different way to see myself, to see this other person or this situation? Can I think of a way that would be more realistic, healthier, more Christian? I must reflect that there are other people who would somehow remain peaceful, optimistic, gentle, and unruffled if they were in my shoes at this time. How would they perceive this moment and circumstance in my life if they were me? How would Jesus suggest that I look at myself, at this other person, at this situation?

From *The Christian Vision*

*H*ow do I revise my vision of reality? How do I change those attitudes that cripple me, that keep me from being a fully alive and happy person?

"Vision Therapy" is simply our term that implies such a revision. It is a habit breaking–new habit making process. If I have an old habit of thought, an old habit of perception, an attitude which proves crippling and destructive, I've got to break that habit. I have to replace it with a new, constructive, life-giving attitude or habit of thought.

Before we can begin this work of change, we must learn to identify those attitudes that distort our vision of reality and cause us serious discomfort. For example, "I must please everyone." Such "people pleasers" are destined for disappointment. This is an impossible ideal that leaves room only for failure and discouragement. It is simply impossible to please everyone. Or to take another example: "I must do everything perfectly." Likewise perfectionists drive themselves into the depths of despair. They can never enjoy personal accomplishments because they don't pass the "white glove of perfection" test.

From the audio program, *The Fully Alive Experience*

*I*n order to eliminate a distorted pattern of thinking, a crippling attitude, we have to work out a simple and direct statement of the truth which will replace the error in our crippling attitude. This statement is called a "counterlogic" or a "counterchallenge." The use or process is called "countering." Recent research calls this method "Voluntary Cortical Inhibition" or "VCI." We voluntarily inhibit old thought or brain (cortical) patterns. When an effective counterlogic is found, it is used as a weapon of attack, to attack the falsehood in our habitual thinking.

For example, if I am tempted to think and feel like a non-person, a nobody, every time this thought or feeling rises in me, I stop or inhibit it with my counterlogic: "I am somebody. I'm the one and only Me!"

Thought and expression are so closely bound together in us that they are like hand in glove. Whenever we are thinking something, we are unconsciously verbalizing our thought. If we change the verbalization, we will change the thought, too. Like hand in glove, if I change the position of my hand inside my glove, the position of the glove will change with it. Likewise, if I verbalize my new attitude, my thinking will move with it. The more I say, "I am somebody," the more I will think it. And the more I think it, the deeper-rooted the new habit will become. Eventually, it will become a part of me. The old, crippling, life-restricting thought patterns are by a conscious decision inhibited and replaced by new, life-giving attitudes.

From the audio program, *The Fully Alive Experience*

*C*ountering" or the use of "Counterlogics" has certainly changed me and my life. I have often repeated to myself the counterlogic: "I am bigger than this." I have always believed that the size of a person is measured by the size of the things that disturb that person. I didn't want to be the size of those trivial things that habitually irritated me. The more I repeated, "I am bigger than this (petty irritation or friction)!" the more I thought and felt that way, the more I grew, and the more free I became.

Another helpful (for me) counterlogic is: "I am an actor, not a reactor." To me this means that I will let no one else decide how I am going to act. If another chooses to be petty, I am not going to be drawn into petty habits of behavior. If another chooses to be angry or malicious, I am not going to let that seduce me from my personal resolve to be a loving person. I am going to decide how I will act. I am an actor and not a reactor.

Finally, a friend who is a psychiatrist once answered an important question for me by asking one. I had always been disappointed whenever I encountered self-centeredness. I really suffered whenever I encountered it. I found it so frustrating. Well, the good doctor asked me: "Did you ever have a toothache?" "Yes, I have," I answered. "And whom were you thinking of when your tooth was hurting?" he asked. "Me, of course," I blurted. "That," he said, "is your answer. People who are self-centered are hurting people. Their pain magnetizes all their attention." I have used that question, "Did you ever have a toothache?" as a counterlogic whenever I have encountered seeming self-centeredness. It has helped me become more compassionate, and certainly much happier.

From the audio program, *The Fully Alive Experience*

*A*nother effective way of revising a crippling attitude is to find a "role model." The supposition is that you have found in yourself an attitude that is shriveling. Then you look for someone, a historical figure or a living person, who models the attitude you would like to make your own. So you study or talk to that person, you ask questions, you try to explore that other person's thinking. Then you try it on for size. You try on the thinking or attitude of that "role model." You get the feel of what it is like to think as that person does. In your exploration of that person's attitude you get a sense of the peace that must result in a person who thinks that way. You sense the enjoyment, the aliveness, the freedom that must result from such an attitude.

Psychologists call this "introjection." We introject the mentality of another. We all do this to some extent. We do this often while watching a movie. We think and feel what the person on the screen is thinking and feeling.

One of my favorite role models is St. Thomas More. There are many saints whose faces look like the bark of trees and who had spiritual bad breath. They do not appeal very much to me. But Thomas More, ah, there was a saint I want to be like. A strong sense of honor and duty coupled with a marvelous sense of humor. He died for his conviction, but he actually joked with the man assigned to behead him. He told the man not to feel bad. Then he added, "We'll all meet merrily in heaven." Whenever I read Robert Bolt's play or see the movie made from it, *A Man For All Seasons*, I think to myself: When I grow up I want to be like that man.

From the audio program, *The Fully Alive Experience*

*S*t. Paul proposes Jesus as a "role model" to the Philippians. The historical background seems to have involved a lot of quibbling, bragging, maneuvering and manipulating for positions of importance. Sometime read over chapter 3 of Paul's *Letter to the Philippians.*

Paul says: Introject the mind of Jesus. Take Jesus for your model. Even though Jesus was God's own Son, he didn't think that the glory of God was a thing to be clung to. He left it behind. He really emptied himself. And he took on the form of a slave, a servant. He took on our human nature. And in his human nature he was obedient, even unto the most shameful of all deaths, death on a cross. Think about it. Think about him. "Have this mind in you . . . the mind of Jesus."

A young girl, the late Simone Weil, once said that when she thought of Jesus dying on his cross, praying for those who nailed him to that cross, promising the "Good Thief" a place in Paradise, expressing concern for his mother, and commending his spirit to his Father: she turned green with envy.

From the audio program, *The Fully Alive Experience*

*A*ll of us have "comfort zones," the areas in which we are comfortable. These comfort zones apply to the way we dress, the emotions we can comfortably express, the things which we will try, the depths to which we reveal ourselves, our openness to change, and so forth.

As long as we stay within these comfort zones, we just keep repeating what we have always done. We don't change. We don't grow. Every day is pretty much like the day before, and every tomorrow is pretty much like today. Our days are all "carbon copies" of one another.

We like our comfort zones, even though they definitely shrink the world in which we live. We know our way around inside our comfort zones. We know how to cope with the things we encounter in our familiar comfort zones. We feel "safe" there.

If you promise me that you are going to stay within your comfort zone, I will be able to tell you what you will be like at the end of your life. You'll be just what you are now, only more so.

If you promise me that you are going to stretch, to step outside your comfort zone, I cannot predict your future. The sky is the limit.

From the audio program, *The Fully Alive Experience*

*T*he third means for changing a crippling, life-diminishing attitude is what we call "stretching." Basically it means that by stepping out of what is called a "comfort zone" we expand our awareness of personal potential. When we "stretch" we (take a deep breath and then) do something right and reasonable, which we have always felt inhibited from trying.

So many times we cop out by saying, "Oh, I could never give a speech before a large public audience!" "Oh, that's not me. I'm a very private person." By saying things like this we are only limiting ourselves. We are burying our potential. Students of human nature say that the average person uses only about ten percent of his or her potential.

In learning to stretch, we shouldn't start out with some giant leap. That might prove discouraging. Apologize, admit you were wrong, express an emotion you were always afraid of, take some time out without feeling guilty, do a favor for someone anonymously, talk to someone you've been ignoring, compliment someone who never compliments you, say "no" to a request without explaining or feeling guilty, hold someone's hand, try something you may well fail at and in this way you will desensitize yourself to the fear of failure, take the first step in starting a relationship, share a secret about yourself that you have always found difficult to open up.

Stretching means a fuller life and a larger world. Don't die with ninety percent of your potential unused.

From the audio program, *The Fully Alive Experience*

*T*here are two ways to change. We can think our way into a new way of acting. Or we can act our way into a new way of thinking.

Stretching is an example of the latter. Whenever we stretch by stepping outside our comfort zones, we expand the awareness of our potential. We think differently after we have stretched. For example, I may think of myself as someone who just can't give a speech in public or tell someone that I love them. So I stretch, I force myself to do it. I step out of my comfort zone.

Afterwards, I think of myself as someone who can give a speech in public or share my love. I can. Yes, I can because I just did it. It was this way the first time we swam without anyone else's support. "I can swim!" we announced to the world. And our concept of ourselves was different after that. Beforehand we thought of ourselves as someone who couldn't but afterwards we thought of ourselves as someone who could.

We had acted our way into a new way of thinking.

From the audio program, *The Fully Alive Experience*

*O*nce a person starts to stretch, to step out of the old comfort zones and try the untried, that person soon develops a "stretch mentality." At least that has been my experience and the experience of others who have confided in me. Every time I stretch I feel myself becoming more of a master of my fears. I feel my world getting larger. I am discovering talents in myself that I never knew I had.

I remember being the shyest child in my kindergarten class. It was a painful existence. I'm really grateful for the people who challenged me to stretch, to get into debating in high school and enter the oratorical contests. Now all the old shyness is gone. I am free to be my real self.

Remembering the successes of the past and enjoying the rewards of stretching have helped me make stretching a way of life. I look forward to the challenges that each day brings because I know every challenge that I am able to meet will bring me a new freedom: to live, to love, to use the talents God has given me.

From the audio program, *The Fully Alive Experience*

*T*he final method of changing an old and crippling attitude is "praying." The practice of prayer has been very important in shaping my life. I think that it has been the most important single source of change for me.

I think of God as an electrical outlet. There is so much power to be tapped. Enough to light a room, heat a room, show a movie and so forth. But you have to get yourself connected to all that power. Prayer does that.

One prerequisite for success in tapping into the the power of God is the willingness on our part to be honest and open in the presence of God. If I play a role with God, tell him what I think he wants to hear, but not what I am really thinking or feeling, there can be no real communication. The same thing is true of our human failures at communication. If I put on a mask or play a part with you, you simply cannot communicate with me. I have not given you a "real me" with whom to interact. It is all play acting.

In prayer I have to open myself completely. I have to expose all my known attitudes to God. I have to stand naked before him. These are my fears, my doubts, and my gifts, as I see them. I can say things to God that I can say to no one else. I can truly tell him what I think, how I feel. And I must do this. Only then can God interact with me, put new ideas into my mind. Only then can God give me new perspectives and attitudes. I am sure that most of the insights that have changed me have been the result of this kind of prayer.

Prayer, then, is opening myself as honestly as I can in self-disclosure, and then opening myself as best I can to receive God's enlightenment.

From the audio program, *The Fully Alive Experience*

*P*rayer should pervade the whole of "vision therapy." We should ask God to enlighten us to locate the attitudes which cripple us and distort our vision of reality. We should pray for the grace to change, to find counterlogics that will truly retrack our thought patterns. We should pray that we will find and take advantage of the role models who are available to us. We must pray for the courage to stretch, to reach for the unreachable star.

Prayer should suffuse our lives. To be honest I have to tell you of the time I was about to address my own Jesuit Community. I was unexpectedly nervous. My mouth was dry. My hands were cold. As the time of my address got closer, I started to pray. After several attempts nothing happened, so I asked God, "Are you trying to tell me something?" God told me unmistakably that I was getting ready to give a "performance." He assured me that he didn't need performances from me but only acts of love. "You are getting ready to perform for your brothers so they will know how good you are. They do not need that. They need you to love them so that they will know how good they are."

It was a Copernican moment in my life. I have done nothing, since that time, including the classes I teach, the things I write and the speeches I give, without asking the Lord: "Help me to make this an act of love. Please don't let it be just another performance."

From the audio program, *The Fully Alive Experience*

I would like to suggest a few practical ways to make "vision therapy" a way of life:

It is very helpful to keep one's "counterlogics" and pictures of one's "role models" in view. I have my own pasted to my mirror, so that I see them first thing in the morning. I keep my "counterlogics" on bookmarks. I have pictures of my role models on the walls of my office.

Make a list in a private journal of the attitudes that are life-diminishing for you. Express in a homemade counterlogic the truth that redresses the imbalance of each crippling attitude. Then put down the names of people who seem to practice the attitudes you would like to have. The people who don't worry, if you are a worrier. The people who are real and authentic, if you feel like a living charade.

Then put these things to work in your life. Remember what the famous William James once said: "It is the most important discovery of our generation, that by changing the inner attitudes of the mind, we can change all the outer aspects of our lives."

From the audio program, *The Fully Alive Experience*

*S*ome time ago a friend told me of an occasion when, vacationing in the Bahamas, he saw a large and restless crowd gathered on a pier. Upon investigation he discovered that the object of all the attention was a young man making the last-minute preparations for a solo journey around the world in a home-made boat. Without exception everyone on the pier was vocally pessimistic. All were actively volunteering to tell the ambitious sailor all the things that could possibly go wrong. "The sun will broil you! . . . You won't have enough food! . . . That boat of yours won't withstand the waves in a storm! . . . You'll never make it!"

When my friend heard all these discouraging warnings to the adventurous young man, he felt an irresistible desire to offer some optimism and encouragement. As the little craft began drifting away from the pier towards the horizon, my friend went to the end of the pier, waving both arms wildly like semaphores spelling confidence. He kept shouting: *"Bon Voyage!* You're really something! We're with you! We're proud of you! Good luck, brother!"

Sometimes it seems to me that there are two kinds of people. There are those who feel obligated to tell us all the things that can go wrong as we set out over the uncharted waters of our unique lives. "Wait till you get out into the cold, cruel world, my friend. Take it from me." Then there are those who stand at the end of the pier, cheering us on, exuding a contagious confidence: *"Bon Voyage!"*

From *Fully Human, Fully Alive*

*I*n order to grow as persons, we need to know that we have someone's unconditional love. There can be no fine print in the contract. There can be no pan scales for measuring input and output. In a love relationship there is no bickering about who is giving more and who is giving less. The only kind of love that provides the needed atmosphere for human growth and personal development says simply: "I love you. No, you didn't earn it. And you don't have to deserve it or prove yourself worthy. You don't have to pay anything to get it. You see, you can't buy it. There is no admission price. You simply have it. It is my gift to you. I love you."

If we ever ask another, "Why do you love me?" we are asking for trouble. The other person might just respond, "I love you because you are so handsome, because you are so beautiful." You will certainly realize that you are not always going to be handsome. You will not always be beautiful. Someday your body will lose its young form. Your hair will turn gray. And your teeth may fall out. Your heart which knows these possibilities will be asking: "Will you love me then?"

The only way I can truly help you is by loving you unconditionally. The only way you can help me is by offering me this same precious gift. And the only pertinent question is not "Why do you love me?" but only "Do you love me?" When the answer is "yes," when this "yes" is unconditional and forever, it will be the springtime of my life. It will be a personal invitation to live fully, and the glory of God is a person who is fully alive.

From the video program, *Free To Be Me*

*T*o all those who are skeptical about love, I would like to say: "Love works for those who work at it." We have to work at love. A work of art is first and foremost a work. Love does not come wrapped in wax paper, fully assembled. Love is a do-it-yourself kit. We have to work at it, put it together day by day, piece by piece, little by little. We have to work at love. It doesn't just happen.

Furthermore, love is not an emotion, a feeling. It is a commitment to another person: "I love you. I am going to be what you need me to be. I am going to do what you need me to do. I am going to say what you need me to say. This is what I mean when I say 'I love you.' If you succeed I will rejoice with you in your success. I will be in the first row of your cheering section, clapping my hands off for you. If you fail, I will be sitting there quietly at your side, holding your hand. This is what I mean when I say I am committed to loving you."

Love is a sweet and beautiful thing. It also will challenge every ounce of determination and courage in us. It is a gutsy commitment that invites another to "take us for granted." Take my love as a given. Love will lead us down roads we could not anticipate. I know that your needs will change from day to day. When you change, I will try to adapt to these changes. I will try to be whatever you need me to be and I know that it will not always be the same thing. And even if you fail, if you should fail my expectations as well as your own, be sure of this: I will always love you. I want my love to be true, and true love is forever. I will never take my love back.

From the video program, *Free To Be Me*

*L*ove should generally be supported by favorable feelings, but it is not itself a feeling. If it were a feeling, love would be a very fickle reality and those who construed it to be a feeling would be very fickle people. Rather love is a *decision* and *commitment*. My Christian vocation is to love all people. This means that I must try to do for each person with whom I interact whatever I can to promote that person's true growth and happiness. However, I cannot enter into an actual and ongoing love relationship with everyone. I must therefore decide—and it should be a careful choice—to whom and at what level of commitment I wish to offer my love.

Having made such a decision, on the presumption that my offer of love has been accepted and reciprocated, I am now by my own free choice committed to the happiness, security, and well-being of the person I love. I will do everything I can to help that person build whatever dreams he or she has. It is this commitment which I make when I offer my love. When I question myself about the place love has in my life, I must therefore ask if there is any person in my life whose growth and happiness is as real or more real to me than my own. If so, love has truly entered my life.

I might even ask if there is any person or cause for which I would give my very life. Jesus has told us that this is the greatest love. "No one can give a greater proof of love than by laying down his life for his friends" (John 15:13).

From *Unconditional Love*

*T*he commitment to love will involve me in much careful and active listening. I truly want to be whatever you need me to be, to do whatever you need done, and I want to say whatever will promote your happiness, security and well-being. To discover your needs, I must be attentive, caring, and open both to what you say and to what you cannot say. However, the final decision about the "loving thing" must be mine.

This means that my love may be "tough" love, not all sweet and coddling. You may ask me for another drink when you are already inebriated, or you may ask me to join you in some deception. Of course, if I truly love you, I must say an emphatic "No!" to these requests. If you are on a self-destructive course, like alcoholism, you will meet in me a firm and confronting love. But, when needed, my love will also be "tender." If you have tried and failed, and you just need a hand in yours in the darkness of disappointment, you can count on mine.

I may read you wrongly on occasion and misjudge your needs. I have done this so often to so many in the past. But know this, that my decision is to love you and my commitment is to your true and lasting happiness. I am dedicated to your growth and fulfillment as a person. If I should fail you, for lack of wisdom or because of the abundance of weakness in me, please forgive me, try to recognize my intention, and know that I will try to do better.

From *Unconditional Love*

*T*here are two "messages" that all human beings need to receive and record. They are the messages of affirmation and of personal responsiblity. These two messages are like the two legs on which a person can walk successfully through life. The message of affirmation is this: "You are a unique human being, the one and only you. You are a creature of God, made in his image and likeness. But after he made you, he broke the mold. There never was and there never will be another you. You are a real gift to this world and a person of inestimable worth." The message of responsibility is this: "As you mature into adulthood you must take your life into your own hands. You must at this time assume full responsibility for your life, your emotions and attitudes. The outcome of your life is in your hands. When you look into a mirror, you are looking at the one person who is responsible for your happiness."

Someone has compared these messages to "roots and wings." We must give to others both roots and wings. The roots of any human existence are the roots of personal worth, of self-confidence, the roots of belief in one's own uniqueness. The message that offers roots is that of an unconditional love. The wings of a human existence are the wings of self-responsibility. Giving a person wings is the message that "You have everything needed to soar, to sing your own song, to warm the world with your presence. The direction of your flight, the song you will sing and the warmth you will bestow on this world are your responsibility. You must take your life into your own hands. You must not blame others and complain about your lack of opportunity. You must assume full responsibility for the course and direction of your life." The message of roots says to an individual: "You've got it!" The message of wings says: "Now go for it!"

From the video program, *Families*

*T*here is no third possibility: love is either conditional or unconditional. Either I attach conditions to my love for you or I do not. To the extent that I do attach conditions, I do not really love you. I am only offering an exchange, not a gift. And true love is and must always be a free gift.

The gift of my love means this: I want to share with you whatever I have that is good. You did not win a contest or prove yourself worthy of this gift. It is not a question of deserving my love. I have no delusions that either of us is the best person in the world. I do not even suppose that, of all the available persons, we are the most compatible. I am sure that somewhere there is someone who would be "better" for you or for me. The point is that I have *chosen* to give you my gift of love and you have *chosen* to love me.

The essential message of unconditional love is one of liberation: you can be whoever you are, express all your thoughts and feelings with absolute confidence. You do not have to be fearful that love will be taken away. You will not be punished for your openness or honesty. There is no admission price to my love, no rental fees or installment payments to be made. There may be days when disagreements and disturbing emotions may come between us. There may be times when psychological or physical miles may lie between us. But I have given you the word of my commitment. I have set my life on a course. I will not go back on my word to you. So feel free to be yourself, to tell me your negative and positive reactions, of your warm and cold feelings. I cannot always predict my reactions or guarantee my strength, but one thing I do know and want you to know: I will not reject you! I am committed to your growth and happiness. I will always love you.

From *Unconditional Love*

*I*n the ten years before my mother's death in 1976, we shared many, many secrets. Once I confided that I had discovered in myself a fear of death. I can still see my dear, bedridden mother, as she slowly turned her head on the pillow and looked at me with soft and understanding eyes. Then she said:

> I have never feared death since you children have been grown up. I didn't want to leave you before that, while you were still little. But now I have no fear of death. But, John, do you know what I do fear? I fear pain. I would find a painful death very hard to endure. So I have asked the Lord (at this point she gazed up at a portrait of the Lord at the foot of her bed), "When you come for me, Jesus, will you tiptoe in here and kiss me softly while I am sleeping? I just don't want to die in great pain."

My mother was eighty-eight years old when she died . . . in her sleep, of course. The Lord tiptoed in and kissed her softly while she was sleeping. He could refuse her nothing. The last twenty-four unconscious hours of her life I sat with her, holding her hand in mine. We waited together for the Angel of Death, for the Lord to tiptoe in. During the time of waiting, I sat there remembering all she had done for me. The touch of her gentle hands was so healing on the head of a sick child. Those hands I held had sewed so many clothes, cooked so many meals, made so many sandwiches and wrapped them in wax paper and put them in little brown bags for school. Those hands tied my first pair of shoes, bathed my body when I was a baby, and put cool cloths on my forehead when I was nauseous. They spanked when spanking was in order and they caressed me when I needed tenderness.

From *The Silent Holocaust*

When we talk about the kind of love with which we want to be loved, most of us would clearly and emphatically specify that it be unconditional. I don't want you to love me for what I can do for you or because I please your expectations. I don't want to have to march to your drums. I want you to love me for better or for worse, in sickness and in health, in good times and in bad, for richer or for poorer, with no strings attached. I can't sell out my person to buy your love.

However, when we are discussing the kind of love which we are willing to give, it is not so clear. Most of us want to be more tentative in case things don't work out. To give my word and promise my unconditional faithfulness to that word is more than a little frightening. We want to leave a back door open, an escape hatch. It is so much easier to be an unencumbered butterfly, flitting from flower to flower. It is so much harder to take the plunge into an unconditional commitment. It seems much less frightening to travel with a tent than to build a permanent home.

From *Unconditional Love*

A time limit on love is one of the conditions we can attach to our commitment. I will love you as long as, until. . . . In the movie *Butterflies Are Free,* the superficial, scatter-brained nymphet played so well by Goldie Hawn is portrayed in the act of running away from her blind lover. She explains her flight: " . . . because you are blind. You're crippled!" In the most profound moment of the movie, the young man replies: "No, I am not crippled. I am sightless but not crippled. You are crippled, because you can't commit yourself to anyone. You can't belong."

The commitment of love, at whatever level, has to be a permanent thing, a life-wager. If I say that I am your friend, I will always be your friend, not as long as or until anything. I will always be there for you. Effective love is not like the retractable point on a ballpoint pen. If I say I am your man, I will always be your man. In the words of another old song, "When I fall in love, it will be forever."

Any other kind of love loses its effect. I need to know that the love you offer me is a permanent offer before I will give up my security operations, my masks, my roles and games. I cannot come out to a temporary, tentative love, to an offer which has all that fine print and many footnotes in the contract.

From *The Secret Of Staying In Love*

*W*hat do we fear in the promise of unconditional love? Perhaps the most disturbing of all fears is that my commitment of unconditional love will somehow be a denial or surrender of myself, a sad farewell to a sense of separate identity. I fear that I will have to give up my individual interests and personal tastes. In fact, if these fears were realized, there could be no relationship of love because relationship means two. Kahlil Gibran in his book *The Prophet* says that unconditional love should not be conceived as making two islands into one solid landmass. A love relationship, he suggests, should rather be like two islands that remain separate and distinct, but whose shores are washed by the shared waters of love. Rainer Maria Rilke says: "Love consists in this: that two solitudes protect and touch and greet each other." A person might possibly surrender his or her own identity to another out of lack of respect for self or out of the need for approval, but one can never do this in the name of true love.

From *Unconditonal Love*

*O*nce there was a time, according to legend, when Ireland was ruled by kings and the reigning king had no sons. So he sent out his couriers to post signs on the trees in all the towns of his kingdom. The signs advised that every qualified young man should apply for an interview with the king as a possible successor to the throne. However, all such applicants must have these two qualifications: They must (1) love God and (2) love their fellow human beings.

The young man about whom this legend centers saw the signs and reflected that he indeed loved God and his fellow human beings. However, he was so poor that he had no clothes that would be presentable in the sight of the king. Nor did he have the means to buy provisions for the journey to the castle. So he begged and borrowed until at last he had enough money for the appropriate clothes and the necessary provisions. Eventually he set out for the castle, and had almost completed his journey when he came upon a poor beggar by the side of the road. The beggar sat trembling, clad only in rags. His extended arms pleaded for help. His weak voice quietly asked, "I'm hungry and I'm cold. Would you please help me?"

The young man was so moved by the need of the poor beggar that he immediately stripped off his new clothes and put on the rags of the beggar. Without a second thought he gave the beggar all his provisions. He loved God and he loved his fellow human beings.

From *The Christian Vision*

*T*he young man in the old Irish legend (yesterday's reading) proceeded somewhat uncertainly to the castle in the rags of the beggar without any provision for his journey home. Upon his arrival at the castle, an attendant to the king showed him in. After a long wait, he was finally admitted to the throne room of the king. The young man bowed low before his king. When he raised his eyes, he was filled with astonishment.

"You . . . you were the beggar by the side of the road."

"Yes," replied the king, "I was that beggar."

"But you are not really a beggar. You are really the king."

"Yes, I am really the king."

"Why did you do this to me?" the young man asked.

"Because I had to find out if you really do love, if you really love God and your fellow human beings. I knew that if I came to you as king, you would have been very much impressed by my crown of gold and my regal robes. You would have done anything I asked because of my kingly appearance. But that way I would never have known what is really in your heart. So I came to you as a beggar, with no claims on you except for the love in your heart. And I have found out that you truly do love God and your fellow human beings. You will be my successor. You will have my kingdom!"

From *The Christian Vision*

*I*n the twenty-fifth chapter of Matthew's Gospel, Jesus describes the final judgment day.

> "Then the King will say to the people on his right, 'Come, you that are blessed by my Father! Come and possess the kingdom which has been prepared for you ever since the creation of the world. I was hungry and you fed me . . .'"

At this the just are puzzled. They ask the Lord:

> "When, Lord, did we ever see you hungry and feed you?"

The reply of Jesus, in effect, is this:

> "I was the beggar by the side of the road of your life. I came to you, not in the majesty and splendor of God, but as a poor and simple beggar. I had no claims on you except for the love in your heart. I had to find out if you could open your hands and heart to the needs of your neighbor. Where your treasure is, there your heart will be, and I had to find out where your heart was. I have found great love in your heart. And so, you shall have a place in my Kingdom forever. You will possess the joy that human eyes have never seen, that human ears have never heard, that the human imagination has never dared to dream. Come, my Beloved, into your Father's house, where I have prepared a special place just for you."

In the end, on that last day and in that final judgment, one thing alone will be important. We shall all be judged by the love that God finds in our hearts.

From *The Christian Vision*

*L*ove works!" I keep saying to myself. But apparently love works only for those who work at it. Love works for those who will take the less traveled road and run the risks of complete emotional openness. It is certainly true that my feelings are unique. They summarize and express my whole life experience and my unique person. If the true gift of love is the gift of myself through self-disclosure, then I must entrust my feelings to those I love.

And to those I love: Please take my feelings into careful hands. And when you hold them, remember that they are a very important part of me. Thank you.

From *Will The Real Me Please Stand Up?*

*O*f course, it is risky to open up our own feelings to another as well as to take in another person's feelings. It is difficult to open up generously and to listen sensitively. But we must do this if we are to say to others what everyone needs to hear: "Here is the gift of me. It is the only real gift I can give you. . . . And thank you for the gift of you. I think I know something of what you are feeling."

When people seem to be obnoxious, they may well be trying to say to us: "You are not listening to how I feel. I am not asking you to agree with me. I don't need you to agree with what I am thinking or trying to say. But I really need you to accept and to understand me and my feelings. Can you? Will you?"

It is likewise a difficult thing to reveal one's own feelings, to run the risk of emotional transparency. It is like undressing in public. You can always put your clothes back on, but others are always going to remember what you looked like. To open ourselves to another person, to stop lying about our loneliness, to stop concealing our fears and hurts, to be open about our affection and to tell others what they mean to us: this is the difficult but essential work of love.

From the video program, *Free To Be Me*

*T*he most common reason for not reporting our feelings is that we do not want to admit them for one reason or another. We fear that others might not think well of us, or actually reject us, or punish us in some way for our emotional candor. We have been somehow "programmed" not to accept certain emotions as part of us. We are ashamed of them. They are simply "unacceptable." Now we can rationalize and say that we cannot report these emotions because they would not be understood, or that reporting them would disturb a peaceful relationship, or evoke an emotionally stormy reaction from the other; but all of our reasons are essentially fraudulent, and our silence can produce only fraudulent relationships. Anyone who builds a relationship on less than openness and honesty is building on sand. Such a relationship will never stand the test of time, and neither party to the relationship will draw from it any noticeable benefits.

From *Why Am I Afraid To Tell You Who I Am?*

*O*pening up my weak and wounded side, my fears and immature habits, even my phoniness and pretenses, will be such a relief. Taking you into my "closed rooms" will be a freeing experience for me. And in the exchange of such communication, you will get to know the real me. Our communication will no longer offer you only an edited and abridged version of me. What you see will be what you get: the one and only, the real me.

You won't be afraid of me or tempted to glorify me as someone who has it all together. You will know that I am a mistake-maker and that I experience in myself the human condition of weakness. I personally like to tell people to whom I am relating, "If you ever get my number, it will certainly be a fraction. Part of me feels certain; part of me doubts. Part of me is loving; another part of me is selfish. Part of me is confident; part of me is insecure. Part of me is proud; another part is humble." I have gradually become more content with being such an ambivalent person, who seems to be split right down the middle.

From *Will The Real Me Please Stand Up?*

*O*nly when we are willing to share our whole selves, warts and all, are we really communicating. But more than this, my openness will have a definite effect on others. Honesty, like everything else that is human, is contagious. My coming out from behind protective walls to meet you face to face will inspire you to do the same. When we are real and honest about our vulnerability, others are immediately relieved. They know that we have taken a risk in exposing our "warts and all" selves. By our honesty, they are invited and encouraged to take off their masks, to reveal their inner selves openly and honestly. They are empowered to take a similar risk and they will experience a similar sense of freedom.

Finally, another bit of wisdom I have gained from a friend in Alcoholics Anonymous is: We are as sick as we are secret. On the other side of the coin is a positive expression of the same truth: We are as healthy and whole as we are open and honest with ourselves and with others.

From *Will The Real Me Please Stand Up?*

*C*ommunication is a free exchange of gifts. The speaker gives the gift of self through self-disclosure. The listener takes that gift into gentle, understanding hands. This response of the listener is itself a gift. It is such an encouraging and reassuring gift that some expression of gratitude is in order.

When you listen to me, the first thing you must do is put your own life aside in order to give me the time I need. By listening to me you offer me what everyone needs most: the encouragement of someone who cares. Sometimes I think of it in terms of physical space. The listener clears a place in his or her life for the speaker to move in, to sit down and spread out the pieces of a personal puzzle. The listener has to make room for the speaker. A good listener is not just a sacrificial lamb, who goes though the motions of virtuous self-sacrifice. The good listener truly wants to know who the speaker is.

"Thank you for turning away from your own needs and concerns. Thank you for wanting to know who I really am. It certainly has made it much easier for me to share with you my own inner spaces."

From *Will The Real Me Please Stand Up?*

A good listener gives me the freedom to be who I am. I am almost painfully aware that you are different from me. My thoughts are not your thoughts and your thoughts are not mine. My fears are not your fears. My worries may not find any resonant echoes inside you. The things that stir anger and resentment in me may well be the things you can take so easily in your stride. And yet you give me the freedom to be different; to fear what you do not fear, to worry about that which would not cause you to worry, and to feel resentment for persons that you would only pity.

A good listener offers us even more than this acceptance of our differences. The good listener goes out to experience vicariously whatever we are trying to share. The good listener makes an effort to get inside us, to look out through our eyes, to feel our fears, to relive with us our reactions. The good listener just says, "Yes, of course," or "I see" and we immediately feel understood.

The good listener offers us this gift of empathy which assures us that we are not alone. This gift of going out of self and somehow standing with us is a very precious gift.

From *Will The Real Me Please Stand Up?*

When I thank you for listening to me, I implicitly make it clear that this was all that I was asking of you. I was not inviting you to solve my problems for me. That would be immature on my part. I was not trying to manipulate you by some subtle accusation, or to put you on trial. I was not even challenging you to evaluate my sharing.

I was only asking you for the great gift of putting aside your own life and agendas for a while and sharing a personal concern with me. I was asking you for the gift of letting me be different from you. I was asking you for the gift of accepting me at the place I am right now. A simple word of gratitude says all this. It lets you know that I appreciate the many gifts involved in the gift of your listening. At the same time, my gratitude reminds me that you are not a thing to be used or a person to be taken for granted.

Very often when we are sharing our so-called "negative" feelings, without intending it we might make it sound like a trial, a challenge, a confrontation. "Thank you very much for letting me be me and for letting me tell you about it!" at the end puts things into perspective. It also supplies a context for our sharing that clarifies and classifies our self-disclosure as a gift of self. Our expression of gratitude makes it clear that this "gift" was not a thinly veiled accusation or manipulation. It was simply a gift, no strings attached.

Oh, and thank you for listening.

From *Will The Real Me Please Stand Up?*

*T*he obvious and primary benefit of honest and open communication will be a real and authentic relationship and what we have called a true "encounter" of persons. Not only will there be mutual communication of persons and the consequent sharing and experiencing of personhood, but it will result in a more and more clearly defined sense of self-identity for each of the parties in the relationship.

Today, many of us are asking: "Who am I?" It has come to be a socially fashionable question. The implication is that I do not really know my own self as a person. My person is what I think, judge, feel, and so forth. If I have communicated these things freely and openly, as clearly as I can and as honestly as I can, I will find a noticeable growth in my own sense of identity as well as a deeper and more authentic knowledge of the other. It has come to be a psychological truism that I will understand only as much of myself as I have been willing to communicate to another.

From *Why Am I Afraid To Tell You Who I Am?*

*W*hat we call "Gut-level" communication will evoke from others a responsive honesty and openness, which is necessary if the relationship is to be interpersonal and mutual. If we want another to be open with us, we must begin by opening up ourselves, by telling the other honestly and openly of our feelings.

"Person is resonant to person," the psychologist Goldbrunner insists. If I am willing to step out of the darkness of my prison, to expose the deepest part of me to another person, the result is almost always automatic and immediate: The other person feels empowered to reveal him or herself to me. Having heard my secret and deep feelings, the other person is given the courage to communicate his or her own self to me.

From *Why Am I Afraid To Tell You Who I Am?*

*Y*our love for me will be effective only to the extent that I confide myself to you. When you say in one of the many ways that love is expressed that you love me, I will want to believe that you really know me. To the extent that I have hidden myself from you the effect of your love will be diminished. I will forever fear that you love only the part of me that I have let you know; and that if you knew the real me, all of me, you would not love me. Love follows upon knowledge, and so you can love me only to the extent that I let you know me.

It is true that, in all communication, kindness without honesty is sentimentality; but it is likewise true that honesty without kindness is cruelty. The genius of communication is the ability to be both totally honest and totally kind at the same time. Although it is one of the stern canons of dialogue that emotions should be reported at the time they are experienced and to the person to whom those emotions are related, kindness should still have much to say about the manner of communication.

From *The Secret Of Staying In Love*

A willingness to learn must be added to a willingness to listen. For most of us this is quite difficult. It asks me to leave where I am, and to go where you are. It even requires that I leave (not give up) my own convictions in order to experience yours. No doubt, if I reflect back to you not only my empathy but also my understanding of your "inner consistency," you will certainly be very grateful. You will feel understood. And this kind of listening in order to learn is a much more valuable gift than listening only long enough to prepare my response.

Sometimes I have thought of this "listening and learning" which we are talking about as comparable to looking for the undiscovered pieces of a jig-saw puzzle. The first installment of self-disclosure is often meaningless by itself. One piece of a puzzle does not make sense by itself. But then will come another piece, if my listening is sensitive and my empathy is real. Slowly, one by one, the pieces will appear and fall together. The picture gradually begins to come clear. Of course, we never totally understand anyone, ourselves included. But we can gain a real sense of what it is like to be "other." We can understand something of the "inner consistency" of the thoughts and feelings of another human being. When this kind of understanding is offered to us, it is a mountaintop moment of consolation. "Thank God, someone finally knows what it is like to be me." The person who has truly been heard and understood will probably be permanently transformed by this magnificent gift.

From *Will The Real Me Please Stand Up?*

*I*f I am in the habit of judging the intentions or motivations of another, I should try very hard to outgrow this adolescent habit. I will simply not be able to disguise my judgments, no matter how many disclaimers I make.

If I really want to know the intention or motivation or reaction of another, there is only one way to find out: *I must ask him or her.*

Perhaps a word should be inserted here about the difference between judging a person and judging an action. If I see someone stealing another's money, I can judge that *action* as morally wrong, but I cannot judge *the person*. It is for God, not for you or me, to judge human responsibility. If, however, we could not judge the rightness or wrongness of an action, it would be the end of all objective morality. Let us not fall into this, that there is nothing objectively wrong or right, that it is all in the way that you look at it. But to judge the responsibility of another is playing God.

From *Why Am I Afraid To Tell You Who I Am?*

*P*eople are very complicated. They are so "other," so different from us that we cannot safely project our thoughts, feelings, or motives into them. We cannot read their interiors by looking at their exteriors.

I hope you can coax out of your memory one instance in which you thought you had correctly read the motives and intentions of another, and then discovered that the hidden reality was quite different. I hope you have been shocked and surprised, for example, to find under a wreath of smiles an empty loneliness. I hope you have found out from personal experience just how mysterious we human beings can be. Just one such discovery can give us pause. Our mistaken judgments make us reevaluate our ability to read minds and judge intentions.

Sometimes by inches but mostly by miles. I have been wrong every time I have tried to read minds and judge intentions. And so I have concluded that the only way to know what someone is thinking or intending is simply to ask that person. Obviously we are all somewhat deceived about ourselves, and so what another would tell us in answer to our questions may not always be accurate or even truthful. But it sure beats our best guesses. Furthermore, asking always promotes an exchange of communication. Just as surely mind reading and judging tend to break down the lines of communication and separate people.

So the next time we feel confident, we should check out our assumptions. Human beings are simply too complicated and too different for guesswork.

Sometimes by inches and sometimes by miles, but there is always a surprise waiting for us in the inner truth of another! Here's hoping you like surprises.

From *Will The Real Me Please Stand Up?*

*P*ersonal presence" implies much more than just being a warm body in the same room. I am personally present to you when I am giving you all my attention. Everything else for the moment has been shut out. The lenses of my mind are focused on you and on what you are sharing with me.

It is difficult for most of us to work up to real honesty and openness. Consequently, we need the atmosphere and support of true presence to attempt a profound sharing of ourselves. I don't want to take the obvious risk of self-disclosure if you look bored or distracted. I don't want to put a tender and sensitive part of myself in your hands only to watch you yawn or notice your attempt to change the subject. I don't want to share my joy or my success with you if you appear to be too preoccupied to celebrate with me.

"Availability" is a closely related concept. All of us know what it is like to knock on a door and get no response. We know what it is like to dial a phone number with a sense of urgency and get a busy signal. There is a similar reaction of disappointment in most of us when we truly wish to share some profound part of ourselves only to notice that our supposed listener does not seem to be available. We sense that this other person would rather not be troubled with us and our sharing. When we get such a "busy signal," we usually just hang up. We are tempted to give up.

From *Will The Real Me Please Stand Up?*

*A*n old American Indian saying reminds us that "to truly understand another human being, we must first walk a mile in his moccasins." To this we would like to add the suggestion that we cannot walk in another's moccasins until we first take off our own. We have to make a real effort as listeners to get out of ourselves, to unshackle ourselves from our personal preoccupations, and to donate our presence and availability to others.

At first this will be very difficult, but as with every other human accomplishment, practice will make it easier and easier until it becomes habitual. Presence and availability are very valuable accomplishments, and certainly worth the effort of our repetition and practice.

So let's exchange our shoes and walk a mile together.

From *Will The Real Me Please Stand Up?*

*I*t seems to me that the key to success in understanding and loving others is empathy. Empathy starts with an attentive listening and an intuitive reading of the uniqueness of another. Empathy asks only one question: What is it like to be you? Empathy is getting inside the skin of another, walking in his or her shoes, seeing and experiencing reality as it looks through the eyes of another. In the end, empathy offers not advice but only understanding. "Oh, yes, I hear you." If the essence of empathy is listening to and living vicariously the life experience of another, the price of empathy is this: It requires a temporary leaving of one's self, one's own thoughts and feelings, one's values and beliefs. When I empathize with you, I leave where I am and I go to be with you where you are.

Carl Rogers suggests that our experience of the human condition often involves feelings like those of a person who has fallen into a deep, dry well. The desperate man trapped in the well can't climb out, so he keeps knocking, knocking, knocking on the side of the well, hoping against hope that someone will hear him and realize his situation. Finally, after a long time of such banging against the side of the well, he hears a responding knock from the outside. Someone has heard him! There is an explosion of joyful relief in the poor man. "Thank God!" Somebody finally knows where I am." Rogers says that when somebody really listens to us and registers understanding, we feel the same grateful explosion of relief: "Thank God! Somebody finally knows where I am. Somebody finally knows what it is like to be me!"

From *The Christian Vision*

*B*y *empathy* we share more totally in another's experience: the thoughts, feelings, attitudes of that person. By empathy we put ourselves in somebody else's shoes. Through the powers of our minds and imaginations we think that person's thoughts, we want what that person is seeking, we feel whatever he or she is feeling. In short, we experience what that person is experiencing.

To develop our powers of empathy we have to acknowledge the unique otherness of every human being. We must be able to leave our own frame of reference and our own instincts and take on those of another. In a sense, empathy is the basic skill of the listener in the communication process.

It is not an easy thing to walk a mile in the moccasins of another. However, if we really want to get inside another's thoughts and attitudes and enter into his or her total experience, we can do it. The first, necessary step is to get out of our own moccasins.

For me the invitation to empahy begins with this question: What is it like to be you? And if I am really asking this question in relating to another, that other will hear my question as a statement of concern: "I care." Whether we are mourning or celebrating, it is difficult for us humans to be alone. An empathic reaction on the part of another is consoling and reassuring. It says in a clear and undeniable way, "You are not alone. I am with you because I care."

From *Will The Real Me Please Stand Up?*

A thousand fears keep us in the solitary confinement of estrangement. In some of us there is the fear of breaking down, of sobbing like a child. Others of us feel restrained by the fear that the other person will not sense the tremendous importance of my secret to me. We usually anticipate how deep the pain would be if my secret were met with apathy, misunderstanding, shock, anger or ridicule. My confidant might become angry or reveal my secret to others for whom it was not intended.

It may have happened that, at some point in my life, I took some part of me out of the darkness and placed it in the light for the eyes of another. It may be that the other person did not understand, and I ran full of regrets into a painful emotional solitude. Yet, there may have been other moments when someone heard my secret and accepted my confidence in gentle hands. I may remember what the other said to assure me, the compassionate voice, the understanding look. I remember what those eyes looked like. I remember the gentle pressure of a hand that told me that I was understood. It was a great and liberating experience, and, in its wake, I felt so much more alive. An immense need had been answered in me to be really listened to, to be taken seriously, and to be understood.

From *Why Am I Afraid To Tell You Who I Am?*

*S*uppose that I am listening to you in an attentive and accepting way. I resist mind reading, trying only to imagine what it is like to be you. However, even with these good intentions and efforts, I am still not sure that I understand. I'm not sure that I really know what you are trying to share. I don't want to bridge this gap by guessing or assuming that I know what you mean. I want you to be assured that I really do understand. So what do I do?

In this case, I have to work to clarify your message. There are three types of clarification. Each of these types deals with a different level of understanding. The first of these types is simply: *Asking for more information*. If the message I am receiving seems indirect or incomplete, I have to look for and locate whatever might be missing. The second type of clarification is: *Checking out word meanings*. It may be a matter of word usage. The meanings you attach to your words may be quite different from those I understand. In this case I must ask you to share your definitions with me. Finally, the third type of clarification we might call: *Verifying my understanding of your experience*. In this case the content and word meanings may be clear, but somehow I am not really sure that I have fully understood the whole tone or emotional impact of your experience.

In seeking a clarification of any of these three levels, the most important thing is that our intentions be clear to the speaker. And our intentions should always be:

- interest in the speaker,
- gentleness and patience with the process,
- and a desire to understand fully the sharing of another.

Passing like ships in the night is a lonely and painful alternative.

From *Will The Real Me Please Stand Up?*

*T*he one sure way not to grow up is to hitchhike on the mind and will of someone else. We will never mature if we let others think for us and make our choices. Consequently, telling another what to think by interpreting reality for him or her is to forestall that person's maturation process. Likewise, telling another what to do is to aid and abet immaturity and a childish dependency.

So what do you say when someone comes to you and you can see the hitchhiking thumb asking for a free ride? I sometimes have to work at stifling my old urge to turn into a computer printer spitting out all kinds of interpretations and advice. I have personally been working on the technique of the well-placed question. It goes something like this: "Gee, I don't know what you should do. What do you think? In your judgment, what are the possibilities?" Sometimes a suggestion can be successfully floated into the conversation by way of a question. "Say, did you ever think of going back to school and getting a degree?" Or, "Do you think your attitude toward authority figures has been affected by your relationship with your father?" But I hope I am old enough and wise enough to know that I cannot think for or choose for anyone but myself. I am an expert only about myself. I must assume the responsibility to do my own thinking and make my own choices. However, I cannot do this for anyone else.

From *Will The Real Me Please Stand Up?*

*A*ll of us, at times, use blocks of one kind or another to prevent ourselves from really listening to another person. We throw up barriers between ourselves and others. Obviously, once these blocks are erected, others can't receive any support or understanding from us. At the same time we also prevent ourselves from receiving the valuable gift of another's sharing. These blocks sabotage any real communication. Consequently, everyone involved is denied the chance to share and to grow.

The following is a partial listing of some common communication blocks.

Advising: "What you ought to do is . . . "

Competing: "I'm sure I look better than . . . "

Computing: "They say that studies have shown . . . "
I never deal with feelings. In fact I rarely hear them.

Distracting: "Say, this is a great place . . . "
I carefully switch the focus of the conversation.

Dreaming: "What? . . . Oh sure . . . I understand."

Filtering: "Another good day at work, eh?"
I filter what you have to say because I want to deal only with certain parts of you and your life.

Gunnysacking: "Yes, but you . . . "
I dump all my carefully collected garbage all over you.

Identifying: "Yes, that's like the time when I . . . "
I use what you are saying as a jumping-off place for my own stories.

Ignoring: " . . . "

Name-Calling (labeling): "Oh, c'mon, you're really paranoid."

Placating: "Oh yes. That's true. Uh huh, you're right."

Rehearsing My Response: ("As soon as he's finished talking, I'm just going to tell him . . . ")

Sarcasm (to cut flesh): "Don't hurry, Honey. You just might lose your image as Miss Holly Come Lately."

From *Will The Real Me Please Stand Up?*

When we are the recipients of another's sharing, it is very important to be explicitly grateful. We have just received an important and valuable gift: part of another human being and another human life. Consequently, we should practice the habit of thanking others for their self-disclosure and for their trust in us.

When self-disclosure is an obvious risk (the confiding of a deep and dark secret), gratitude comes most easily. It is likewise pleasant and easy to acknowledge a self-disclosure that affirms us and our worth. It gets a bit more difficult when the sharer offers to take us into the valleys of his or her sadness or depression. It is also difficult to feel grateful when others share with us their problems, personal labyrinths that seem to have no exit.

The situation in which it is the most difficult to be openly grateful, I would think, is one created by a self-disclosure that is directly or indirectly critical of us. And yet most of us know how hard it is to express our negative reactions. When someone does bring up an issue that implies some failure on our part or some negative reaction to our persons, we can be sure that this person has probably had to work up extra courage to share these negative-type feelings. It is therefore especially important for us to be explicitly grateful for such a sharing.

If I do think of you as a gift to be given and if I do think of your sharing with me as the giving of that gift, I will certainly want to thank you. In addition to the contents of your sharing, you also give me your trust. I could react badly, looking hurt and angry or expressing disappointment in you. I might even refuse to listen to your sharing. Yet in sharing yourself you hold out your offering in uncertain, trembling hands. Thank you, thank you, thank you.

From *Will The Real Me Please Stand Up?*

*I*t is extremely important that you and I insist upon our right to have fully and to express freely all our feelings. "This is me: for better or for worse, in my sickness and my health, whether I have a long or short life. This is me." It is only when we have made this kind of commitment to honest communication, only when we have put ourselves on the line rather than putting some phoney act on the stage, that we can be loved effectively. When we have been open and honest in our communication and someone tells us that we are loved, we've got it made. Then and only then can we really believe in the love that is offered. Then and only then can we say: "You really know me and you really love me." This is the beginning of a true and healthy self-image. And it is only a healthy self-image that will free us, move us into the fullness of life, to join the dance of life and sing the songs of life. Only when we have been honest and subsequently loved can there be a real, internal resonance between what we are truly feeling inside and what people are saying to us from the outside. It is vitally important to internalize whatever love is offered to us, but love can be effective in us only after we have put ourselves on the line, after we have told others who we really are. Once someone said to me, "I would love you even if you were evil." I swallowed hard. I had no idea about what to do with that. But I remember that it felt good, reassuring. Later I reflected that it was indeed one of those rare expressions of unconditional love. There was no price of admission. There was nothing I had to do. I didn't even have to be good. I just had to be myself. I was simply loved. I deeply believe that it is this kind of unconditional love that is the beginning, the wellsprings of all real life. Our lives are indeed shaped by those who love us . . . and by those who refuse to love us.

From the video program, *Free To Be Me*

*W*hatever else love may ask of us in a given case, there are two indispensable gifts that are always part of loving. We can always be sure that these two gifts are needed. The first is the gift of self through self-disclosure. All the other gifts of love—like flowers, jewelry, cigars, and candy—are mere tokens and symbolic expressions. The essential gift of love is always the gift of myself. If I do not give you my true and authentic self, I have given you nothing. I have given you only pretense and sham. I have let you watch my charade.

The second essential gift of love is the affirmation of the other person's worth. If I am to love you, somehow I must appreciate and reflect back to you my appreciation of your unique goodness and giftedness. I cannot interact with you without making some contribution, either positive or negative, to your all-important self-image. Nor can I so interact with you without taking away some increase or decrease in my own sense of personal worth. We are all like mirrors to one another. We perceive ourselves largely in the "feedback" of one another's reactions. We are always contributing, positively or negatively, to one another's self-image. I can know that I am worthwhile only in the mirror of your smiling face, only in the warm sound of your voice, and in the gentle touch of your hand. And you can understand your worth only in my face, my voice, and my touch.

From *The Christian Vision*

*I*n Christian theology there is only one priest, and that is Jesus. I am sure that you know that a "priest" is associated biblically with the one who offers sacrifices or gifts to God. But in an even more profound sense, a "priest" means a mediator, a mediator between God and mankind. In a real sense, we are all priests because we are all baptized into Jesus, the one high priest. You and I are priests because by our baptism we now bear the person and share in the priesthood of Jesus. We share in his role as mediator. Obviously, Jesus fulfilled his role as mediator perfectly. He was deeply in touch with the heart of his Father and deeply in touch with the human heart. It was his calling. It is also ours.

Sometimes we emphasize one of these two connections more than the other. Those of us who concentrate only on the God connection become persons of supposedly deep personal union with God. But the temptation of this emphasis is: "Jesus and I and let the rest of the world go by." This kind of "God and I" spirituality slowly loses a compassionate feeling for the human heart. And when we lose this connection, we lose the essence of priesthood. Obviously, Jesus never lost this connection. It is part of the comfort that he will always be to us: he understands the human heart; he asks us to do likewise.

From the video program, *Jesus As I Know Him*

*S*ometimes I think that God is something like an electrical outlet. There is a lot of power waiting to be tapped in an electrical outlet. There is enough power to light a room, to heat a room, to turn on music or produce a television picture. But unless we get plugged in, all that power is wasted. And the plug-in, the way we get plugged into the power of God is through faith. Faith is our God-connection. It is our faith that taps into and releases the power of God.

There is a story in the Gospels that illustrates this. One day Jesus was walking along a crowded road with his Apostles. There was all kinds of jostling and pushing on the crowded streets. Suddenly, however, Jesus stops and asks, "Who touched me?" The Apostles are astonished. "Who touched you? You've got to be kidding. Everybody's pushing and shoving, and you ask 'Who touched me?' Are you serious?"

Jesus thoughtfully explains, "Yes, I am. I mean that someone touched me with a very special touch. Someone touched me with the touch of faith." The Apostles are still puzzled. "And how did you know that?" they ask. Jesus replies: "I felt my healing power go out from me." Then he looked down and saw a little lady who was looking up at him. She said almost apologetically, "I did. You see, I have had these hemorrhages for so many years. I have been to doctors and spent all I had on their remedies. But nothing has helped. I've wasted all my money. I have nothing left. But then I thought that if I could just touch the hem of your garment, I would be healed." Jesus smiled at her, "You are healed. Oh yes, you are indeed healed. Your faith has healed you."

From the video program, *Jesus As I Know Him*

I am haunted by the idea that no one should ever be famous as a Christian. It is Christ who should be famous. He is the great reality. I should want you to know my Christ. I should want you to know and love my Jesus, not me. At least, this is the way it should be. I say "my Jesus," although he really isn't my exclusive possession. I say "my Jesus" because he is the Jesus I know. He is the Jesus who is my best friend and constant companion. My whole day and life is a running conversation with this Jesus. If others could "bug my brain," they would be astonished. "He is talking to someone all day who isn't really there." To which I would respond: "He is there only to the eyes and ears, to the mind and heart of faith. He said he would take up his abode in those who would believe in him and love him. And I do believe in him and I do love him." Would you believe that Jesus and I actually have "nicknames" for each other? Special names for special friends. It is this Jesus that I want to share with you. This is what the early Christians felt: "We want you to know our Jesus." So they wrote the story of his life, the Gospels, because they wanted us to know their Jesus. St. John begins his first Letter: "I want to tell you what my eyes have seen, what my ears have heard, and my hands have touched. I want you to know my Jesus." The Gospels themselves were intended as a faith-portrait of Jesus. It was indeed a portrait that was born of faith. The only way to know Jesus is to believe in him. We can know him only to the extent that we believe. Of course, the Gospels are not objective history. The evangelists couldn't write an objective history about someone they loved so much. No one could write an objective history of his or her mother. Jesus was their life and their hope. They wanted to share him, not themselves, with the whole world. You see, no one should ever be famous, not as a Christian.

From the video program, *Jesus As I Know Him*

I would like to suggest that the questions we are asking as we go through life are leading us to the feet of God. I would like to suggest that our questions help us to understand the importance of the word of God and the personal Word that God uttered into this world, his Son, Jesus. Jesus alone offers us assurance of a correct version and vision of reality. In the eighth chapter of John's gospel, Jesus encounters a group of fellow Jews, and they have a little discussion about freedom. His contemporaries say to Jesus in the dialogue recorded by John: "We are free." "Oh no!" replies Jesus, "You're not really free." But they come back: "Yes, we are. We are the sons of Abraham. We are the slaves of no man. We are truly free." And then in effect Jesus tells them, "No, you are not free. Until you accept me and my message you cannot be free because only the truth can set you free. Your tyrants are not outside you, but inside you in all the false and crippling notions that imprison you." It is indeed only the truth of Jesus that sets us free. Only when we know who we are and how much God loves us, only when we know that other people are really our brothers and sisters, and only when we know that life is for loving can we be truly free. Only when we know that this world is God's world and that it is good can we feel at home in it. Finally, only when we know that God is our Abba, the Hebrew for "Papa" or "Daddy," can we understand our own identity, our own worth, our own hope and grounds for security. Only this truth can truly set us free.

From the video program, *Free To Be Me*

*L*ord God of my life: Here I am again, filled with a thousand thoughts and feelings, desires and plans, joys and sorrows.

I see two worlds, painfully distant from each other. They are the worlds of psychology and theology: the worlds of the human and the divine. I see so many of my brothers and sisters trying desperately to make a savior of psychology. They are always playing "growth games." They dig into the darkest corners of their minds and the softest parts of their hearts. What they are doing is mostly good, but so much of the pain goes on and on. And sometimes it seems like a case of the blind leading the blind. I want to say to them: "You are not just body and mind. You are spirit, too! You can't make it without God. You can't be truly fulfilled unless your spiritual hungers are also filled." We are, as you said, Jesus, the branches of your vine. Cut off from you, we begin to die, inch by inch, day by day. There is an emptiness in us that only you can fill.

But I also see the world of religion. I see some of my brothers and sisters trying to be religious without being fully human. They seem a little rigid and narrow at times, wanting to be holy, but not human. They seem to be winning a place in heaven, without realizing or enjoying the beauty of earth. They keep the ten commandments, but their observance looks so joyless. Such a world seems small and the air in that world is stale.

From the video program, *Free To Be Me*

*L*ord God of my life: Sometimes we "religious people" seem afraid to love ourselves, as though that would be a sinful violation of some divine commandment. Any concession to humanity seems to be a compromise of humility. Some of us seem to do good for others without really caring about the broken, bleeding humanity around us. We seem to be crawling through a dark tunnel on bleeding hands and knees to get an eventual reward. Heaven is not cheap, we seem to be saying.

Oh Lord, when I catch myself thinking and acting this way, and when I see others taking this course, I want to protest: "We can't be truly holy unless we are willing to be truly human! We can't really say a yes of love to you, Lord God, unless we have first said it to ourselves (body, mind and spirit!) and to our very human brothers and sisters."

Lord God, I feel called by you to make some contribution to the effort of bringing these two worlds together, and I know where I must begin—with myself. I must bring both worlds together in me, if I am to be all that I can be—free to be me! For this I need your healing power: to enlighten whatever is dark in me, to mend that which is broken, to straighten whatever is twisted, and to revive whatever of life and love may have died in me.

And, as I work at this, under the gentle influence of your love and grace, make me a channel of life and love for my brothers and sisters. Make me an announcer of good news, a bridge over troubled and dividing waters. Help me bring together humanity and divinity, the heart of man in all its splendor and the heart of God in all your magnificent beauty.

From the video program, *Free To Be Me*

*I*t is the Jesus who promises us his peace that you and I must get to know. But we have our doubts, don't we? We wonder if Jesus is real, and, if he is real, is he really available for us. Is he really there? Our struggle with doubts is reminiscent of a dark night when the Apostles were out in a boat on the Sea of Galilee.

> When evening came, Jesus was there alone, while the boat, by now far out on the lake, was battling with a heavy sea, for there was a head-wind. . . . When the disciples saw him walking on the water, they were terrified. "It is a ghost," they said, and cried out in fear. But at once Jesus called out to them, saying: "Courage! It is I. Do not be afraid." It was Peter who answered: "Lord," he called out, "if it is you, tell me to come to you across the water."
>
> "Come to me!" called Jesus. (Matthew 14:23–29)

Maybe this is the heart and soul of faith. Maybe we have to be out in a boat, battling the heavy sea of life. Maybe we have to peer out into the mist to see his figure, a figure of mastery and mercy that walks on the distant waters. Maybe we have to be filled with a million memories of the human lives that have been touched and transformed by his healing hands, of all the mortal misery that has been redeemed by his mercy. But even then Jesus could be a ghost, a delusion. Maybe we have been brainwashed. Maybe the Gospels are only fiction. That figure of mastery and mercy, out there in the distance, over the sea, may be a mirage born of insecurity. How can I be sure? "Lord Jesus, if it is really you, tell me to come to you. Tell me to step out in faith across the waters of my life." "Come! Come to me!" says Jesus.

From *A Reason To Live, A Reason To Die*

*D*uring the depression years in this country, an elderly Jewish gentleman named Mike Gold ate every day at a Catholic Charities house in New York City, run by Dorothy Day. Dorothy Day once said of him, "He eats every day at the table of Christ, but I don't think he will ever really understand Jesus because of his first introduction to him."

In his earlier years, Mike Gold had been an author. He wrote a book called *Jews Without Money*. In his book Mike Gold tells the story of how as a little boy he lived in a Jewish ghetto in New York City, and how his mother repeatedly warned him: "Mikey, don't ever go beyond these four streets. Mikey, don't ever go outside our neighborhood." But one day, with a child's curiosity, he crossed the streets of prejudice. He went outside his neighborhood. There he was accosted by a group of older boys, who accused him: "Say, you're a Christ killer, aren't you?" Then they added: "You killed Jesus."

When little Mike Gold returned home, beaten and bloodied, his mother asked: "Mikey, what happened?" The small boy answered, "I don't know. I don't know. The older boys . . . they beat me up." "But why?" his mother asked. But the child could only say, "I don't know."

So his mother cleaned him up and put him in fresh clothes. And as she was rocking him, holding him tenderly in her arms, he raised his little bruised lips to her ear and asked:

"Mama? Mama, who is Jesus?"

From the video program, *Jesus As I Know Him*

*K*nowing and loving Jesus is not a simple matter. Knowing and loving are never simple. We are creatures of delusion, and, like the people of Israel in the course of their exodus to the promised land of God, we are tempted by idolatry. Knowing and loving demand choice and resolution. There is a detachment in every attachment, an emptying that precedes every filling, a death in every life. No one can serve two masters. And so we must be aware of our divided hearts and of the possibility that there are other forces at work in our lives which can make our faith-commitment anemic and half-hearted. There are idols, some beautiful and some ugly, which dilute our love and stifle our union with Jesus. Self-hatred as well as pride, puritanical prudishness as well as selfish overindulgence, fear and recklessness, adoration and detestation of one's mind or body—are all idolatrous forms of self-preoccupation that turn our eyes inward and away from Jesus. The answer to the many problems involved in a life of faith is always the same: Get to know Jesus.

Only he can help us see our lives and everything we do as part of our relationship with him. As we come to know Jesus, the false dichotomy between faith and life will disappear. Our joys and sorrows, successes and failures, gains and losses will all be recognized as part of God's loving plan, unfolding itself in our lives and in our world. This coming alive in faith, this renewed vision of the meaning of ourselves, this achievement of identity in Christ is possible only through a living, loving relationship with Jesus.

From *A Reason To Live, A Reason To Die*

*H*ow do we freely accept the gifts of God? How do we correspond with his initiatives and cooperate with his work in us? I am personally convinced that the answer is both in human nature and in God's revealed word: Getting to know Jesus. Notice that we are not urged to know about Jesus but to know *him*. As Cardinal Newman once said: "We do not build cathedrals to intellectual principles but to persons. It is only by persons that we are subdued, melted, won over." Faith is not something that must be intellectually understood as much as it is something that must be experienced and lived. It is in its deepest essence a living relationship of love with God in, with and through his Son, Jesus. St. John writes:

> This, then, is the witness (of God) about his Son: God has given us eternal life, and this life is in his Son. Whoever has the Son has this life; whoever does not have the Son of God does not have life. (1 John 5:11–12)

Jesus himself said: "I am come in order that you might have life, life in all its fullness (John 10:10) . . . . I am the way, the truth, and the life; no one goes to the Father except through me" (John 14:6). And Peter, preaching to his Jewish contemporaries, says this of Jesus: "Salvation is to be found through him alone; for there is no one else in all the world, who has been given by God to us, by whom we can be saved" (Acts 4:12). This, then, is the secret of faith and the genius of the believer: to cultivate a deep and warmly personal relationship with Jesus, so that everything one does becomes an act of love for and faithfulness to Jesus. Constructing arguments for the plausibility of faith and debating the rationality of faith does not produce lovers, saints or heroes. The heart of the matter is knowing and loving Jesus.

From *A Reason To Live, A Reason To Die*

*J*ohn Steinbeck once said, "All men's sins are attempted shortcuts to love." All the sinners portrayed in the New Testament (like all of us sinners) were looking for love in the wrong places. Then Jesus entered their lives. He taught them what real love is by loving them. He gave them someone they could love. Of course, he is the same Jesus: yesterday, today and always. He is the Jesus who enters our lives with kindness, encouragement and sometimes with challenge.

Most of the gospel people whom he loved, especially Mary Magdalen, turned out to be tremendous. When the Apostles were afraid to go to Calvary, Mary Magdalen stood there with great faith and courage. She was, no doubt, taunted. We can easily imagine that the men on Calvary would have mocked her. "Hey, look who's here! It's Mary, Mary Magdalen. You all remember 'Naughty Mary'? C'mon, Mary. We know you. What's all this pious stuff? We knew you when. You're not fooling us, Mary." But for Mary all this really didn't matter; because she had been loved and she had found someone to love. She and her life had been changed forever by Jesus.

When Jesus enters a life, he transforms that life. He leads us in unpredictable ways to personal greatness. Jesus looks beyond all those external qualities and past records that throw most people off. He finds the goodness that few others ever look far enough to find. He loved Mary Magdalen into life, the Mary out of whom he had once cast seven devils. He will love you and me into the same fullness of life and love and personal greatness.

From the video program, *Jesus As I Know Him*

*T*hen there was a little fellow named Zacchaeus. Zacchaeus was up a tree in more ways than one. Zacchaeus was a runt and much worse he was a publican. He had two strikes against him. A publican was a Jew who collected taxes from fellow Jews to send to Rome. Obviously, publicans were not well loved. Everybody hated poor little Zacchaeus. He was a loner and not by choice. But then one day he was walking alone along a sideroad, when he saw crowds lining up. So he asked someone who didn't recognize him: "Hey, what's happening?" He was told that "It's Jesus, the great Jesus of Nazareth. He's coming down the road." Now because he was so small, he couldn't possibly see over the heads of those lined up in front of him. So he climbed up in a sycamore tree. Then, as he passes, Jesus notices the little fellow up in the branches of the tree. He asks the line of people to allow him through. He goes to the base of the sycamore tree, and calls up to Zacchaeus: "Zacchaeus, I have to stay for the night in this town. Do you suppose I could stay with you?"

Can you imagine the little man's surprise? "With me? He wants to stay with me? Nobody even talks to me, and he wants to stay with me? Say, how did he know my name anyway?" When I think about Zacchaeus and how his life was changed by this day, I think of the verse:

> I love you, not only for what you are, but for what I am when I am with you. I love you not only for what you have made of yourself, but for what your love is helping me to make of myself. I love you for passing over all the foolish, weak things that you can't help dimly seeing there, and for drawing out into the light all the beautiful belongings that no one else had looked quite far enough to find.

From the video program, *Jesus As I Know Him*

We should be grateful to God for coming into our world as a little baby. No one is afraid of a little baby. A baby is just a gurgling little bundle of humanity in its mother's or father's arms. So that we wouldn't be afraid of him, he came to us as a baby. Furthermore, Jesus lived in a little town that would never have appeared on any map if he hadn't lived there. And he lived there most of his life in absolute obscurity. Then, when he came to die, he died on a cross, the worst and most shameful form of punishment in the world in which he lived. After he died Jesus was buried in another man's tomb because he apparently could not afford one of his own. It almost seems that when God walked into our human history, he came to us in helplessness and obscurity. He came as a baby and died with crowds laughing in his face. I guess he didn't want us to be afraid to approach him. Nobody is afraid of babies. And no one is afraid of people who are suffering. Jesus has made it so easy to feel comfortable, to feel "at home" with him. In his whole life he seems to be asking us the question he once asked his Apostles: "Why were you afraid? Didn't you know that I was with you?"

From the video program, *Jesus As I Know Him*

T

he Prostitute (Luke 7:36–50): On an occasion, when Jesus was dining with a Pharisee named Simon, a very strange episode interrupted the meal. A woman entered the room. The presence of a woman was not permitted at such banquets. But she was not only a woman; she was one of the local prostitutes. The Roman liturgy identifies this woman as Mary Magdalen. The prostitute flings herself at the feet of Jesus, and her warm tears bathe his feet. She wipes them with her hair, and anoints them with a fragrant balm. Simon, being an exacting Pharisee with little compassion for human weakness, is beside himself with self-righteous indignation. So Jesus asks him the question about who loves more, the one who has been forgiven more or the one who has been forgiven less. When Simon gives the obvious answer, Jesus tells him quite plainly:

> "Simon," Jesus said, "you see this woman? I came into your house, and you poured no water over my feet, but she has poured out her tears over my feet and wiped them away with her hair. You gave me no kiss of greeting, but she has been covering my feet with kisses ever since she came in. You did not anoint my head with oil, but she has anointed my feet with balm. For this reason I tell you that her sins, her many sins, must have been forgiven her or she would not have shown such great love. It is the one who is forgiven little who shows little love." Then Jesus said to her, "Your sins are forgiven." Those who were with him at the table began to say to themselves, "Who is this man, that he even forgives sins?" But Jesus said to the woman, "Your faith has saved you; go in peace."

If the Roman liturgy is right in identifying this woman as Mary Magdalen, what a testimonial to the forgiving love of Jesus she became! It was Mary who stood at the foot of Christ's cross, remembering perhaps that he had once consoled and defended her when she was a woman of public shame.

From *A Reason To Live, A Reason To Die*

*I*n the gospel narration about the evening Jesus spent at the home of the Pharisee, Simon, there is one special line which I love. You will remember that the meal is interrupted when a prostitute enters the room and prostrates at the feet of Jesus. Simon glares at her. He is furious. Jesus looks up at him and asks simply (this is the line I love): "Simon, do you see this woman?" Most of us (probably Simon also) like to reduce persons to problems. We refer to them as "problems" and "cases." We even do this to ourselves. We think of ourselves as "problems." Why do we do this? Probably because a "problem" can be solved. A "case" can be reviewed and judged. But we can't solve persons. We can't review persons. We can only understand them. In the gospel narration Jesus is saying: "Simon, this is not a *case*. This is not a *problem*. This is a *person*. Do you see this *woman*? She is a human being. This is a woman, Simon. Can you see that?"

It is a tragedy to mistake persons for cases or problems. Sometimes medical personnel do this. They say things like, "There's a case of ulcers in Room 301." We might think that if we were to pull back the sheets, we would see a case of ulcers lying in the bed. But we know better, don't we? It is a person who has worried a hole in his or her stomach. It is not a case. He or she is a person, a worried person.

"Do you see this woman?" The Jesus who asked Simon this question does not approach us as cases. "I have here an accurate tab of your record," as though we are mere statistics (cases) in his book. To Jesus we are not cases or problems. We are persons. And Jesus knows: You can solve problems, but you can only understand persons. And, of course, each of us is unrepeatably and uniquely . . . a person.

From the video program, *Jesus As I Know Him*

*T*he renowned English author and wit, Gilbert Keith Chesterton, was once asked: "If Jesus were living in our world today, what do you think he would be doing?" Chesterton thought for a moment and then replied: "He is living in our world today. He is living and loving in us."

The import of this question and answer is very important. Is Jesus a dead Rabbi or a living Lord? That's the basic question, isn't it? Do I really believe in his assurance: "I will be with you all days, even till the end of the world!"?

If I do believe in his living presence in my life, I will gradually develop a personal relationship with him.

From the audio program, *The Growing Edge Of Life*

*A*ccording to our Christian theology, the way we get saved is by being "in Jesus." We get baptized "into Jesus." We become an engrafted part of his Mystical Body. It is something like this: Jesus comes down from heaven to our earth; and then we all attach ourselves to him. So then when he goes back into heaven, we go with him. (This is an analogy, of course, and every analogy limps a little.) The important realization is that it is our connection with Jesus that is the source of our own salvation. We are not saved by what we do. We are saved by what he does. What we do gets us into Jesus.

Jesus himself puts this a number of ways. "I am the vine and you are the branches." He insists that "Unless my life somehow flows into you, you cannot have life." "Cut off from me, you can only die." "If you remain united to me, you will bear much fruit." "I have come that you might have life, and have it in abundance." To the woman at the well, he promised "a fountain of everlasting life."

It is therefore extremely important that we each have a personal relationship with Jesus.

From the audio program, *The Growing Edge Of Life*

*W*hen I was a newly ordained priest, I was riding in a car with another priest who was many years my senior. In our conversation, I told him a story I had read about St. John of the Cross. It seems that John had been seriously misunderstood by others and had endured much suffering as a result. In the end, our Lord appeared to him, and thanked John for his spirit of faith. Then he promised to grant any one wish that John might ask. The little saint asked our Lord: "To be further humiliated and despised for your sake."

My old priest friend, Charlie, moaned loudly: "What a terrible wish. Why would John ever ask for that?" So I asked him: "If you were promised any one wish, what would you ask for?" His reply has stayed with me all these years. And I must say that it makes more sense to me than the request of St. John of the Cross. He said simply: "I would ask that Jesus might be known and loved by everyone."

(I promised him that if I ever told the story of St. John of the Cross, I would tell Charlie's story too.)

From the audio program, *The Growing Edge Of Life*

*J*esus tried to make this clear to his contemporaries: Love will ask much more of us than the Law could ever require. When a person enters into a legalistic relationship, that person can come to a point where he or she says, "I have now done enough. I have fulfilled all my obligations." The person can then prove it by citing chapter and verse in the provisions of the contract. However, true love can never say, "I have done enough. I have now fulfilled all my obligations." Love is restless, drives us on. Love asks us to walk many miles not demanded by justice or legalism. In effect, Jesus was saying, "When I confront your legalism with the law of love, I am not asking less. I am not diluting the demands of your relationship with God. Pan-scale justice can only regulate a human life; love will encompass and energize that life. And in the end, love is the only response that you can appropriately make to the loving invitations of my Father, who is love."

I think that Jesus was asking the people of his generation and is today inviting us to drench our minds and spirits in the knowledge of God's love for us. We are the delight of his smiling eyes, the children of his warm heart. God cares for us more than any mother has ever loved her child. If we could only realize how much we are loved, we would of course want to respond, to make some return. "What can I ever do for the Lord in return for all the things he has done for me?" the psalmist asks in Psalm 116. When we have opened our minds and hearts to God's love we will go far beyond the requirements of what we have to do. Justice and observance of the Law say that I must go just this far. Love will ask me to walk many undemanded miles beyond that point. If we love, we will want to do more than what we must. We will want to do all we can. Love is like this.

From *The Christian Vision*

*W*herever you are in your development, whatever you are doing, with a strong affirmation of all your goodness and good deeds, with a gentle understanding of your weakness, God is forever loving you. You do not have to change, grow, or be good in order to be loved. Rather, you are loved so that you can change, grow and be good. Your realization of this unconditional love is extremely important. You must remember people like:

Peter the Rock, who was often a sandpile, a man who had denied even knowing the one who had loved him the most.

Zacchaeus, who was a runt, who offered to collect taxes for Rome from his own people for a "kickback" from the take.

Mary Magdalen, who was a "hooker."

Andrew, who was pretty naive. He thought that five loaves and two fish were enough for five thousand people.

Thomas, who was an all-star bullhead.

Martha, Martha, who was a twitch, worrier, and complainer.

The thief on the cross, who said what might have been his first prayer and was promised immediate paradise.

The blind man, who did not know who Jesus was but only that he himself was blind and now he could see!

Saul of Tarsus, who was hellbent on destroying Christianity until he took that road to Damascus and found a loving Lord.

God was in Jesus, loving them, affirming them, forgiving them, encouraging them, challenging them all the way into greatness, peace, and the fullness of life: and millions more like them, and like us.

From *Fully Human, Fully Alive*

*J*esus would die as he had lived, unconditionally loving. Under every crucifix, depicting the Lord with his heart opened and his hands stretched out as if to embrace all the weak and the wounded of the world, there should be a caption reading:

"This is what I mean when I say I love you!"

If the parable of the Prodigal Son is the story of unconditional love, Jesus on his cross is the portrait of such love. Like love itself the person of Jesus is both a comfort and a challenge. The comfort is more profound than anything we have ever experienced. The "Shalom! Be at peace. I understand." is always held out to us, and especially at those times when we feel like old Peter the Rock and sometimes sandpile: "Depart from me, Lord," Peter moaned, "for I am a sinful man!" But, of course, unconditional love doesn't ever depart. Jesus asked Peter, as he asks us, only this: "Do you love me?" He does not ask about our weakness but only about our love. It is comforting.

His challenge is: "Love one another as I have loved you!"

From *Unconditional Love*

*I*n the so-called temptation narratives which are recorded in Luke 4:1–13, we find Jesus, at the beginning of his public life, clarifying his own life principle. More specifically, we find him rejecting three life principles suggested to him by the Devil.

The first temptation, we might say, was to accept the life principle of *pleasure*. Jesus had fasted, a total fast from all food, and was very hungry. The promise of the Devil was the satisfaction of his physical hunger. The reply of Jesus was: "Other things in life are more important than bread!"

So the Devil takes Jesus up to a high place and shows him all the glittering kingdoms of the world and promises him *power* over all these places and peoples. Jesus firmly rejects this life principle: "We must worship God, and him alone." Jesus will give his heart neither to the pursuit of pleasure nor to the flattery of power.

So Satan takes Jesus up to the pinnacle of the Temple and urges him to throw himself off. "Let your Father catch you in the arms of his angels!" the Devil taunts, but Jesus is resolute. He will not abdicate his personal responsibility for his life. I see this third temptation precisely in this way. It implies that we are not really free anyway. It asks us to accept a kind of determinism that rationalizes an *avoidance of responsibility*. Jesus is firm: "Don't experiment with God's patience."

In this clarification of his own life principle, Jesus is stating firmly: "I will not live for pleasure! I will not live for power! I will not surrender responsibility for my life and my actions!"

From *Unconditional Love*

*G*od's plan means this: Jesus will live in each of the members of his Church. This is the way that the people of this and of all generations to come can meet Jesus: in us, in you, in me! We are the flesh and blood, the bones and skin of Jesus, whose members we are. We are God's planned way of sharing himself and his love.

There is a familiar, post-World War II story about a statue of Jesus in the shell of a bombed-out German church. The figure of Jesus was portrayed in this statue as reaching out to the world. However, in the devastation of the bombing, the hands of the statue were broken off. For a long time afterward, the statue without hands stood as it was found. However, a sign was hung from the outstretched arms: "He has no hands but yours!" In a very real sense this is true. We, the Church, the members of his Body, are his only hands, his only mouth, his only mind and heart. We are indeed the extension of Jesus in space and the prolongation of Jesus in time. We will continue his work of redemption, loving this world into life, or it will not be done at all. The Kingdom of God marches at the pace of our feet.

From *The Christian Vision*

*O*f course, this could send shock waves through the nervous system. "I am Jesus to the world? Oh, no! I can't be that." After we get over the initial dread and the impulse to make a disclaimer, I think we all have to realize very calmly that this is not a call to walk on water. However, it is a call to stand up and be counted. Again, we recall the haunting question: If you were being arrested for being a Christian, would there be enough evidence to convict you? The Jesus who asks to be recognizable in me isn't the perfect and all-good and all-powerful Jesus. I could never manage that. However, it is rather the Jesus who labors in me, who consoles me and supports me in my human weakness, that must shine out of me. It is the Jesus who said to Paul: "My strength will work through your weakness."

All of us carry the treasure of this loving Jesus, residing within us and working through us, in fragile vessels of clay. We cannot be expected to exhibit perfection, but we must be willing to stand up and to offer our personal testimonials to grace. You and I should want to say to the world, as best we can, by our words and way of living, by our work and our worship: "Jesus has touched my life. By his kindness, by his encouragement, and by his challenge, Jesus has made all the difference in my life. I was blind and now I see. I was lost and now I'm found!" However, for myself I feel an inner urgency to add to this witness: "But please be patient. God is not finished with me yet."

From *The Christian Vision*

*I*t was this, I feel sure, that Jesus wanted so much to make clear to Peter and the disciples. In all his days with them, but especially at the Last Supper, in his last moments with them, he wanted to underline the truth: My Kingdom is a Kingdom of love! It is not a place where power rules or people compete. It is not a playground of pleasure or a haven for those who have no heart to try. The solemn and solitary requirement for entrance into the Kingdom of God is the choice of love as a life principle. There is only one badge of identification: "By this shall all know that you are my disciples, that you love one another as I have loved you" (John 13:35).

"If you cannot accept this," Jesus insisted with Peter, "you cannot be my partner. The only power in my Kingdom is the power of love!"

Jesus wants to know if the lesson has come through. He apparently found in the Apostles the same lack of understanding that I so often find in myself. In Mark's Gospel, Jesus asks the Apostles seventeen times (I once counted them!): "Are you still without understanding?"

I must ask myself the same question again and again: Do I really understand? Do I really believe that Jesus calls me to accept as my own the life principle of love? Do I really understand that such a commitment is the only way to true and abiding happiness? These are the questions whose answers lie deep inside of me. I must at least attempt a search of those deepest parts. My whole life is at stake.

From *Unconditional Love*

Autumn

*M*y Brothers and Sisters: I am sure that the most persistent and restless desire of my life is to be fully human and fully alive. On the other side of the coin, my deepest and most haunting fear is the possibility of wasting the glorious opportunity of my life. My personal prayers vary according to the experience and needs of each day, but one prayer is never omitted: "O God, my Father, don't let me die without having really lived and really loved!" This is my hope and my prayer for you, too.

Over the course of my own life and in my quest for the full experience of human life, the most fulfilling and transforming moments have been moments of "insight." Sometimes these precious insights, that have widened the dimensions of my world and intensified my participation in life, have exploded like the 4th of July. Sometimes they have come like the dawn, slowly and gradually bestowing a gift of light and life. I felt the joy of recognition and the warmth of kinship for the great psychiatrist, Carl Jung, when he added insight to the three traditional theological virtues; he said that the most meaningful moments in his own life were the moments of faith, hope, love, and *insight (Man in Search of a Soul)*.

It is necessary, of course, to test insights in the laboratory of life. Any knowledge that does not change the quality of life is sterile and of questionable value. On the other hand, if the quality and emotional patterns of life are changed, the change is usually traceable to some new insight or perception. This has been the story of my own life, and I am sure that it is the story of all human lives.

From *Fully Human, Fully Alive*

*T*he famous Viennese psychiatrist, Viktor Frankl, says that the most important thing psychology can and should do in the next fifty years is to impress us with our own powers, especially with our powers to change and to grow. We are never beyond change. Psychology needs to stimulate the defiant powers of the human spirit, to tell us: You can do it. The one thing I am most saddened to hear from another is: "This is the way I am. I was this way in the beginning, am now and ever shall be." I want to plead with such people: "Oh no! Please don't say that. Don't even think that." I believe in change with every muscle, fiber and brain cell of my being. We are all capable of change. We must believe in the defiant powers of the human spirit, as Viktor Frankl would say. There is admittedly a strong current of determinism in modern psychology. It is a kind of computerized, behavioral scientism that says: "No, sorry. It's all over for you. You were once programmed to be what you are, and your whole life is just a phonograph record spinning itself out. What will be, will be." The people who buy into this life-principle of determinism find in it a convenient way of avoiding personal responsibility. Personal responsibility means making decisions, choosing, suffering, enduring, risking, and changing. People who don't want to take risks often like to talk endlessly about what happened in the past. They enjoy interpreting dreams and reading horoscopes, with the hope that this will explain what free will refuses to revise. They say: "Well, I was not loved as a child," as though this would explain everything, especially the final outcome of their lives. Others say: "Well, I've made so many mistakes in the past. There can't be much future for me." To this type of person, Jesus says: I am the Divine Physician. I came for the weak and the sick not for the well. I am the Good Shepherd. I am looking for the lost ones. At some time we are all confronted by this Jesus, who believes in change and conversion even more than I do, even more than Viktor Frankl.

From the audio program, *My Vision And My Values*

I remember a time, many years ago, when I was in Germany trying to master the language of the "natives." I was privileged to serve for a while as chaplain in a remote Bavarian convent. The dear little Sister who was assigned to care for my room was eighty-four years old. Every time I left my room, even for a moment, she cleaned it. And I don't mean a superficial cleaning. She would wax the floors, polish the furniture, and so forth. On one occasion when I left my room for a short walk, I came back to find "Schwester" on her knees, putting a final sheen on her waxing job. I laughingly teased her:

"Schwester, Sie arbeiten zuviel!" ("Sister, you work too much!")

The dear and devoted little Sister straightened up (still kneeling) and looked at me with a seriousness that bordered on severity. She said:

"Der Himmel ist nicht billig!" ("Heaven isn't cheap, you know!")

God bless her. She was no doubt educated to believe, and she believed with all her heart, that life was supposed to be an ordeal, the price of eternal bliss. Heaven must be bought, and it is not cheap. I feel sure that heaven now belongs to that dear soul, who lived so faithfully according to her lights. (In fact, I think that there must be a roped-off section for special souls like "Schwester.") But I can't believe that this kind of joyless purchase of a place in heaven is really the life to which God is calling us. I do not believe that he intends that we should crawl through a tunnel on bleeding hands and knees to have a so-called "pie in the sky when we die." God is not a Shylock, demanding his pound of flesh for eternal life. In fact, I believe that, theologically speaking, eternal life has already begun in us because God's life is already in us. We should be celebrating this.

From *Unconditional Love*

*J*esus challenges us to replace our crippling attitudes with his Be-attitudes. He asks us to make our lives an act of love. Now to set out on such a course we must be sure that we are hearing this challenge as "good news," not as a call to crucifixion. God isn't calling us to a lonely, joyless existence with the promise of a delayed reward. God is calling us to live, to love and enjoy the challenge. God's formulas are roadmaps to freedom and peace. God is saying to us: "The only way to live is to be free. So save your heart for love and save your love for persons. Don't ever let any 'thing' own you. Don't let money or fame or power or the pursuit of pleasure put a ring in your nose and lead you around. Love persons and use things." And, of course, this is the only way to live, to be free. The reassurance of God is indeed good news. The English author, Chesterton, once remarked "The problem is that, for the most of us it isn't news; and to many of us it doesn't sound like good news." Yet that is precisely what the gospel is: the good news of God, given to us by Jesus: the call to live fully!

There is a story about a priest meeting the comedian, Groucho Marx, on the street one day. The priest recognizes him and asks, "Excuse me. Aren't you Groucho Marx?" The comedian replied, "Yes, Father, I am." "Well," the priest continued, "I just want to thank you for all the joy that you have brought into this world." Groucho is supposed to have replied, "And I would like to thank you, Father, for all the joy you have taken out of this world."

Maybe we just haven't read and reported the gospel message as good news. Maybe we have forgotten that Jesus came that we might have life in all its fullness. Maybe we have to revise our own attitudes in the light of the beatitudes of Jesus. After all, they are the call to happiness.

From the video program, *Jesus As I Know Him*

I had come, in my own way, to the realization that love is the essential ingredient in a program of full human living and that love works if people are willing to work at it. I had come to see that communication is the lifeblood of love and that the experience and expression of emotions is the essential "stuff" of communication. I had also come to realize that no one can cause emotions in another but can only stimulate emotions that are already there waiting to be aroused.

After moving through these insights like milestones of understanding into ever new and exciting territory, I was left with a lingering question. Supposing that a person were to act on all these insights, feeling perfectly free to experience and in a mature way to express his loneliness, fear, anger, and so forth. Where does the person go from here? Will the simple and open expression of these negative and burdensome emotions be sufficiently healing to change the patterns of his or her reactions? My own experience, with myself and with others, leads me to believe that a change in undesirable emotional patterns can come only with a change in thinking—with a change in one's perception of reality or vision.

It now seems obvious to me that our emotional reactions are not permanent parts of our makeup, the way we were in the beginning, are now, and ever shall be. Rather they grow out of the way we see ourselves, other people, life, the world, and God. Our perceptions become the habitual frame of reference within which we act and react. Our ideas and attitudes generate our emotional responses. Persistently negative emotions are an indication that there is a distortion or delusion in our thinking, an astigmatism in our vision.

From *Fully Human, Fully Alive*

*F*ully human beings can go outside of themselves, can be committed to a cause, and they do this *freely.* Of course, the fully human being must be free. There are many philanthropists among us who give of their goods or their time addictively or compulsively. There seems to be some driving need that leaves them restless; some guilt or anxiety that is an obsessive ring in the nose, leading these people from one good deed to another. The fully human being goes out to others and to God himself, but not by a kind of obsessive-compulsive neurosis, but actively and freely, and simply because he or she has chosen to do so.

Fully human beings in their efforts to love do not identify themselves with what they love. They do not think of others whom they love as though they were somehow extensions of themselves. Gabriel Marcel, in his book, *Being and Having,* laments that our civilization teaches us how to take possession of things, when it should rather initiate us into the art of letting go; for there is neither freedom nor real life without an apprenticeship in dispossession.

From *Why Am I Afraid To Tell You Who I Am?*

*T*he fully human person is an *actor,* not a *reactor.* The syndicated columnist, Sydney Harris, tells the story of accompanying his friend to a newsstand. The friend greeted the newsman very courteously, but in return received gruff and discourteous service. Accepting the newspaper which was shoved rudely in his direction, the friend of Harris politely smiled and wished the newsman a nice week-end. As the two friends walked down the street, the columnist asked:

"Does he always treat you so rudely?"

"Yes, unfortunately he does."

"And are you always so polite and friendly to him?"

"Yes, I am."

"Why are you so nice to him when he is so unfriendly to you?"

"Because I don't want *him* to decide how *I'm* going to act. I am an actor not a reactor."

From *Why Am I Afraid To Tell You Who I Am?*

*H*ave you ever felt that you were standing with another at an important fork in the road of that other person's life? If so, you probably sensed that if the person chose the less traveled road it would make all the difference. I have felt the same feeling. Each of us stands, I think, at the fork of a road in life. I can take the road of blaming: the other people in my life, the "way I am," the situation in which I find myself, the weather, the stars, and so forth. This road of assigning responsibility for my reactions to others is a dead-end road. At its end there is only death: the death of my growth and development as a Christian, the death of peace, the death of what might have been. Growth begins only where blaming ends.

I have a sense that we can also choose the less traveled road marked, "What's in me?" Of course, there are some zigs and zags, some bumps and sharp turns in that road. There will be mountains to be climbed, waters to be crossed. Along that road we may feel burdened at times with the tasks that honesty imposes upon us. But if we choose that road, we will eventually become whole by becoming profoundly Christian. We will become more like the Christ of our faith. And we will experience his peace, and possess the fullness of life that Jesus has promised as his gift and legacy to believers.

From *The Christian Vision*

*A*s "fully human" persons "we are our own persons." We do not bend to every wind that blows. We are not at the mercy of all the pettiness, the meanness, the impatience and anger of others. Atmospheres do not transform us as much as we transform them.

Most of us, unfortunately, feel like a floating boat at the mercy of the winds and waves. We have no ballast when the winds rage and the waves churn. We say things like, "He made me so mad." "You really get to me." "Her remark embarrassed me terribly." "This weather really depresses me." "This job really bores me." "The very sight of him saddens me."

Note that all these things are *doing something to me and to my emotions.* I have nothing to say about my anger, depression, sadness, and so forth. And, like most people we are content to blame others, circumstances, and bad luck. The fully human person, as Shakespeare puts it in *Julius Caesar,* knows that: "The fault, dear Brutus, is not with our stars, but with ourselves. . . ." We can rise above the dust of daily battle that chokes and blinds so many of us; and this is precisely what is asked of us in the process of growth as a person.

From *Why Am I Afraid To Tell You Who I Am?*

*G*od calls us to the fullness of life. A deep, personal peace is the promise and legacy of Jesus to his followers. When the fullness of life and personal peace are interrupted by discomfort, whether it be physical or emotional or behavioral, the experience of discomfort is an invitation to personal introspection and reflection. "What is in me?" is the necessary and sometimes painful question that must be asked. I cannot change others, the world about me, the weather, or the position of my stars. I can change myself. In reflection and prayer, I can trace my discomfort to its attitudinal roots. I can look clearly at what is in me. And this is the area of my attitudes which I can control and change. There may be times when my attitude is found to be in full harmony with my Christian faith. But most of the time, if you are like me, you will find a neurotic and un-Christian attitude at the source of your discomfort.

And so I have to ask myself about alternative attitudes. I have to go out to others in my need, to explore the mind and attitudes of another who does not seem to be afflicted with my discomfort. It may also help to record in a journal a written description both of the old attitude to be unlearned and the new attitude to be acquired.

From *The Christian Vision*

*T*he whole process of maturation depends on *how we react* to the difficulties or challenges of life. The immature person sees only the difficulties: they are so close to his near-sighted eyes that he can see only the problems and pays very little attention to his own reaction which is, in fact, the critical and definitive thing. Difficulties pass, but our reaction to them does not. Each reaction, mature or immature, lingers on in us as the beginning of a habit. Repeated mature reactions tend to produce the formed habits of maturity which define us. Repeated immature reactions dig their own grooves.

The Christian must always accept him or herself in the present, pilgrim and human condition, which will inevitably involve failure. Ideals must always be introduced to the test of actual experience. In this introduction our ideals, which very often sound beautiful, require of us a struggle, a renunciation, a battle for control of self, a willingness to start again in the wake of failures, a lucid acceptance of the mystery of the cross.

It is not the problem, and in this case not the isolated *failure* that is critical, definitive or paramount. It is our *reaction to it*. The reaction of Christians must always be suffused with a confidence nourished by the conviction that God and oneself are a majority, even stronger than one's own weakness. The process of maturation as a Christian and as a human being will inevitably be marked by failures, but the only real failure is to quit. When the situation gets tough, the Christian must get tougher. We must become bigger than our problems. In the end, such determination to love will bring us to the feet of Love itself, which is our eternal victory in the victorious Christ.

From *Why Am I Afraid To Love?*

I keep thinking about all the great men and women in our human history. Imagine Joan of Arc whimpering, "But I can't ride a horse, let alone lead an army!" What if Christopher Columbus had said, "I can't be right and all those people wrong. What if I fail and get lost on the high seas? What will other people say about me then?" Suppose that Thomas Jefferson had caved into his fears: "Write a Declaration of Independence for a new country? You're kidding. I've never written a Declaration before."

Now you might react by saying, "Yes, but they were great and famous people. I'm neither great nor famous." To which I am tempted to reply, "Right. But neither were they before they stretched."

From *Will The Real Me Please Stand Up?*

*E*very person has a natural built-in tendency to grow. Personal growth is something like physical growth. When we look at the body of a small child, we know that all the child needs is time and the proper nourishment. In time the small child's body will grow into its full development. Likewise, when we find another human being somewhere in the course of his or her personal process or progress, we have to have faith that with time and the proper nourishment that person will grow into full maturity.

The proper nourishment for personal growth is a loving acceptance and encouragement by others, not rejection and impatient suggestions for improvement. Human beings, like plants, grow in the soil of acceptance, not in the atmosphere of rejection. We have said that personal growth resembles physical growth: all the energies and tendencies are there.

If you will accept me wherever I am, all my energies and desires to grow will be released and energized. If you will reassure me that it is all right to be where I am now, I will have the courage to move beyond where I am. With your loving acceptance of me, I will gradually grow into the fullness of life.

From *Will The Real Me Please Stand Up?*

*B*y way of general description, fully alive people are those using all of their human faculties, powers, and talents. They are using them to the full. These individuals are fully functioning in their external and internal senses. They are comfortable with and open to the full experience and expression of all human emotions. Such people are more vibrantly alive in mind, heart and will. There is an instinctive fear in most of us, I think, to travel with our engines at full throttle. We prefer, for the sake of safety, to take life in small and dainty doses. The fully alive person travels with the confidence that, if one is alive and fully functioning in all parts and powers, the result will be harmony, not chaos.

Fully alive human beings are alive in their external and internal *senses.* They see a beautiful world. They hear its music and poetry. They smell the fragrance of each new day and taste the deliciousness of every moment. Of course their senses are also insulted by ugliness and offended by odors. To be fully alive means to be open to the whole human experience. It is a struggle to climb a mountain but the view from the top is magnificent. Fully alive individuals have activated imaginations and cultivated senses of humor. They are alive, too, in their *emotions.* They are able to experience the full gamut and galaxy of human feelings—wonder, awe, tenderness, compassion, both agony and ecstasy.

From *Fully Human, Fully Alive*

*F*ully alive people are also alive in their *minds.* They are very much aware of the wisdom in the statement of Socrates that "the unreflected life isn't worth living." Fully alive people are always thoughtful and reflective. They are capable of asking the right questions of life and flexible enough to let life question them. They will not live an unreflected life in an unexamined world. Most of all, perhaps, these people are alive in *will* and *heart.* They love much. They truly love and sincerely respect themselves. All love begins here and builds on this. Fully alive people are glad to be alive and to be who they are. In a delicate and sensitive way they also love others. Their general disposition towards all is one of concern and love. And there are individuals in their lives who are so dear to them that the happiness, success, and security of these loved ones are as real to them as their own. They are committed and faithful to those they love in this special way.

For such people life has the color of joy and the sound of celebration. Their lives are not a perennial funeral procession. Each tomorrow is a new opportunity which is eagerly anticipated. There is a reason to live and a reason to die. And when such people come to die their hearts will be filled with gratitude for all that has been, for "the way we were," for a beautiful and full experience. A smile will spread throughout their whole being as their lives pass in review. And the world will always be a better place, a happier place, and a more human place because they lived and laughed and loved here.

From *Fully Human, Fully Alive*

*T*he fullness of life must not be misrepresented as the proverbial "bowl of cherries." Fully alive people, precisely because they are fully alive, obviously experience failure as well as success. They are open to both pain and pleasure. They have many questions and some answers. They cry and they laugh. They dream and they hope. The only things that remain alien to their experience of life are passivity and apathy. They say a strong "yes" to life and a resounding "amen" to love. They feel the strong stings of growing—of going from the old into the new—but their sleeves are always rolled up, their minds are whirring, and their hearts are ablaze. They are always moving, growing, beings-in-process, creatures of continual evolution.

How does one get this way? How do we learn to join the dance and sing the songs of life in all of its fullness? It seems to me that the contemporary wisdom on this subject can be distilled and formulated into five essential steps to fuller living. Briefly, these five steps are: (1) to *accept* oneself (2) to *be* oneself (3) to *forget* oneself in loving (4) to *believe* (5) to *belong*.

These steps are normally taken in the order suggested and each one builds upon the previous accomplishments. While each one builds on and grows out of the previous steps, none is ever fully and finally completed. Each will always remain an ideal to keep us reaching. In terms of a vision, or basic frame of reference, each of the five steps is essentially a new awareness or perception. The more deeply these perceptions are realized, the more one is enabled to find the fullness of life.

Bon Voyage!

From *Fully Human, Fully Alive*

To Accept Oneself. Fully alive people accept and love themselves as they are. They do not live for the promise of some tomorrow or the potential that may someday be revealed in them. They usually feel about themselves as they are the same warm and glad emotions that you and I feel when we meet someone whom we really like and admire. Fully alive people are sensitively aware of all that is good in themselves, from the little things, like the way they smile or walk, through the natural talents they have been given, to the virtues they have worked to cultivate. When these people find imperfections and limitations in themselves they are compassionate. They try to understand, not to condemn themselves. "Beyond a wholesome discipline," *Desiderata* says, "be gentle with yourself." The wellsprings for the fullness of life rise from within a person. And, psychologically speaking, a joyful self-acceptance, a good self-image, a sense of self-celebration are the bedrock beginning of the fountain that rises up into the fullness of life.

From *Fully Human, Fully Alive*

*T*o *Be Oneself.* Fully alive people are liberated by their self-acceptance to be authentic and real. Only people who have joyfully accepted themselves can take all the risks and responsibilites of being themselves. "I gotta be me!" the song lyrics insist, but most of us get seduced into wearing masks and playing games. The old ego defense mechanisms are built up to protect us from further vulnerability. But they buffer us from reality and reduce our visibility. They diminish our capacity for living. Being ourselves has many implications. It means that we are free to have and to report our emotions, ideas, and preferences. Authentic individuals can think their own thoughts and make their own choices. They have risen above the nagging need for the approval of others. They do not sell out to anyone. Their feelings, thoughts, and choices are simply not for hire. "To thine own self be true . . ." is their life principle and lifestyle.

From *Fully Human, Fully Alive*

*T*o *Forget Oneself in Loving.* Having learned to accept and to be themselves, fully alive people proceed to master the art of forgetting themselves—the art of loving. They learn to go out of themselves in genuine caring and concern for others. The size of a person's world is the size of his or her heart. We can be at home in the world of reality only to the extent that we have learned to love it. Fully alive men and women escape from the dark and diminished world of egocentricity, which always has a population of one. They are filled with an empathy that enables them to feel deeply and spontaneously with others. Because they can enter into the feeling world of others—almost as if they were inside others or others were inside them—their world is greatly enlarged and their potential for human experience greatly enhanced. They have become "persons for others," and there are others so dear to them that they have personally experienced the "greater love than this" sense of commitment. They would protect their loved ones with their own lives.

Being a loving person is far different from being a so-called "do-gooder." Do-gooders merely use other people as opportunities for practicing their acts of virtue, of which they keep a careful count. Loving people learn to move the focus of their attention and concern from themselves out to others. They care deeply about others. The difference between do-gooders and people who love is the difference between a life which is an on-stage performance and a life which is an act of love. Real love cannot be successfully imitated. Our care and concern for others must be genuine, or our love means nothing. This much is certain: There is no learning to live without learning to love.

From *Fully Human, Fully Alive*

*T*o *Believe.* Having learned to transcend purely self-directed concern, fully alive people discover "meaning" in their lives. This meaning is found in what Viktor Frankl calls "a specific vocation or mission in life." It is a matter of commitment to a person or cause in which one can believe and to which one can be dedicated. This faith commitment shapes the lives of fully alive individuals, making all of their efforts seem significant and worthwhile. Devotion to this life task raises them above the pettiness and paltriness that necessarily devour meaningless lives. When there is no such meaning in a human life, one is left almost entirely to the pursuit of sensations. One can only experiment, looking for new "kicks," new ways to break the monotony and boredom of a stagnant life. A person without meaning usually gets lost in the forest of chemically induced delusions, the alcoholic fog, the prolonged orgy, the restless eagerness to scratch without even having an itch. Human nature abhors a vacuum. We must find a cause to believe in or spend the rest of our lives compensating ourselves for failure.

From *Fully Human, Fully Alive*

*T*o Belong. The fifth and final component of the full life would no doubt be a "place called home," a sense of community. A community is a union of persons who "have in common," who share in mutuality their most precious possessions—themselves. They know and are open to one another. They are "for" one another. They share in love their persons and their lives. Fully alive people have such a sense of belonging—to their families, to their church, to the human family. There are others with whom such people feel completely comfortable and at home, with whom they experience a sense of mutual belonging. There is a place where their absence would be felt and their deaths mourned. When they are with these others, fully alive people find equal satisfaction in giving and receiving. A contrary sense of isolation is always diminishing and destructive. It drives us into the pits of loneliness and alienation, where we can only perish. The inescapable law built into human nature is this: We are never less than individuals but we are never merely individuals. No man is an island. Butterflies are free, but we need the heart of another as a home for our hearts. Fully alive people have the deep peace and contentment that can be experienced only in such a home.

From *Fully Human, Fully Alive*

*T*his is just fiction, okay? However, the little story I am about to share is very illustrative of what I would like to suggest, namely, that the way we look at things regulates our reaction to them. Anyway, the story is about two little boys, identical twins, one of whom was an incorrigible optimist and the other an equally incorrigible pessimist. Now the parents were concerned about this so they took the boys to a child psychologist. The psychologist said: "I think I know what to do. On their next birthday, give the little pessimist the best toys you can afford, and give the optimist a box of manure. That will level them off."

So the parents did this. They put the little boys in separate rooms with their "presents." When the parents peeked into the room of the little pessimist, they saw the boy looking dejectedly at his beautiful toys, complaining. "I don't like this color. This will probably break. I know a boy who has a better calculator than this one." The poor parents looked at each other and groaned.

Then they stepped across the hall and looked in on the little optimist. He was gleefully throwing the manure up in the air, saying, "You can't fool me! Where there is this much manure, there's got to be a pony somewhere."

"Keep your eye upon the doughnut and not upon the hole."

From the video program, *Free To Be Me*

*F*ully alive people find enjoyment in what others regard as drudgery or duty. They don't *have* to; they *want* to. They are aware of the thorns but concentrate on the roses. Each day has a newness about it; it is never a carbon copy of yesterday. No person, including themselves, is today who he or she was yesterday. Since their vision is always tentative and open to modification, fully alive people eagerly await new insights. These insights will renew them and their vision of reality.

Caution! In describing fully alive people, their visions and basic questions, I feel a certain uneasiness. I don't want to seem to be describing an ideal that is essentially unrealistic. There are many pop-psychologists who will tell us authoritatively that all we have to do is think positively and optimistically. We should ignore our failures and just streak along the primrose path. This will change everything! This is obvious and dangerous nonsense. The danger in the "keep smiling!" quackery is that such romanticism and glamorization always end in sad disillusion when reality intrudes.

Also, I have the feeling that the enthusiasts can force the positive mental attitude kind of happiness on people whose basic vision is, in fact, negative and pessimistic. This is really quite cruel. It amounts to urging the person to put a smiling mask over his or her essential sadness.

From *Fully Human, Fully Alive*

*O*ne of the most persistent and widely believed delusions is that one person can make another happy. You cannot confer on me the fullness of life. That has to be my choice. Sometimes in relationships one party can twist himself or herself into a pretzel trying to make the other happy and always without complete success. The fact is that no one can make me happy; nor can I make someone else happy. We each have to do that for ourselves. Trying to educate myself to this fact, I see the sign in my mirror every morning that reminds me, "You are looking at the face of the person who is responsible for your happiness today." The clenched fists that open to the full experience of life are a matter of my own decision, my own choice. If I am to love happily and fully, it will be because I have decided to do this. Happiness is indeed an "inside job." I have chosen to make Christ's vision my own. I have chosen to join God in his pronouncement about creation: "It is very good!"

From *The Christian Vision*

A black evangelist friend of mine told me that when Jesus first became real to him as a teen-ager, he sneaked into his high-school classroom before the start of the school day and printed on the chalkboard in huge letters: JESUS CHRIST IS THE ANSWER! When he returned later, he discovered that someone else had printed under his statement: YEAH, BUT WHAT IS THE QUESTION? "Yeah," he thought, "what is the question?"

As his life progressed, my friend found that there isn't only one question. Life asks how much we can love, enjoy and endure. Life asks us to distinguish between what is really important and what is unimportant. Life asks us to exercise the judgment of conscience. But perhaps the most profound question asked by life is the question of significance and meaning. We need to believe that our lives will make a difference for someone or for something. "What's it all about, Alfie?" Of course, there are no patented, simple answers that flow out of automated machines. The German poet, Rainer Maria Rilke, counsels us to be patient toward all that is unsolved in our hearts. He suggests that we must learn to love the questions themselves while waiting for and working out the answers.

My evangelist friend, now an old man, tells me that he now knows much more about the many questions which life asks. Life has questioned him about his values and priorities, about his vision and dreams, about his courage and capacity to love. "But," he said to me, looking over his glasses, "to all the questions that life asks: JESUS CHRIST IS THE ANSWER!"

From *Fully Human, Fully Alive*

W̵hen they ask, "Will the Jesus People please stand up?" I want to stand tall. I want to stand and be counted as one of the Jesus People. But I must share this with you: It would be very frightening to stand alone. I need you to stand with me in the ranks of the Church, the Jesus People. I need my weak voice to be joined by yours in the chorus that sings the Lord's praise and says the Lord's prayer. Yes, I have felt the touch of the Lord upon my life and I have felt the hand of the Lord in mine. But I would be very doubtful about my own experiences if you did not stand at my side and confirm me in my faith by your own testimonial to grace.

This is the deepest meaning and the fundamental function of the Church, as I see it. As mentioned, the question is not, *What* is the Church? The real question is, *Who* is the Church? "You are" (UR) is the heart and center of the very word *Church*. If we, if you and I, are to be the Church, then I know that I need you, and need you badly, to stand next to me, a God with skin. I need to hear your voice being raised with mine in prayer. I need to know by the experience of your nearness that God has made you my sister, my brother, and that we are together his family. I need to pray with you for the coming of his Kingdom. I need to hear you saying your "yes" which braces my own "yes" with a new strength. There is an inevitable contagion in everything human. And so I need the support of your presence, your love, and your person. God reaches out to me through you and out to you through me. And if, somehow and for your own reasons, you should choose to "leave the Church," please do not think that you have simply walked out of a building or an organization marked with weakness. The fact is that you have left us who need you and who will miss you and your love.

From *The Christian Vision*

*T*he basic question for me is: Do you really want to love? Are you willing to be the "public utility," the town pump which is there for all to use? Do you really want to let Jesus be reincarnated in your humanity? Jesus is the "man for others." If you give yourself to him, he will immediatly put you in the service of others in one way or another. Do you really want to volunteer for this life of loving? You can't do it on your own. He must do it in you. Will you have enough faith to release his power into your life? These are the only pertinent questions.

I am now deeply convinced that the power of love is from God. I believe that no humans can truly love unless God is active within them. I hear Jesus say, "Without me you can do nothing. You can bear no fruit. I am the vine and you are the branches. Cut off from me you are dead." I hear St. John say that only the person who knows God can know the meaning of love. I hear St. Paul describe love as the highest and greatest gift of the Spirit. Wherever I have found love I have felt the presence of God, God at work in the minds and hearts and muscles of us human beings.

My experience of God has been working this transformation in me, too. Oh, I am still a very selfish person. God is not finished with me yet. Others may not think of me as a very effective lover, but they do not know the before and after; they cannot read the motives of the heart. The process of divinization, in which God makes us more and more to his image and likeness, is a slow, gradual, and often painful process. I am still a pilgrim. But I have been touched and I am partially transformed. This is the basis for my hope. The God who has touched me in the past will act again and again in my life. Over again I will feel his finger and find him.

From *He Touched Me*

*I*n various moments of my life, when I am relating to and communicating with others, I observe myself in action, and I ask, "Is this the person I would like to be?" With this I quietly ask God to help me become my ideal. I ask him to empower me to practice what I preach. Help me to be real. If I am not real, I am nothing. My life will only be a charade. I dread this thought, that death will come to me like the final curtain of a command performance. I will then wipe off my stage makeup, take off my costume, give back my lines to the author, while the audience continues to applaud me for being someone I never was. I know that when I come to die, God will look for scars, not medals. When I am dying, I want to remember the times when I was real and honest, when I shared myself in an open self-disclosure as an act of love. I want to remember the times when I gave to those who were hungry the food of my sharing, to those who were thirsty the drink of my listening and understanding, to those who were locked inside themselves the gentle, extended hands that said, "Come out. You will be safe with me." I want to remember the times when I offered the healing gift of loving and caring to those who were in need.

From *Will The Real Me Please Stand Up?"*

*A*bout five years ago my Jesuit Provincial Superior asked me and two other theologians to speak at all the Jesuit houses in our area. I was personally very comfortable with this situation because I have a lot of mileage on my mouth and am never nervous in a speaking situation. However, when we came to Loyola Univeristy, my own community of 120 Jesuits, I was very nervous. My mouth was dry. My hands were cold. And of course, I knew why. I wanted to impress my fellow Jesuits. I wanted them to know what a "Fulton Sheen" they had in their midst.

So I prayed (while the other two speakers were giving their presentations): "Jesus, please extend over me the hands you once held out over the sea of Galilee when it was turbulent. Bring about in me a great calm. I need poise if I am going to impress the boys." Nothing happened. And so I prayed again, reminding Jesus that he promised to produce whatever we asked in his name. But still nothing. Then I remembered that someone once counseled, "If you keep asking God the same question and you don't get an answer, try another question." So I did. "Jesus," I asked, "are you trying to tell me something?"

Now I should have told you at the beginning that God speaks to me. (I figure that, if I am going to drop names, I might as well drop the really big one.) Let me say simply and directly, that on this occasion God spoke to me. Inside me somewhere I heard clearly: "You are getting ready to give another performance. (I knew my life had been cluttered with perfomances.) And I don't need any more performances from you. Only acts of love. You are getting ready to perform for your brothers so they will know how good you are. They don't need that. They need you to love them so they will know how good they are." I know it was from God. That night and that message have changed my life.

From the video program, *Free To Be Me*

A meaningful life can result only from the experience of love, and this implies a commitment and dedication to another. Love rejects the question "What am I getting out of this?" as the only criterion of fulfillment. Love understands by direct experience those often quoted words of St. Francis of Assisi: "It is in giving that we receive." Egoistic concern and concentration on self can lead only to the loss of self. It is a strange and painful paradox that we all must learn. The most perceptive insight of contemporary personalism is that I become a person only if I receive my personhood from someone else through the gift of affirmation. If I never see myself valued by others, I will never value myself.

Giving the gift of myself in love leaves me with a deep and lasting satisfaction of having done something good with my life. I live with the sweet memory of having contributed a gift of love to the lives of others. Likewise I am left with a sense of having used well the gifts which God has invested in me. Love takes time, demands a history of giving and receiving, laughing and crying, living and dying. It never promises instant gratification, only ultimate fulfillment. Love means believing in someone, in something. It supposes a willingness to struggle, to work, to suffer, and to join in the rejoicing. I doubt that there has ever been one recorded case of deep and lasting fulfillment reported by a person whose basic mind-set and only question was: What am I getting out of this?

It is, of course, the paradox of the Gospels: satisfaction and fulfillment are the by-products of dedicated love. They belong only to those who can reach beyond themselves, to whom giving is more important than receiving.

From *Unconditional Love*

*S*everal years ago my mother lay dying. She had lapsed into a coma and was apparently unconscious. The doctor told us, "She will not recover from this. She will die in her sleep." I immediately decided that I would spend as much time as I possibly could at her bedside. While I sat there, listening to her labored breathing, my mind went back over all those years and over all that my mother had meant to me. I combed through years and years of sweet memories. I would like to tell you about one such memory that came back to me at that time.

As boys we used to go over to the nearby park and put what was called "dry ice" into our mouths. We had to keep moving it inside our mouths, of course, because otherwise it would "burn" us. However, when we exhaled a steamy vapor, we thought everyone was looking at us, mistaking us for Puff the Magic Dragon. On one such occasion, in the crush of people at the park, I was blowing the vapor out of my mouth when somebody jostled me and . . . I swallowed the chunk of dry ice! I *knew* I would die. Of course, I went running home and told my mother what had happend. "I swallowed . . . I swallowed the dry ice. I am going to die."

She handled my announcement quite serenely. "Well, not just yet, maybe." She called the doctor who lived next door. He encouraged my mother to "Flood his stomach with milk," which she did. Then I remember that she held me on her lap. I remember the sweet feel of her arms around me. I remember the rocking of the chair. And also I clearly remember thinking: "I can't die. It would break my mother's heart. She loves me so much, it would break her heart if I died." As I was sitting next to my mother in her own last moments of life, I remembered all that. I thought about those arms that once held me. I cried quietly tears of appreciation.

From the video program, *Families*

*T*he kind of world we live in is governed to a large extent by the consensus ethic of that world. There are at the present time two ethics competing for domination in our contemporary American society. There is the traditional, humane, pro-life ethic, which sees every human life as valuable in itself. It offers loving acceptance and care to every human being, without distinction of size, shape, skin color, or self-sufficiency. It assumes that every life is worth living.

Under this ethic, everyone who comes into this world comes as part of our human family. Everyone comes as a unique and unrepeatable gift. There will be, in this world, people like the late Helen Keller: deaf and blind and unable to communicate until "Annie" Sullivan comes along. Anne Sullivan will attain the stature of a tremendous human being only because there is the challenge of a Helen Keller to call greatness out of her. You climb the mountain because it is there. There will also be in this world retarded and deformed people. There will be schools for "exceptional children" and "Special Olympics."

There will be sympathetic and compassionate treatment of the aged and the senile, who are also a part of our family and who motivate us to be human and loving. The message that the aged deliver will be a request, an invitation, and a challenge to our capacity for love and endurance. When we rise to this challenge, like muscles that grow strong with exercise, our societal capacity for mutual love and concern will also grow. We will become more and more humane toward one another. The world under the pro-life ethic may not be as neat and clean and pain-free as the world ruled by the quality-of-life ethic, but it is far more humane and compassionate and a much more loving world.

From *The Silent Holocaust*

*I*n rendering to love its required "work" or effort, it is important that we seek unity, not happiness. Those who set out upon the journey of love must strive for that transparency, that sharing and community of life which is the heart of love. Would-be lovers must not be constantly taking their temperatures and counting their pulsebeats to keep an up-to-the-minute check on how well they feel or how happy they are. A sense of well-being and happiness, as Viktor Frankl so often warns us, can come into a human life only as a by-product. You have no doubt heard this verse:

> Happiness is like a butterfly.
> The more you chase it, the more it will elude you.
> But if you turn your attention to other things,
> It comes and softly sits on your shoulder.

To be truly happy in love, a person must want and seek unity, oneness, sharing. Sometimes this unity involves many things that are painful: honesty, when you would rather lie a little, talking-out when you would rather pout, admitting embarrassing feelings when you would rather blame someone, standing there when you would rather run, admitting doubt when you would rather pretend certainty, and confronting when you would rather settle for peace at any price. None of these things which are among the just demands of love, brings immediate peace and happiness; they bring immediate pain and struggle. Yes, love works if we will work at it. The work of love is to achieve a total honesty and transparency, and these are very difficult attainments. So people who run in a direct chase after the butterfly of happiness in love relationships will be empty-handed and empty-hearted in the end. Unity not happiness is the stern condition of success at love.

From *The Secret Of Staying In Love*

*I*n the process of loving there are three important stages or moments: (1) *Kindness*: a warm assurance that "I am on your side. I care about you." (2) *Encouragement*: a strong reassurance of your own strength and self-sufficiency. (3) *Challenge*: a loving but firm exhortation to action. "Go for it."

Just as an artist-painter uses canvas and oils to achieve certain desired effects, so the artist-lover must try to sense when the need of the loved one is for more kindness, more encouragement, or more challenge. It is never easy to know.

Kindness. Someone has wisely said that "people do not care how much you know until they know how much you care." To build a relationship on any foundation other than kindness is to build on sand. I have to know that you really want my happiness and my growth, that you really are "for me," or I won't open at all to your influence.

Encouragement. What all people need most is to believe in themselves. They need confidence in their own ability to take on the problems and opportunities of life. To "en-courage" means to put courage in. Encouragement instills into the recipient a new and fuller awareness of his or her own powers. Encouragement says: You can do it!

Challenge. If encouragement makes the one loved aware of his or her strength, challenge is the loving push to use this strength: "Try. Stretch. Do it. If you succeed, I will be in the front row clapping my hands off. If you fail, I will be sitting right at your side. You won't be alone. Go ahead now. Give it your best shot. Go for it!"

From *Unconditional Love*

*I*n trying to love another person, the questions that love asks are: What do you need? What can I be for you? Love says: If you need me to be tough, I can be tough. Love isn't always sweet and tender. If you will be helped by a tough confrontation to accept your responsibilities, count on me. But please know this: If I am tough and unrelenting, it is because I love you. I can't let you con me out of my toughness because that would not be loving. But, please believe me: I really want to do, to be, to say whatever I think would be best for you. Sometimes you will have a lot on your mind and will want to talk. I'll try to be there to listen. At other times you will just want to be alone. I will try to read and recognize your need and I will leave you alone in your solitude. I know your needs will change from day to day. I will try to respect this reality, to recognize your changing needs.

This is the genius, I think, of loving: To do, to be, to say what you need and *at the same time* to affirm you. I must communicate to you a strong sense of your own worth. I am aware that the self-image, one's sense of personal worth, is the radical source of all human behavior, of all moods. A sense of personal worth is also the radical source of emotional and mental health. I know that if you truly believe in your own worth, everything else will seem to harmonize in your life. So, whatever else love asks of me, I will try to leave you with a sense that you are a uniquely valuable and irreplaceable person.

If I should fail, fail to recognize and respond to your needs, please forgive me. I am often weak and shortsighted. My own personal aches and pains often obscure my vision of your needs. But have faith in me. My deepest and most sincere intention is to love you.

From the audio program, *My Vision And My Values*

*O*ur lives are shaped by those who love us, and by those who refuse to love us. I teach at Loyola University in Chicago. I am especially interested in two types of students. I look for those who seem to need special help, but I am also very interested in those who are well. I am as interested in knowing the sources of personal health and happiness as I am in the sources of human damage and destruction.

A few years ago a young woman was enrolled in my class who appeared to be the personification of personal health. She had a marvelous attitude toward everything and everyone. One day, as she was leaving the classroom, I asked her: "Noreen, how did you ever get the way you are?" She knew I meant this as a compliment, and replied: "Whatever way I am, it is because of my family. I have a wonderful family. You will have to meet them sometime." I eagerly accepted.

The occasion was a party, a celebration. I could feel the atmosphere of contagious affirmation everywhere. Everyone seemed to appreciate and affirm everyone else. A verbalization of the messages exchanged in various ways would have been: "You really count. When you come into this house, you are special. Everyone here is special." It was a beautiful experience. I left feeling about ten feet tall. As I was leaving, I said to the parents: "You are really doing a great thing here in your family. I am very grateful to have an experience like the one I had tonight." Noreen's father replied rather modestly, "Well, we are doing what we can. You know what I tell these kids? I tell them that we don't have much else, but *we* are the riches in this family. *We* are."

I left thinking: "You're right, Noreen. It's your family!"

From the video program, *Families*

*T*he truth about love, I think, is that it is indeed a profound comfort, but it is also a monumental challenge. Love immediately challenges me to break the fixation I have with myself. It will drag me all the way from my infantile *id* to a complete self-donation to a cause or person in freely given love. Love demands that I learn to focus my attention on the needs of those I love. It will ask me to become a sensitive listener. At times, love will insist that I postpone my own gratifications to meet the needs of those I love. The kind of communication which is the lifeblood of love will require me to get in touch with my most buried thoughts, and to share these in the frightening act of self-disclosure. Love will make me vulnerable. It will open me to the honest reactions of others whom I have allowed to penetrate my defenses. If I have built protective walls around my vulnerable places, love will tear them down.

Love will teach me to give and to receive without panscales. Love transcends pan-scale justice. If love divides the burdens of life in half by sharing, it also doubles one's responsibilities. Two do not eat as cheaply as one, unless one of the two does not eat. It is also true that two cannot make decisions as quickly as one, and so forth. If you prefer to be an island, a recluse, a narcissist, preferring to live in a world that has a population of one, love would rip out of your hands everything that you hold dear and clutch tightly.

And yet, it seems obvious to me, as I feel sure it will seem to you, that these very challenges of a true love relationship, which assault our self-centeredness, are in fact the bridge to human maturity and ultimate human fulfillment.

From *Unconditional Love*

I think weathering the storms of the love process is the only way to find the rainbows of life. The comfort that one finds on the "less-traveled road" of love are found nowhere else. Life has a much deeper meaning when I truly love another. The loneliness of a world that has a population of one is filled by a new and warm presence when love enters a life. The self-alienation that results when we do not interact intimately is replaced in us by a healthy sense of self and of self-worth when we have been renewed by love. It is what we call today a sense of "identity." It has become a truism that we can know and love only as much of ourselves as we are willing to share with another in love. The aimless wandering of the loveless person finds in love a sense of belonging and a place called home.

Going out to another in love means risk—the risks of self-disclosure, rejection, misunderstanding. It means grief, too, from the temporary separations, psychological or physical, to the final separation of death. Whoever insists on personal security and safety as the non-negotiable conditions of life would not be willing to pay love's price or find love's enrichments. Whoever shuts himself or herself up in the cocoon of self-protective defenses, keeping others always at a safe distance and holding on tightly to personal possessions and privacy, will find the price of love far too high and will remain forever a prisoner of fear.

From *Unconditional Love*

*W*hen God created this world, he saw in his mind's eye an infinite number of other possible worlds which he might have created. You and I were in some of those other possible worlds. We were not in others. But God did not want a world without you or me, because of his special predilection and love for us. It was as if God were saying "Oh, I could have made a world without you, but I didn't want a world without you. No world for me would have been complete . . . without you."

It is also true that God could have chosen a world in which you did exist, but in circumstances and with gifts different from the actual circumstances of your life and with gifts other than your own. But he did not want a "different you." It is *this you* that God loves: the you with your actual fingerprints, hair color, voice and heart, with your unique and unrepeatable immortal soul.

God does not love us as one big glob of humanity. He loves each of us individually. In his own eyes there is no one and there never will be anyone like each of us. Our lives, and the other individual circumstances and personal determinations of those lives, are God's special gift. His providence has chosen and destined you and me, by a special act of love, to deliver a message, to sing a song, and to confer an act of love on this world which no one else can. Each of us is a unique and unrepeatable image and likeness of God, a unique and unrepeatable mystery of his love. The bottom theological line in this is that you and I have been known and loved by God from all eternity and through all eternity. Each of us has always been a part of the mind and heart of God. The "I" of God has been saying to the "Thou" of you and me an eternal "I love you."

From *The Silent Holocaust*

*T*ommy had been the resident atheist in my Theology of Faith course. As he was turning in his final exam, he asked me if I thought he would ever find God. "No!" I blurted, and then as he turned to leave, I added: "You won't find Him. He will find you, Tom." He did not seem to be much impressed or affected. I thought he missed my point.

Five years later he came into my office. He was dying. His body was badly wasted with a terminal cancer. He had only a few weeks to live. He reminded me of that last day in class. He told me how, when he learned that he had terminal cancer, he pleaded with God to come and console him. Then he related that one day he gave up all hope of making contact with God. But he remembered another day in class. I had said that there were two essential life tragedies: one was to live without loving, and the second was to love without sharing that love with others. They need our love and we withhold it.

So he told me how he went trembling to tell his father: "I love you, Dad." Then to his mother and little brother. He added: "Then, one day I turned around and God was there. He didn't come to me when I pleaded with him. Apparently he does things in his own way and at his own hour. But the important thing is that he was there. He found me. You were right. He found me even after I had stopped looking for him."

I invited Tom to come to my class, to tell them his story, how opening our hearts to those we love is God's open door into our lives. Love is indeed God's port of entry. Tom said he would come to my class, but he didn't make it. However, just before he died, we had one last talk. He told me that he wouldn't be coming to my class. Then he asked me: "Will you tell them for me? Will you . . . tell the whole world for me?" I promised I would. "I'll do my best, Tom. I'll tell them."

Thank you for listening.

Condensed from *Unconditional Love*

*T*here are some things that all of us find very painful, like loneliness. Loneliness is the prison of the human spirit. When we are lonely we pace back and forth in small, shut-in worlds. We believe that no one understands us and we don't really care very much about understanding others. On the other side of the coin, most of us have at least fleetingly experienced the joy of sharing. Maybe we have stood with another on the shore of an ocean, watching a gorgeous sunset. It meant so much to be able to turn to another and say, "Isn't it beautiful!" Or we may have shared a secret joy or pain with another. We remember the profound consolation of feeling understood. It felt so good to know that someone cared, that we were not alone.

In other words, there is a reward system and a sanction system built into human nature. We have an inner need to know and to be known, and the satisfaction of this need brings us a sense of human fulfillment. When we build walls of separation between ourselves and others, our immediate inner reaction might be a sense of security. But the eventual result is starvation of spirit, a pervasive sense of loneliness. We have built our own prisons. We care about no one and no one cares about us. We are alone.

From *Will The Real Me Please Stand Up?*

*S*omeone who counts such things has written that the average child, during the first five years of life, receives 431 (!) negative messages on an average day. "Stop making that noise . . . Get down from there . . . What are you doing with my scissors? . . . No, you're too small . . . Look at the mess you've made . . . You've got dirt on your shoes and I just cleaned the kitchen floor!" And so forth (x 431).

As a result of these messages, we develop instincts of self-protection. We try to cover or pad our egos to prevent further damage. Psychologists call these protective efforts "ego-defense mechanisms."

The sadness is that they camouflage the "real me."

From *Will The Real Me Please Stand Up?*

*T*he most common "ego-defense mechanisms" are the five described here:

(1) Through *compensation* we lean over backward to avoid falling on our faces. Freud calls it *reaction formation*. For example, we try to hide our uncertainties by pretending to "know it all." The little boy "whistles in the dark" as he walks through a cemetery at night.

(2) By *displacement* we construct a psychological detour, an alternate course or outlet for impulses that we can't let out directly. For example, I can't express my hostility to my boss whom I find obnoxious so I go to a baseball game and yell, "Kill the umpire!"

(3) By *projection* we cleverly disown undesirable qualities in ourselves, but attribute these repugnant qualities to someone or something else. For example, Adam blamed Eve and Eve blamed the serpent. Or we blame our poor work on poor tools.

(4) By *introjection*, we claim as our own the good qualities or deeds of others, sharing vicariously in their achievements and basking in the rays of their glory. In another form of introjection, we imagine ourselves as heroic victims of persecution.

(5) By *rationalization* we find good reasons to justify what we basically know is wrong. When I steal I imagine myself as Robin Hood stealing from the rich (them) to give to the poor (me).

They are all impediments to good communication because they somehow conceal us and our vulnerability. They are barriers to authenticity.

From *Will The Real Me Please Stand Up?*

*T*here is such a strong desire in most of us to shed our pretense, our sham, our phoniness. We all would like to be real. Phoniness requires so much effort. And once we start playing the game, we have to keep playing it. We would like to be able to put our real selves on the line rather than put an act on the stage. What a relief it would be to tell it like it truly is, to feel safe and secure in just being ourselves.

Such honesty would challenge us to stretch, to step out of our comfort zones. To tell our truth openly to everyone seems very frightening. The consequences of honesty sometimes seem to carry too high a price. But not to worry. It takes about three weeks, according to the experts, to get in the groove of a new habit, if we practice it every day. The open admission of our human woundedness and weakness may well look like a mountain until we start the climbing. In fact, we immediately experience and recognize in ourselves a new honesty and realness.

At the same time others sense and reflect back to us their recognition of our authenticity. Our relationships become real, grounded in an honest self-disclosure.

From *Will The Real Me Please Stand Up?*

*T*he peace that comes with honest self-disclosure is an immediate and undeniable reward. People who are willing to share their vulnerability don't have to keep up the exhausting effort of repression. They don't have to tie masks over their faces. They don't have to go through the contortions of compensation, projection, and rationalization. They make what Dag Hammarskjold called the "longest journey," the inward journey into self. What they see and hear in this exploration of their inner spaces they put out on the ticker tape of communication. "This is me. This is all of me, no more, no less. If you can come and celebrate it with me, fine. I must tell you this: I don't have to please you. What I have to do is be myself, my own true self."

From *Will The Real Me Please Stand Up?*

W e are, each of us, a conglomeration of mysterious needs and impulses which need to be ventilated. We need to be able to express ourselves, to talk ourselves out without fear of rejection by others. Too often the problems that we keep submerged within us remain in the darkness of our own interior, undefined and therefore destructive. We do not see the true dimensions of these things that trouble us until we define them and set lines of demarcation in conversation with a friend. Inside of us they remain as nebulous as smoke, but when we confide ourselves to another we acquire some sense of dimension and growth in self-identity and the capacity to accept ourselves as we are.

It may well be that our walls and masks will make this difficult. Our real fear is that we would be rejected, that the other person would not understand us. And so we wait and wait and wait behind our walls for the sufficient sound of reassurance in another, or we gaze out of the windows of our towers looking for a Prince Charming to come and rescue us. In the meanwhile, we can only perish. We will very likely "act out" the problems that remain submerged within us if we refuse to "talk out" these problems. We will act out our hostilities by destructively criticizing those around us, or act out our need to be loved by an emotional overdependence upon others.

And we must remember, if we want to love others truly, that these repressed and suppressed problems are very definitely impediments to love. They are our toothaches which keep us converged on ourselves, keep us from being ourselves, and keep us from forgetting ourselves.

From *Why Am I Afraid To Love?*

I would like to introduce here a distinction, based on content, between two types of communication. The first is the communication or sharing of emotions or feelings, which I would like to call *dialogue*. The second type of communication is the sharing of thoughts, values, the making of plans or decisions together, and, in general, things of a predominantly intellectual nature. This I would like to call *discussion*. Of course, this is an arbitrary distinction, and I am sure that not everyone would want to make it or would accept my usage of the words. It really is not important if others like or want to use the distinction, as long as what I am trying to say is clear. I need this or some such distinction to make a point which I think is tremendously important.

My point is this: There must be an emotional clearance (dialogue) between two involved partners in a love-relationship before they can safely enter into a deliberation (discussion) about plans, choices, values. The assumption behind this distinction and the priority given to dialogue is that the breakdown in human love and communication is *always* due to *emotional* problems. Two people in love can continue to deepen in their affection for each other while holding opposite opinions in almost any area of life. These contrary intellectual persuasions do not become an obstacle to love until one or both of the parties feels emotionally threatened.

From *The Secret Of Staying In Love*

*I*t is absolutely necessary to realize that nothing justifies me in becoming a judge of others. I can tell you who I am, report my emotions to you with candor and honesty, and this is the greatest kindness I can extend to myself and to you. Even if my thoughts and emotions are not pleasing to you, it remains the greatest kindness to reveal myself openly and honestly. Insofar as I am able, I will try to be honest with myself and communicate myself honestly to you.

It is another thing to set myself up as judge of your delusions. This is playing God. I must not try to be the guarantor of your integrity and honesty; that is your work. I can only hope that my honesty with and about myself will empower you to be honest with and about yourself. If I can face and tell you my faults and vanities, my hostilities and fears, my secrets and my shames, perhaps you will be able to admit to your own and confide them to me, if you wish.

It is a two way street. If you will be honest with me, report your triumphs and tragedies, agonies and ecstasies to me, it will help me to face my own, and to become an integral person. I need your openness and honesty; you need mine. Will you help me? I promise that I will try to help you. I will try to tell you who I really am.

From *Why Am I Afraid To Tell You Who I Am?*

*I*n sharing ourselves with others, we must always take full responsibility for our own actions and reactions. As a consequence of this, we will make "I statements," not "You statements."

Most of us grew up as "blamers." We accused others of making us angry. We rationalized many of our reactions by telling others, "You had it coming." Or we insisted that they had provoked our response. "I just couldn't help it." "I would have been all right if she hadn't started it." It is difficult for most of us to look back and acknowledge that our actions and reactions were not caused by others but rather by something in us. Yet this is always the fact. If I can only cross over the line that separates the "blamers" from those who accept the full responsibility for their behavior, it will probably be the most mature thing I have ever done. At least it will bring me into an honest contact with reality, and this is the only way to grow into a mature human being.

From *Will The Real Me Please Stand Up?*

*S*ometimes we don't feel like it, but each of us is a unique mystery. The mystery of you and the mystery that is me have never existed before. No one exactly like you or me will ever exist again. The combination of qualities and giftedness that is you is a package that has never been put together before. It is as unique as your fingerprints. And only you can share your mystery and giftedness with me. It is also true that just as every snowflake and every grain of sand on the seashore has a unique structure, so am I different from every other human being in all of human history. The treasure of my uniqueness is mine to give or to withhold.

If you choose to withhold your gift from me, I will be deprived of sharing in the unique mystery and experience of you. Likewise, I can deny you the vicarious experience of what it is like to be me. Just as we will forever be deprived by such mutual withholding, the opposite possibility is also true. We can be forever enriched by a mutual openness and sharing. The vicarious participation in another's unique human existence is always enriching. This is the great gift of communication.

When you tell me who you are, when you share with me your uniqueness, you will take me into a different world, a different time and place, a different family. You will share your old neighborhood with me, and tell me the stories that you listened to as a child. You will take me into valleys and to the tops of mountains I have never seen. You will lead me into the secret vaults of experiences that were not part of my life. You will introduce me to emotions, hopes, and dreams that were never mine. And this can only widen the dimensions of my mind and heart. I will be forever enriched by our sharing. The size of my experienced world will be permanently enlarged because of your goodness to me.

From *Will The Real Me Please Stand Up?*

*I*f we are to help each other, I must open myself and my world to you for your entry. And you must open yourself and your world to me for me to enter. I must allow you to experience me as a person, in all the fullness of my person. And I must be allowed to experience you in this way. For this, I must tell you who I am and you must tell me the same about yourself.

This kind of communication is the only avenue to the deepest riches of a human relationship. True and deep sharing with another is absolutely necessary for our growth as persons. Most of our relationships are primarily concerned with practical things like solving problems and making plans. The primary emphasis should rather be on this deeper sharing of our persons.

From *Why Am I Afraid To Tell You Who I Am?*

*A*ll of us experience breakdowns in communication now and then. It's part of relating. To say that this will never happen would be to deny the facts of life. Those breakdowns do not necessarily signal the end of a relationship. They are simply communication crises. They are much like situational crises when a person is temporarily overwhelmed by an event.

First and foremost, my *attitude* toward such crises will have a considerable effect on the *outcome* of the crises. If I think there could not and should not be communication crises, I will often be painfully surprised as well as frustrated. I will be spared much of this gloom if only I learn to accept crises as a normal, inevitable part of communication. After all, two absolutely unique persons are trying to share their very different and highly personalized views of reality. The fact that communication often works is almost more amazing than these occasional crises.

Second, it is very important not to view these inevitable crises as failures. Otherwise we're digging another hole of disappointment for ourselves. In order to work through these crises profitably, it's important to understand when and why they occur. Sometimes they are simply a natural part of the growth process. The emotional lives of all human beings move through cycles of intimacy and distancing. It is normal and natural. The entire world of nature evolves through cycles in the growth process. If I accept this cyclic evolution, I will be able to work within it in creative ways. I will recognize crises as milestones of growth. I will see these crises as chances to be creative rather than as catastrophes of destruction.

From *Will The Real Me Please Stand Up?*

*F*riendship and self-revelation have a newness about them with each new day, because being a human person involves daily change and growth. My friend and I are growing, and differences are becoming more apparent. We are not growing into the same person, but each into our own. I discover in my friend other tastes and preferences, other feelings and hopes, other reactions to new experiences. I discover that this business of telling another who I am cannot be done once and for all. I must *continually* tell you who I am and you must *continually* tell me who you are, because both of us are continually evolving.

From *Why Am I Afraid To Tell You Who I Am?*

*I*t may be that the very things which first attracted me to you now seem to work against communication. In the beginning, your sentiment seemed to balance off my more intellectual inclinations; your extroverted ways complemented my introversion; your realism counterbalanced my artistic intuition. It seemed like such an ideal friendship. We seemed like separate halves that needed each other to become one whole. But now, when I want you to share my intellectual vision, I am annoyed that you take no interest in my objective arguments of reason. Now, when I want to show you that you are not logical in your sentiment, it does not seem to matter to you at all. In the beginning we seemed to fit together so well. Now your desire to go out to others and my more introverted inclinations which seek solitude seem to be divisive.

Of course, our friendship can still be. We are standing within arms' reach of that which is most humanly rewarding and beautiful. We must not turn back now. We can still share all the things we once shared with such excitement, when first I told you who I was and you told me who you were; only now our sharing will be deeper because we are deeper. If I will continue to hear you with the same sense of wonder and joy as I did in the beginning, and you will hear me in this way, our friendship will grow firmer and deeper roots. The tinsel of our first sharing will mellow into gold. We can and will be sure that there is no need to hide anything from each other, that we have shared everything.

From *Why Am I Afraid To Tell You Who I Am?*

*T*o become more effective communicators we must "stretch" beyond our "comfort zones." The problem is that we huddle carefully inside that comfort zone; and if it is small, then we are imprisoned in a small world. However, most of us would rather stay in our prisons than pay the price of discomfort for venturing out. We allow ourselves to be painted into a small corner of life. We never find out the limits of our abilities because we never explore them. We don't enjoy our full capacities because we never really test them. It has been said that the average person uses only ten percent of his or her abilities. The other ninety percent gets buried in graves of fear. We fear failure. We fear making a fool out of ourselves. We fear the ridicule of others. We fear criticism. So we cave in and settle down in our comfort corner, and every day begins to look pretty much like yesterday and tomorrow. We wear the same clothes, say the same things, meet the same people, go through the same routines because that is where we are comfortable.

"To stretch" as we use the term here, means "to step outside our comfort zones." It means to dream the impossible dream, to reach for the previously unreached, to try the untried, to risk the possibility of failure, to dare to go into places where we have never been.

From *Will The Real Me Please Stand Up?*

I have often imagined our emotions as children surrounding their parents, Mother Mind and Father Will. Often children try to walk tightrope on high fences, to peek over cliffs, and to pet grizzly bears. They kick and cry and squeal when they are not allowed to start dangerous bonfires or throw sharp knives. Mother Mind and Father Will have to be strong and determined. Some parents have insisted that insanity is, in fact, inherited: You get it from your children.

When a person first attempts this challenge of stretching, of stepping out of old comfort zones and into new areas, the children (the emotions) will certainly act up. They will start kicking and screeching, crying and protesting. The imagination (an interior sense) will paint ugly pictures of embarrassment and failure. It will make frightening sounds. "The world will end with a 'big bang!' At least there will be a big explosion. Someone, probably me, will definitely faint. Murphy's Law ('What can go wrong will go wrong!') will once more prevail."

But if Mother Mind and Father Will are strong enough, they will prevail. And believe it or not, the world won't go up in smoke. There will be no explosion. No one will faint or die. And old Murphy won't even show up. But that's only some of the things that won't happen. What will result from our stretching is that the world will be widened for us, and our lives will become fuller and more satisfying. Talents will be revealed that we didn't even know we had. Do you remember the first time you swam without someone holding you afloat or the first time you hit a home run? "I can do it!" you announced to yourself and to the world. You didn't drown and you didn't strike out. You did it! A new self-confidence and a new world were created for you in that moment. It always happens when we stretch.

From *Will The Real Me Please Stand Up?*

*G*ood communication requires that the communicators spend special or quality time together. Quality time implies that there is no time crunch and there is no crush of a crowd around you. In quality time we can search confidently for just the right words that express what we are thinking and feeling. Most of us find self-disclosure difficult, even when we don't have to worry about a time deadline and other distractions.

It is scary to tell another person the things we have kept hidden in the darkness for a long time. And so it helps to find a time and place where there is no rush and there are no distractions. It is easier to locate the hidden pieces of our human puzzle while sitting together at the close of the day.

We also need an unhurried and undistracted listener, one who can provide us with "presence" and "availability." It is always much easier to share ourselves when we know someone cares enough to listen. In a very real sense the quality of the time regulates the quality of listening. And the quality of listening directly affects the quality of sharing. The desire and determination to set aside such special time will be proportioned to our desire for communication.

Special times may be the wisest investments we can make.

From *Will The Real Me Please Stand Up?*

*T*ouching is an important form of communication. At times the slightest touch can say something, can express a warmth that words cannot convey.

There are those of us who feel threatened by touch. Probably under all our real or imagined fears is the fear of true intimacy. The fear of intimacy is always with us. Somehow we sense that touching can be a strong bonding force. Bonding leads to and results from commitment. Commitment, of course, implies obligation. And the obligation of commitment is scary to most of us. So we sense and fear the consequences of affectionate touching.

We should think of our senses as gifts of God and antennas of learning. In fact, one of the laws of learning is that the more senses involved in the learning process, the deeper the lessons will penetrate and the longer they will be remembered. Please take a moment and recall the sensory images of your own childhood: being carried up to bed and tucked in, being kissed and consoled when you fell down, riding high up on Daddy's shoulders or holding on tightly to Mama's hand in a crowded department store. Images of safety and security.

When it comes to self-esteem and security, we need all the assurances we can get. And so we need to hear kind words, to see smiles and feel the tenderness of loving touches. Somehow touching bridges our feeling of separateness and aloneness more effectively than words.

From *Will The Real Me Please Stand Up?*

*I*t is not strictly a part of dialogue, since it involves judgments and a decision, but is is an almost magical enabler and facilitator of dialogue. It is the simple request: "Will you forgive me?" The beginning of most human rifts that sabotage love and dialogue is what I have called a "wounded spirit." For example, I speak to you in a manner or I say something to you that hurts. I may or may not realize the effects of my manner or words on you, but to a greater or lesser degree you are crushed. It may also happen that you do not tell me of your pain, but act it out on me. We can then easily be trapped in a getting-even game, a back and forth contest. When this begins, the lines of communication are down, the relationship is bleeding and there is a great need for healing.

What I am suggesting here is that most ailing relationships can be restored to health almost miraculously by this simple but sincere request: "Will you forgive me?" In asking the question, I am not assuming all the blame. I am not deciding who was right and who was wrong. I am simply asking you to take me back into your love from which I have been separated. The acknowledged need for forgiveness is the most effective means of restoration for wounded spirits. No relationship should go on for very long without it.

From *The Secret Of Staying In Love*

*A*dmitting our failures and asking to be forgiven will help to remove many of the obstacles to good communication. A sincere apology instantly dislodges all the defensive techniques which are the death of dialogue. Also an apology shares, as nothing else can, our personal vulnerability. Yet most of us find it very difficult to apologize. Some fear lurks deep within most of us that makes an honest admission of our mistakes difficult.

Certainly part of our difficulty with apologizing is the problem we have with interior honesty. To get to the moment and act of apologizing, I must first be very honest with myself about my failures and limitations. We need all the help we can get to be honest with ourselves. The spirit of truthfulness must be present in all sincere apologies. Then we must strive to make an honest admission of our failures to others who have been hurt or offended by our mistakes. "I was wrong. I am sorry. Please forgive me." I think it is very rare that forgiveness is ever withheld when one sincerely admits a mistake and asks for forgiveness. When sought and granted, this forgiveness then becomes a source of release. The record book has been wiped clean. The person forgiven no longer has to bear the burden of guilt. The person forgiving no longer bears the burden of resentment.

From *Will The Real Me Please Stand Up?*

When rationalizing, we cannot look at the truth objectively. We are too busy working out a construct of self-justification. "You had it coming. You did the same thing to me three weeks ago. I'm only giving you a taste of your own medicine." Most of us get lost in the endless circle of rationalization. We twist the truth, launder our language, and even falsify the facts. And all this labor is designed simply to justify ourselves and to whitewash our mistakes. And once the rationalization is completed, there is no more need for an honest admission of failure or an apology.

To avoid the dishonesty of the rationalization process, I must ask myself: Do I accept the real me, the flawed imperfect me, the one who limps, the broken me? Do I really accept myself as a mistake-maker? Have I learned how to laugh at myself and my "klutziness"? I have to think about this very seriously. Unless and until I do so accept myself, I cannot be truly honest or real. And if I am not real, my life will become one prolonged charade.

From *Will The Real Me Please Stand Up?*

*N*o matter how romanticists have tried to color it ever-sweet, and despite the sardonic claim of cynics that it is overrated, love is the tough, essential answer to the riddle of human existence, of human wholeness and happiness. To live is to love. Still it must be conceded that the cynics have a good set of statistics. It's not just the backlog of business in the divorce courts. It's the general fragmentation of the human family, parents against children, brothers against brothers, and so forth. If love really is the answer, it seems quite certain that the efforts of humans to find the answer in love-relationships have a high mortality rate. Love works if people will work at it. But why does love so often fail? What is the "work" which love demands, and why are we sometimes unwilling to undertake it?

Love supposes, is, and does many things, but basically it is practiced in the act of *sharing*. To the extent and depth that two people are committed to each other in a love-relationship, to that extent and on that level they must actively share each other's life. Another word for sharing is *communication*, the act by which people share something or have it in common. If I communicate a secret of mine to you, then we share it, have it in common. To the extent that I communicate myself as a person to you and you communicate yourself to me, we share in common the mysteries of ourselves. Conversely, to the extent that we withdraw from each other and refuse mutual transparency, love is diminished.

From *The Secret Of Staying In Love*

*T*wo *Solitudes that protect, touch and greet each other.* Here we find the only reality worthy of the name love. The two partners drop, however gradually, the projected image which was the first source of attraction to find the even more beautiful reality of the person. They are willing to acknowledge and respect *otherness* in each other. Each person values and tries to promote the inner vision and mysterious destiny of the other. Each counts it a personal privilege to assist in the growth and realization of the other's vision and destiny. Rilke's brilliant poetic insight seems to capture the nature of the true love relationship:

> Love is . . . a high inducement to the individual to ripen, to become something in himself, to become world, to become world to himself for another's sake. It is a great, an exorbitant demand upon him, something that chooses him out and calls him to vast things. Love consists in this, that two solitudes protect and touch and greet each other.

From *The Secret Of Staying In Love*

A good working definition of interpersonal love is that of psychiatrist Harry Stack Sullivan: "When the satisfaction, happiness, and security of another is as real to you as your own, you truly love that person." This desire to see you satisfied, happy, and secure is *not* just a feeling. Feelings are instant, transient, and ambivalent. Love is rather a *decision* (I am going to love you) and a *commitment* (I will say, do, and be whatever you need for your satisfaction, happiness, and security). In other words, I decide that I am going to love you as I love myself. And I am going to provide as best I can whatever promotes your true happiness.

This is what love really is. And this is the love that must be the motive of all communication. Like many other things, a motive can be recognized by its consequences or results. "By their fruits you shall know them." If my motive is love, the first thing I will do is to observe you, to look at you with the supersighted eyes of love. Love is not really blind; it is supersighted. A loving person sees things in another that nonloving eyes can never see. I make this observation of you in order to read your moods and recognize your needs. On one day you may need me to celebrate a recent success with you. On other days you may need me to sit silently with you in a dark room of grief. It may be that you will need my tenderness at times. At other times you may need my toughness. But whether you need blue velvet or blue steel, I will try to supply it.

Sometimes it is difficult to know what is the loving thing to do, to say, to be. Each of us is a profound mystery. It is not easy to read another's mood and recognize another's needs. At times I will be flying blind. Sometimes love is blue velvet—tender and gentle. Sometimes love is blue steel— firm and tough. Consequently, love is an "art," not a "science."

From *Will The Real Me Please Stand Up?*

I am continually experiencing the evergrowing, ever-new reality of you. And you are experiencing the changing reality of me. And, through each other, we are together experiencing the reality of God, who once said that ". . . it is not good for a human being to be alone."

your slightest look
easily will unclose me
though i have closed
    myself as fingers,
you open always petal
    by petal
myself as Spring opens
(touching skillfully, mysteriously)
her first rose

        e.e. cummings

From *Why Am I Afraid To Tell You Who I Am?*

I think that the most harmful deception that most of us fall into is this. We get deluded into thinking that if we change (for the better) God will love us more. Have you ever felt that way? Have you ever felt that if you tried a little harder, ran a little faster, prayed a little more, God would love you a little more? When we think this way, we are always running hard, but we never make it into the comfort of God's arms.

When I was a novice in the seminary, each morning I would promise God a perfect day. This is going to be it. And somehow I really believed it. But at the end of the day I was apologizing for my fragile humanity. In my own misguided way I was saying to God: "If I change, if I really make it to that perfect day, you will love me, won't you?" Of course, I never made it to the promised improvement because I was always restrained by the thought that God really loves only the perfect. He doesn't really like us human fractions. Of course, this delusion stifles the human spirit. Such discouragement is the strategy of the devil.

Now I am sure that God is trying to straighten out this delusory thinking. I imagine God saying, "Hey, you've got it backwards. You don't have to change so I will love you. If you ever realize how much I do love you, oh, then you will change! Change will be automatic and inevitable. The knowledge that you are loved will empower you. But if you are always trying to change in order to win my love, you will wear yourself out. You will use up all of your energies trying to measure up. Eventually you will get discouraged and give up. Then, of course, you can't change. Just know this: I have given you all my love as a gift. You can't really win it or be worthy of it. All you can do is simply accept it. And when you do, then you will certainly change."

From the video program, *Free To Be Me*

*I*t is a historical tragedy that Christian preaching of God's word has somehow inverted its priorities. It has stressed the particular truths which Christianity has espoused rather than the person of its Lord, as the Apostles and early Christians did. It is not that Jesus did not have specific teachings, but these teachings will not make much sense to the person who has not first accepted Jesus himself.

God's ways are not our ways, and God's truth is often difficult for us. There is some pertinence here of the axiom that you can only know as much of another as you love. We have always said so glibly that love is blind. The real fact of the matter is that love is supersighted. Often we ask, with an adolescent naiveté, what so and so sees in his wife (or vice versa); he seems to love her so much. It is precisely because he does love her that he can know her in a way that is not available to anyone who does not love her. He sees things in her that only the eyes of love can see. So it is that only those who have been led over the unchartable course of faith to the threshold of God's love stand any chance of understanding him and his unique ways of dealing with us. We are not equipped to understand the truths of God—much less debate them—until we first understand the central truth of his person and of his love for us.

From *A Reason To Live, A Reason To Die*

*M*any of us wonder if we haven't put too much distance between ourselves and the love of God. We wonder if the warm rays of his love can still reach us. The Word of God reminds us of the parable Jesus used to explain how God feels about us when we have left him, left him in pursuit of our own dreams and plans, confident in our own formulas for happiness. We read in the Word of God the well known parable of the Prodigal Son. In this parable the Word of God depicts God's love and goodness as a constant. God is ready to embrace and to welcome us whenever we are ready to say "yes," whenever we are open and willing to be loved. God's patient love doesn't really care where we have been or what we have done. He is forever holding out wide and loving arms waiting to embrace us. The invitation is always the same: Come to me! Still there is something in most of us that keeps asking the wrong question: How could you ever love me?

Once a study was made of people who had given up faith in God. The reasons of these various people for giving up their faith were catalogued. Some ceased to believe because they felt churchgoers were "a bunch of hypocrites." I have always been personally unmoved by this reason. I always feel the impulse to say, "Oh, come on in. There's always room for one more hypocrite." However, the one reason that struck me as truly profound was this: "Faith did not *ask* too much; it *promised* too much. It was not that God's Word was too *hard* to believe; it was rather that it was too *good* to believe. Could a God of infinite power and majesty really lean out of heaven to take me in his arms, to claim me as his child, the child of his heart and the apple of his eye? I don't think so. It is just too much." The Word of God which we accept in our act of faith is indeed very good news—not too difficult but almost too much.

From *The Christian Vision*

*I*t is a highly personalized outlook or vision of reality that shapes the dimensions of our lives and our world. It is this vision of reality that ushers us into a fuller life or shackles us into a shriveled life. Our vision of reality either releases us into a large and lovely world or paints us into a small corner. One of the most important parts of this vision is our perception of God. Each of us has a different "felt sense" of God. Though it is hard to admit, some us are really frightened by God. We are afraid of what he might ask of us or do to us if we really turned over our lives to him. Can I ask you for a moment now to reflect on your own personal perception of God. If you were dying and the doctors were to tell you that "it will be just a short time now," would you be happy to be "going home" or would you be filled with a disappointed terror? Jesus compares death to two very different things. He says that death can either be for us a bridegroom coming to claim his bride, or a thief coming to rob us of all that we treasure. I often ask myself: What will death be for me: a bridegroom or a thief? Somehow I think it is my concept of God which most forcefully shapes my reactions to living and to dying, to life and to death.

Now we have to be careful when we test our perceptions of God. We can't ever expect to get an imagined "photograph" of God. A "felt sense" of God is not the same thing as a photograph. One of the reasons the Jewish people forbade graven images of God was their knowledge of God's infinite being. If we try to shrink God into the proportions of a photograph or statue, it has to be blasphemous. We have to experience God in his enormity, in his majesty, in his mystery. God is an infinite love which surrounds us. He is outside us and he is inside us. His loving presence pervades everything. What is your "felt sense" of him?

From the video program, *Free To Be Me*

*I*s there such a thing as "sin"? The Gospels leave us Christians no doubt about the reality of sin. Still, it is dangerous to reflect on this reality of sin without understanding that God is love. I would like to suggest an analogy. God is like the sun. The sun only shines. It gives off its warmth and light. Now we can stand in the light and warmth of the sun or we can leave the sun. But when we leave the sun, we know that the sun does not go out. The sun goes on shining. We can leave the sun, we can lock ourselves in a dark dungeon where the sun cannot reach us. We may grow dark and cold there, but we know that the sun does not change. We change. But we also know that we can always walk back into the sunlight. It is always there for us. It is the same thing with God's love. It is unconditional, constant and continuous. It is like the light and warmth of the sun. It is always there for us.

Have you ever loved someone who did not want your love? Have you ever said to someone, "I just want to love you, to help you. I want what is best for you!"? Do you remember what it felt like when the other person said, "No thanks!" and walked away? As the person walked away from you, you called out: "If you ever want to come back, my love will be here waiting for you. I will always love you." I am sorry if you have had such an experience, but if you did, this analogy of God's love and the reality of sin will mean a little more to you. God says exactly this to each of us: "I love you. If you choose to leave me, I will not stop you. I will always leave you free, but I will always be here for you. There may be a time when you will separate yourself from my love but never believe that you have lost my love. You can only refuse, but you can never lose my love. I will always be here for you."

From the video program, *Free To Be Me*

*W*hen Jesus was asked who God is and how he thinks of and reacts to sinners, Jesus told the story of the Prodigal Son. Perhaps we should really call this parable the Parable of the Prodigal Abba, because the central message concerns the father and his prodigal (extravagant), unconditional love.

In the story itself, it seems that a man and his two sons live and work together on a farm out in the country. The younger boy more and more comes to think of his father as outdated. He gradually comes to be disenchanted with, even to resent, life with his father. He has had it with the chickens in the morning and the crickets in the evening. The boy dreams about the delights of the big city with its darkened lights and wicked delights. One day he comes to his father to demand his inheritance and to announce his impending departure. The father is sad, of course, but he finally gives his son the inheritance. The boy, without looking back over his shoulder, sets off to realize his high hopes and to actualize his daring dreams.

Jesus portrays the father as allowing his son to leave, but the father's heart is heavy with regret. During the long interval of the son's absence, the father sits nightly on the front porch of the farmhouse, watching with sad and longing eyes the road from the city. He cannot forget his son. He will always remember his little boy, the apple of his eye and the delight of his dreams. There will always be a special place in the heart of the father for his son. Only when the boy discovers the hollowness of his hopes and the delusion of his dreams, only when his inheritance has been spent and his friends desert him, does he come back down the long road homeward.

From *The Christian Vision*

*I*n his parable of the Prodigal, Jesus pictures the father, looking as usual down the road that leads from the city, and suddenly recognizing the distant figure of his son. The father's heart pounds wildly, almost breaking with excitement. Overcome with joy, contrary to all the traditions of the time, the father runs down the road and gathers his lost boy back into his own finding arms. He doesn't even hear the boy's suggestion, "I can't hope that you will take me back as a son." After saying this, the boy feels the tight arms of his father encircling him, and hears the relieved sobs in the father's chest. He feels his father's warm tears washing down the furrows of his own cheeks. The father moans softly, over and over again, "You're home . . . you're home!" Then the father gathers himself together, summons his loudest voice, and calls for rings and robes "for my boy." He gives an instruction to call in the music makers, to kill the prized fatted calf. There will be a party to end all parties. He repeats the joyful proclamation: "My son is home! My son is home!"

When he finishes this story, Jesus looks squarely into the eyes of the Scribes, the High Priests, and the Pharisees. "This," he adds, "is who God is. This is how God feels about and reacts to a sinner." (See Luke 15:11–32) Of course, his story sealed the fate of Jesus. They would now set into motion the machinery of his death. It would come as no surprise. Jesus knew all the time what the result would be even before he started his parable. And he would gladly die for love. "I have a baptism wherewith I am to be baptized and I am anxious to see it accomplished." (Luke 12:50) Under every crucifix commemorating his death, the followers of Jesus might well see an indelible caption: "This is what I mean when I say 'I love you!'" And down through the arch of the centuries, and out to the ends of the earth, the story would be told and the message would be repeated, and people would gradually come to understand: *God is love!*

From *The Christian Vision*

*W*e know God in knowing Jesus. Jesus is the Word that was with God from all eternity, the Word that is God: Jesus. St. Paul calls Jesus "the visible image of our invisible God." (Colossians 1:15) Theologians have called Jesus our "window into God." And Jesus himself assures Philip, "Whoever sees me sees the Father." (John 14:9) Also, St. John writes in his prologue:

> The Word became a human being and, full of grace and truth, lived among us. We saw his glory, the glory which he received as the Father's only Son . . . No one has ever seen God. The only Son, who is the same as God and is at the Father's side, he has made him known. (John 1:14, 18 GNB)

God not only was in Jesus, reconciling the world to himself (see 2 Corinthians 5:19), but was also revealing himself to us in Jesus. God was speaking our human language, as it were, in becoming a human being, like us in all things except sin. In uttering his Word into the world God was telling us everything he could about himself. The divine person of Jesus is the surest way to a more accurate attitude toward God, even though we can never hope to have a totally adequate view or concept of God. Again, it is obvious that God is simply too big, too magnificent, too infinite for the finite lenses of our minds. However, we can get clearer and clearer insights into the mind and heart of God by reflecting on the mind and heart of Jesus. The wisdom and power, the might and majesty of God reside in Jesus. Through Jesus they are revealed to us.

From *The Christian Vision*

*O*nce upon a time I used to think: "If I improve, become more charitable, eliminate my frequent faults of commission and omission, if I pray more and so forth, God will love me more." I am now convinced that this kind of thinking involves a serious misconception of our loving God. It is simply incompatible with a true vision of God. Again, it is making God to our human image and likeness. It ascribes to God that kind of "you have to earn it" type of conditional love with which we humans often pretend to love one another.

Almost all of our human experience has been with conditional love: "If you change . . . if you do this or don't do that . . . I will love you." So we have to sit with this thought of God's unconditional, freely given love, and think about it for a long time. We have to soak in the realization of God's love in prayerful meditation. The truth of covenant, the truth that God could have made a world without you or me, but that such a world would have been incomplete for him—these are truths that are taken in slowly and realized only with the help of grace. God wanted you and me just the way we are, because . . . simply because this is the you and this is the me he has always loved. God *is* love. This is all God ever does.

From *The Christian Vision*

*S*ooner or later the question always arises: What about the so-called "wrath of God," mentioned in the Bible? Biblical scholars assure us that there is no wrath *in* God. God does not get angry, as we do. The scholars tell us that this "wrath of God," mentioned in the Scriptures, is a figure of speech, an anthropomorphism. In such a figure of speech we ascribe human qualities or reactions to God. And while this particular anthropomorphism was probably intended to emphasize the incompatibility of God and sin, it has too often been used in a misleading way. It is true that we can't choose a sinful life, apart from God, and have a loving relationship with God at the same time. But it is likewise true that our sinning does not change God or arouse wrath in him.

It would be seriously misleading to imply that God gets angry because of something we have done. If that were true, we would be in control of God's reactions, which is unthinkable. It is likewise impossible to imagine that the Jesus who insists that we should love our enemies and forgive without limit would add, "But my Father will be very angry if you don't love him!" The only Father revealed by Jesus runs down the road, takes his son into his arms, and sighs with great relief, "You are home! It's all I have ever wanted. Wherever I am I want you with me, and wherever you are I want to be with you. If a mother would ever forget the child of her womb, I could never forget you!"

From *The Christian Vision*

*I*t is extremely important to realize that God's love is a *covenanted* and not a *contractual* love. In a business contract, if one party fails to meet its commitment, the second party of the contract is released from all the binding effects of that contract. For example, I promise to pay you five dollars to cut the grass in my yard. However, you do not cut the grass, and so I am not bound to pay the promised five dollars. It is not this way in a covenant. A covenant implies a promise of unconditional love, a promise that is never canceled. A covenant promises a love that will go one hundred percent of the way at all times, no matter what is the response of the beloved. Covenanted love is not earned or won by the person to whom it is given. It is always a free gift. Covenanted love walks undemanded miles, goes far beyond the demands of justice and reciprocity. Covenanted love is never taken back or withdrawn. Covenanted love is forever.

In our human experience, there is usually very little to help us understand this kind of love. Sometimes we think that only a mother loves in this way. However, our great God assures us: "If a mother were to forget the child of her womb, I would never forget you . . . I have carved your name on the palms of my hands so that I would never forget you." (Isaiah 49:15–16) "I will never leave you, nor will I ever forget you!" (Hebrews 13:5)

From *The Christian Vision*

*I*n the master vision, provided by the message, life, and person of Jesus, we Christians are called to be channels of love to one another. God, who is love, created us in an act of love. All goodness is somehow self-diffusive. In the act of creation God's goodness diffused itself. We all know what this diffusion of goodness means from personal experience. When we have something good—like a good joke, a good recipe, or even a bit of good news—the instinct of love is to share it. So our Father-God, experiencing in himself an ecstasy of love and happiness, wanted to share his life, his happiness, and even his home with us. From all eternity he planned this and picked out each of us to be the special recipients of his love. We are the chosen children of his family and of his heart. Each of us was conceived and born into this world only because we were loved and wanted by our Father-God.

From the beginning there was a human network of veins and arteries through which this love was to be carried to all the parts of God's human family. However, somewhere, somehow, something went wrong. We call it "original sin." Sin and selfishness, hatred and homicide became a part of our human inheritance. But the call has always remained the same.

In the Christian vision these two commandments are really linked together. I cannot say my "yes" of love to God unless I say my "yes" of love to each and every member of God's human family. There are to be no exceptions. The French poet Charles Peguy once said that if we try to come to God alone, he will certainly ask us some embarrassing questions: "Where are your brothers and sisters? Didn't you bring them with you? You didn't come alone, did you?" These yeses of love, required by the two great commandments, are inseparable. Jesus himself made this very clear: We can refuse our love to no one.

From *The Christian Vision*

I have often thought about what I would have done if God had put me in charge of planning the Nativity, the birth of Jesus. First, I would have brought to Bethlehem a battery of gynecologists and obstetricians. I would have built a magnificent hospital and a palace for the reception of the dignitaries of the world. Of course the palace would have made the palace of the Roman Emperor look like something out of Woolworth's. I would have blazed huge headlines in all the papers. I would have hired the best public relations people available. I would have provided music. Music always lends a special dimension to celebration. I know that historically this Nativity will happen only once. I would have felt obliged to put on a Nativity to be remembered forever.

But God, planning from all eternity with all his infinite wisdom and with all his infinite power, arranged to have his Son born in a manger. It was actually a cave in the side of a mountain. An odorous, damp and ugly little cave. God did not even provide a place for his Son in the local inn. And the first people God invited to see his son were simple shepherds. They were considered the outcasts of society. They could not testify in court or even vote. They were the lowest class in a class conscious society. They were the least of his children.

I don't even have the nerve to tell God of my proposed plans for the Nativity. If I had been in charge, the whole message of Jesus would have been lost in the magnificence of my trappings. Christmas really brings me to my knees and helps me to realize much more clearly what is important and what is unimportant. I suppose that this is why God, whose thoughts and ways are not mine, arranged a cave in Bethlehem.

From the video program, *Jesus As I Know Him*

I believe that God has spoken to others before me, that his inspirations have resulted in many beautiful lives and deeds for God and mankind. I have always believed this, that he stopped Saul of Tarsus short on the road to Damascus, that he pursued the reluctant St. Augustine down the labyrinths of human weakness, that he inspired the founder of my own order, St. Ignatius Loyola, to hang up his soldier's sword and to do battle only for the Kingdom of God. Oh yes, God did these great deeds in these great men.

But would he come to me? This was harder for me to grasp until I stopped asking the wrong question and began to ask the meaningful question. I had been asking: "Who am I, O my God, that you would come to me in tenderness and intimacy? How could I ever be so important to you? What do I have to offer?" I was trapped in my old preoccupation with self. The real question is, of course: "Who are you, my God? Who are you that you would come to me and speak to me, that you would fill my poor finite mind with your thoughts and perspectives, that you would enable me to see this world through your eyes, that you would put your strength and desires into my frail will, that you would pour your divine grace into this vessel of clay? Who are you that you graciously accept the loaves and fish of my life to feed the hungry throughout the world? Who are you? Show me your face, fold me and my life into your loving arms, let me feel your fire and the soothing touch of your hand on the face of my thirsting soul."

From *He Touched Me*

*G*od's love for each of us is just as unsolicited, unmerited, and unconditional as was his love for the People of Israel. Jesus is the Word of this love, uttered into the world. God comes to us in him, wanting to share, to communicate the goodness, the joy, and the love that is his. He wants to love us into the fullness of life.

On the human level all of us have at some time experienced this kind of inner urge and insistence to share something good with a friend. At an even deeper level it is the inner urge of artists to share with others a vision of beauty, the music that they have heard inside themselves. At the deepest human level it is the desire of procreation: when two people love each other very much, they want to share their love and their lives with a new life, fashioned by God from their own flesh and blood. It is something like this with God. The impetus of God's love comes from within himself, to share with us his life and love. It is a free gift, freely given, not earned or deserved or claimed by any right of ours. It is a beautiful, eternal gift, held out to us in the hands of love. It is an unconditional covenant.

All we have to do is say "Yes!" All we have to do is open ourselves to receive this pearl of great price, this love that will transform us and every moment of our lives. The key word is openness. The little child who is inside me wishes that openness were simple. The fact is that the big "Yes!" of openness has many other little "yeses" inside it. Some of them will be very costly. Some will call for great courage. Some will be uttered in darkness.

From *Unconditional Love*

*E*ach of us has his or her own unique and very limited concept of God, and it is very often marked and distorted by human experience. Negative emotions, like fear, tend to wear out. The distorted image of a vengeful God will eventually nauseate and be rejected. Fear is a fragile bond of union, a brittle basis of religion.

It may well be that this is why God's second commandment is that we love one another. Unselfish human love is the sacramental introduction to the God of love. We must go through the door of human giving to find the God who gives himself.

Those who do not reject a distorted image of God will limp along in the shadow of a frown, but they certainly will not love with their whole heart, soul and mind. Such a God is not lovable. There will never be any trust and repose in the loving arms of a Father, there will never be any mystique of belonging to God. The person who serves out of fear, without the realization of love, will try to bargain with God; and will do little things for God, make little offerings, say little prayers, and so forth. Fear-riddled people try to embezzle a place in the heaven of their God. Life and religion are more like a chess-game, hardly an affair of love.

From *Why Am I Afraid To Love?*

*I*n the last year a computerized study was made on one hundred persons who were considered to be very successful in their personal and professional lives. All available information on these people was fed into a sophisticated computer in an effort to find out what all of them might have in common. What is the common denominator of human success? Education and environment were ruled out. Most of them (seventy percent) did come from small towns with a population of fewer than 15,000 people. Finally, however, a universal quality was discovered: Every single one of these highly successful people was a resolute . . . *"good finder."*

By definition, "good finders" are persons who look for and find what is good: in themselves, in others, and in all the situations of life. Good finders are actively aware that God who is mighty has done uniquely beautiful things in themselves. Good finders look for and find what is good in others, and vocally affirm these others. Good finders are explicitly and gratefully appreciative of the goodness and giftedness in others. Finally good finders look for what is good in all the situations of life. Good finders know that the best blessings almost always come into our lives disguised as problems. Good finders know that there is a promise in every problem, a rainbow after every storm, a warmth in every winter.

God is the original good finder. Once he looked upon a cold and cruel world, where gladiators entertained others by killing one another. Two thirds of all people lived in dehumanizing slavery. God's reaction was to send his only begotten Son into this world, not to condemn it, but to love it into life.

(A Christmas message to his friends)

*I*t was at the end of my fifteen years of Jesuit training. I had accumulated so many academic degrees I felt like "Father Fahrenheit." However, as I entered St. Thomas Hospital in Akron, Ohio, to serve as chaplain for a short time, a startling thought occurred to me. I had never seen anyone die. I had never seen anyone born. Scenes of suffering and raw grief had all been quarantined out of my academic existence. I somehow sensed that St. Thomas Hospital would be an initiation into areas of life I had never previously entered. I would experience the loves and the hurts, the joys and the sorrows of human existence as never before.

The most educational of all the experiences was the birth of a baby boy. A retired nursing Sister, who took pity on my inexperience and who took charge of my hospital-life education, told me that, before leaving the hospital, I had to see a delivery. I warned her that she was apparently wearing her wimple too tight, and that it would alarm the delivering mother if a chaplain were brought in to witness the birth of her child. I also rehearsed a litany of other reasons why this would be imprudent if not impossible, but she saw through them and through me. The next morning I was in the delivery room. The atmosphere was casual and chatty until the actual moment of delivery. Then the room became very still . . . until a baby boy came wriggling into the world. A doctor cleared the baby's breathing passages of mucous with suction tubes and briskly rubbed his chest and back. Then it happened. The baby cried.

When I heard that first wail of life, something very profound happened to me. I simply turned numb. I was utterly overwhelmed by the beauty and sacredness of that moment and what I was seeing. A new life had begun.

From *The Silent Holocaust*

*D*uring and after the birth of that baby, it was as if my mind were saying, "Cannot compute! Cannot compute!" What I was witnessing was too big, too beautiful, too sacred to fit easily into my mind. My mental machinery simply short-circuited. In a daze I stumbled out of the delivery room, and as I walked down the long corridor of the hospital, my theological education began to connect to what I had just experienced. In the Judeo-Christian tradition, God does not come to know you and me at conception or birth. God does not get such new ideas, nor does he lose old ones. He has known and loved each of us from all eternity.

God had waited from all eternity for that moment of birth. And now he would show his little boy the adoring face of the mother that had carried him so lovingly. He would show that little boy the magnificent stars he had strung in the sky. He would introduce him to the music of lullabies and the softness of his mother's arms, the gentleness of his father's hands. The "I" of God had been saying to the "Thou" of that small baby: "With an everlasting love I have loved you. This is why with loving kindness I created you" (from the prophecy of Jeremiah, 31:3). Cannot compute. Cannot compute. The miracle of life. The Good News of God's love for his world and for each of us. Every new child is a sign that God wants the world to go on.

From *The Silent Holocaust*

*A*fter my term as chaplain at the hospital, I sorted through all the profoundly human experiences that had been mine. I found that people die as they have lived: afraid or angry, believing or despairing. The human condition with all its superficial foibles and throbbing needs. Goodness mixed with evil. Evil softened by goodness. But the mountaintop experience was certainly witnessing the birth of that baby boy. In the long and arduous process of my own psychosexual maturation, it was an undeniable milestone. I understood in that tremendous and insightful experience the miracle of human reproduction. Theologically I felt as though I had touched the smiling face of God, who had lovingly dreamed of that little boy from all eternity and who had conferred upon him the inestimable gift of life.

That child was indeed a unique and unrepeatable image and likeness of God himself. God does not make carbon copies. In the whole history of the human race that little boy had never occurred before, and in the entire course of human history still to be, he will never occur again. No one has ever had or will ever have his fingerprints, his unique combination of gifts, his immortal soul. It is a realization that can enter the mind only gradually. It is a mystery of love that we can only dimly appreciate and never fully understand.

From *The Silent Holocaust*

*T*here is an old Christian tradition
that God sends each person into this world
 with a special message to deliver
 with a special song to sing for others,
 with a special act of love to bestow.
No one else can speak my message,
 or sing my song,
 or offer my act of love.
These are entrusted only to me.

According to this tradition, the message may be spoken, the song
sung, the act of love delivered
 only to a few,
 or to all the folk in a small town,
 or to all the people in a large city,
 or even to all the people in the whole world.
It all depends on God's unique plan
 for each person.
At this holy time of Christmas, when we are recalling the fact that God
so loved the world that He sent his Son into the world for us, I want
to say this to you:
 Your message has been heard in my heart,
 Your song has warmed my world,
 And your love has brightened my darkness.
Thank you, thank you for your message, your song, your love.
You will always be in my own grateful heart and prayers.

(A Christmas Message to his friends)

*I*f God had a specific will for each of us and for every detail of our lives, I'm afraid that God would be aiding and abetting infantile delinquency. We would never grow up. We all know what happens to the child whose parents insist on making all of his or her decisions. The child grows up into a very immature adult. We humans grow up by struggling through and making decisions for ourselves. Now God would not do this to us: He would not preempt all our decisions. That would predestine us to a helpless form of immaturity.

What God rather holds out to us is a general will: Do something loving with your life and your talents. Do something beautiful for your brothers and sisters. Make love your life principle. This will involve us in many decisions. We will be constantly confronted with the ever-present question: What is the loving thing to do? But it is in struggling with and making these decisions that we shall become mature sons and daughters of God.

From the audio program, *The Growing Edge Of Life*

I also believe that, in addition to God's general will, there is operative at definite times in our lives a specific will of God. I think it is certain that God has sent you or me into this world with a specific thing to do: a definite message to deliver, a song to sing, an act of love to bestow.

When we come to that point of time in our lives, when God wants us to do something specific, he will nudge us with his grace. He will put into us a deep attraction, a sense of vocation. To us it may seem like a vague conviction, "I am supposed to do this." It may be that God will make us uncomfortable until we say "yes." He comes to comfort the afflicted but also to afflict the comfortable.

I think that I was called to be a priest by such a specific will of God. I think that God chose me to be a priest and so tailored the graces of my life that I would be attracted to the altar of my ordination. There have, of course, been other moments in my life when I somehow knew that God wanted something specific of me. He wanted me to help this person, to do that thing, to become involved in this cause, to be concerned about a given situation. In each of these times, I felt that God was asking me for a specific "Yes!"

From the audio program, *The Growing Edge Of Life*

*G*od, my Father: Create in me a heart that hungers for your will alone—a heart to accept your will, to do your will, to be whatever you want me to be, to do whatever you want me to do.

When you chose to create this world, you knew the blueprint and the design of my life: the moment of my conception, the day and hour when I would be born. You saw from all eternity the color of my eyes and you heard the sound of my voice. You knew what gifts I would have and those that I would be without. You knew also the moment and the circumstance of my dying. These choices are all a part of your will for me. I will try lovingly to build an edifice of love and praise with these materials which you have given me. What I am is your gift to me. What I become will be my gift to you.

As to the future, I ask for the grace to sign a blank check and trustfully to put it into your hands, for you to fill in all the amounts: the length of my life, the amount of success and the amount of failure, the experiences of pleasure and of pain. I would tremble to do this except for one thing: I know you love me. And, of course, you know much better than I what will truly and lastingly make me happy.

From *The Christian Vision*

*I*n response to your will, O God, I want my life to be an act of love. Wherever there is a choice, help me to ask only this: What is the loving thing to do, to say, to be? To make the decisions that love must, I seek and need your enlightenment. Touch my eyes with your gentle and healing hands that I might find my way along the winding course of love. Strengthen my will and direct my feet to follow that course always.

And whenever there is something special your love has designed for me to do in my life, let me be found ready and waiting. Help me to become a sensitive instrument of your grace. I believe that you have a providential master plan for this world, and I want to be part of it. I want to make my contribution to your Kingdom, the contribution you have entrusted only to me. I want you to use me to help love this world into the fullness of life.

Finally, my Lord and my God, let me be faithful to my commitment and dedication to your will, faithful until the end. Let "faithfulness" be the summary of my days and of my nights. Let the inscription on my tombstone read:

> He said his "yes!" to God,
> He was faithful to the end.

From *The Christian Vision*

*R*ecently I heard an appealing analogy for the faith experience. It seems that a small boy was flying a kite high up in the sky. Soon a low-drifting cloud encircled the kite and hid it from view. A man passing by asked the little boy what he was doing with that string in his hand. "Flying my kite," the child responded. The man looked up at the sky and saw only the cloud in an otherwise clear sky. "I don't see a kite up there. How can you be sure that there is a kite up there?" The child replied, "I don't see it either, but I know my kite is up there because every once in a while there is a little tug on the string."

In the same sense I know that there is a guiding hand in mine as I proceed along the path of my life. I know that there is a light, not mine, that shows me the way I am to go, one step at a time. I know that the Lord walks with me. And there is a deep and warm sense of gratitude in my heart to walk this way with you, my Sisters and Brothers, as my companions. With the Lord's guidance and your company, "every once in a while there is a little tug on the string." Thanks for letting me tell you about it.

From *The Christian Vision*

The greatest gift of God,
I would think,
is the gift of life.

The greatest sin of humans,
it would seem,
would be to return that gift
ungratefully and unopened.

From *The Silent Holocaust*